Men Are PiGs, But We Love Bacon

Men Are PiGs, But We Love Bacon

Not-So-Straight Answers from
America's Most Outrageous
Gay Sex Columnist

MICHAEL ALVEAR

KENSINGTON PUBLISHING CORP.
http://www.kensingtonbooks.com

KENSINGTON BOOKS are published by

Kensington Publishing Corp.
850 Third Avenue
New York, NY 10022

All Kensington titles, imprints and distributed lines are available at special quantity discounts for bulk purchases for sales promotion, premiums, fund raising, educational or institutional use.

Special book excerpts or customized printings can also be created to fit specific needs. For details, write or phone the office of the Kensington Special Sales Manager: Kensington Publishing Corp., 850 Third Avenue, New York, NY 10022. Attn. Special Sales Department. Phone: 1-800-221-2647.

Kensington and the K logo Reg. U.S. Pat. & TM Off.

ISBN 0-7582-0285-7

First Kensington Trade Paperback Printing: May 2003
10 9 8 7 6 5 4 3 2 1

Printed in the United States of America

To Richard Banconi,
for teaching me how to lie about my age

Acknowledgments

Great things can come from someone saying "no." This book is a testament to that. Three years ago Dan Savage's syndicator told the publisher of a gay entertainment magazine that he would not sell the gay author's column to gay newspapers. How's that for irony?

The editor was Chris Crain, the visionary editorial director of Window Media, the largest chain of gay newspapers. Chris called me up one day and said, "I want you to write about sex."

"Fine," I responded. "Send me your cutest employees and I'll get started."

So, my first thank you is to Dan Savage's syndicator. The second goes to Chris Crain, not just for making the column—and therefore this book—possible, but also for standing up to enormous pressure from easily-offended gay schoolmarms to pull the column on account that it made so much fun of easily-offended schoolmarms.

I'd also like to thank my distinguished and often sober panel of experts, starting with Richard Banconi, MSW. His warped yet flawless logic ("beauty is only a light-switch away") significantly affected the way I wrote the column.

Shouts also go out to Brad Thomason, Ph.D., who was literally my psychologist-in-residence. We lived together as boyfriends for the first two years that I wrote the column. I depended on him to give me the clinical view of my psycho readers and for that I thank him. And also because he let me steal his best lines. Like the title of this book. It was his response to a friend wondering how he could have dated me.

I'd also like to thank the three board-certified family practice physicians who made themselves available for my impertinent questions: Jim Braude, M.D., the funny, fresh-faced scion of the busiest gay practice in the southeast. Manuel Patino, M.D., my own personal physician. If I had his bedside manner, I'd be too busy fucking to write this book. And finally, the bright and beautiful Kris Johnson, M.D., a hottie doc if you ever saw one. Thanks guys for making me sound like I knew what I was talking about.

Lastly, I'd like to thank Dan Savage, the master of the rip-and-chew advice column. No, Dan, you're not imagining it. My column is a complete rip-off of yours.

Contents

Introduction

If you're looking for warmth and compassion, you've picked up the wrong book. Try *Chicken Soup for the Cock*; it's three aisles over.

This is a sex advice book with fangs. It's a collection of columns appearing in over twenty gay newspapers under the title "Need Wood? Tips for Getting Timber."

Throughout the four years I've been writing the column I've managed to ENRAGE just about every gay group in existence. There's a reason for that. I make fun of people who aren't used to being made fun of, I'm judgmental as hell, I leer (if it's possible to leer in print), and I brag a lot.

Oh, and I give accurate medical advice.

That's what enrages critics the most, I think. Yanking threads off the fabric of gay piety would be one thing, but I do more than that. Thanks to my panel of board-certified physicians, therapists, and psychologists I club my politically correct victims with medical facts, not just common sense. And if there's one thing the easily offended hate, it's being clubbed with common sense.

I write this column the way men talk about sex—brutally, with a sense of entitlement, and a breathtaking gift for the gratuitous insult. Sound familiar? It's you and your friends at brunch.

When the column first started, almost no one knew what to make of it. Gay sex advice, when it's published at all, has that kind of "everyone-is-beautiful-in-his-own-way" and "isn't-it-all-wonderful"

1

kumbayah hogwash that makes even the biggest dick pigs cough up what they shouldn't be swallowing in the first place.

At first, it was hard to get papers to carry "Need Wood?". "It's too controversial," said one editor, worried about all the headaches that come with controversy. "Can't you tone it down?" Well, no. I offered to throw in a year's supply of Advil and a bottle of Insta-Spine, but he declined. Years later, the column became one of the most successful syndicated properties in the gay press.

If you're wondering why every letter addresses me as "Woody" when my name is Michael, it's because you've never heard of Eppie Lederer, may she rest in peace. She was known in many circles as Ann Landers. I write the column under the pseudonym "Woody" because hell hath no fury like a gay man dissed. I just didn't want to be the victim of a drive-by doiling.

But with this book, I'm throwing caution to the wind the way my readers throw their legs in the air—with wild abandon. Now everyone will have a shot at boiling my pets in an exquisite tarragon, rose petal and saffron demi-glace, with pecan-crusted hearts of palm and a delicate mint-fennel sauce.

You won't really learn how to be a better lay with this book. I mean, there's plenty on techniques but that's not the point of the book. The point is to show the real struggles, the real problems, and our real behavior (or rather misbehavior) in the face of our all-consuming desire.

In other words, this isn't a manual; it's theater.

From the inane to the insane, from the sad to the bad, from the ingratiating to the infuriating, the questions and answers in this book will leave you laughing, crying, and sometimes spitting nails.

Many of the questions come from guys who are not "out" to their doctors, making honesty and forthrightness a scarce commodity during office visits. They're also too embarrassed to ask their friends, particularly if it's a painful and potentially shaming problem like having a small penis or being HIV positive.

The letters give you a voyeuristic glimpse of other people's sex lives. The questions tend to run a lot longer than those in other advice columns because, in my humble opinion, the questions are often more interesting than the answers.

I said "often" not "always." Give me some credit, for Chrissakes.

Critics—and there are many—loathe my column because they feel society at large already judges and ridicules gay men, and here I am joining them.

If I were making fun of men loving each other, they might have a point. But I don't make fun of male love. I make fun of the way we go about getting it, maintaining it, losing it, and looking all over for it again.

Nothing is more entertaining to me than watching gay men rationalize the excesses of their vanity and their promiscuity. That's why I relish whacking the piety piñata. I love watching the canonized candy that sprays out of it.

Look, when straight men don't tell the truth about their sexual lives we call them liars. When gay men don't, we call them "dissidents." The HIV "dissidents," for example, want to keep *shtuuping* everything that moves, but that doesn't sound too good in the middle of a plague, so they adopt an absurd crusade against medical facts.

The homo holier-than-thou hypocrisy can also be seen in sex panic types who cloak their compulsive need for anonymous sex in public restrooms with high-minded talk of sexual freedom. The truth is, we won't allow ourselves to be honest about our sexual natures. We won't allow ourselves to say that we're sexual beings, and that the organizing principle for most of us is to get us some man-meat.

We're not allowed to say, for example, "Yeah, we hit on this idea to use abandoned warehouse space, awful music, and mind-whacking drugs to get laid more often." Instead, we say bullshit things like "I go to circuit parties because it gives me a sense of belonging," or because it's a "difficult and necessary spiritual journey."

We're the only group I know that can make the pursuit of plain old dog-yard scrumping sound like some noble, spiritual quest for a better life.

Both gay men and straight men are afraid to admit we want to have as much sex with as many people as we can. Where we diverge is in the strategies we use to cover up our inconvenient natures. Straight men pretend they don't really feel that way; gay men admit they feel that way but for righteous reasons.

I constantly get letters from people who marinate in what Phillip Roth called the "ecstasy of sanctimony." No group drips with this kind of moist sexual self-righteousness like the kink crowd. Well, with the possible exception of the "Safe Sex Nazis." Or the "Just Say No to Drugs" crowd, or the "Monogamy Mommas" or the . . . wait, I'm running out of groups.

My point, and I do have one, is that we're humorless hypocrites when it comes to sex and I consider it my life's mission to poke fun of the hypocrisy till it goes away.

When it comes to sex all of us, at some point, fall off the stupid tree and hit every branch on the way down. Consider me the guy who helps you up, dusts you off, and shows you a better tree to climb. While making fun of you the entire time.

Hey, it's enough that I'm helping. I have to be nice, too?

I get a lot of satisfaction from writing this column. What could be more rewarding than liberating people from their fears, their preconceptions, their hesitancies? What could be more rewarding than helping people achieve a deeper understanding of their nature, their problems, their struggles? What could be better than knowing you helped someone overcome their shame and have a more rewarding sex life?

Other than fucking them, I mean.

Chapter 1

How Your Dick Works: How to Work Your Dick

This chapter is about the brain between our legs.

You don't need to write a sex advice column to know that the Great Male Decision-Maker suffers from a low IQ and a large appetite, a sometimes deadly but mostly comic combination. If you did, you'd know what most of the questions in this chapter are about. I wouldn't have to spell it out in big, long, and (did I mention) thick, letters.

Yes, the size of the prize is what draws the most letters. So let's put the subject to rest: Yes, size matters. To size queens. To the rest of us, it's right up there with six-pack abs and chiseled cheeks—nice, but nothing we'd throw you out of bed for if you didn't have it.

First, a fact: Condom manufacturers say only 6 percent of the male population needs extra-large condoms. You can imagine how that makes the other 94 percent feel.

If big dicks mean better sex then that means only 6 percent of all men have great sex. I don't think so. And neither do you, but it doesn't matter. We know great sex has little to do with size yet we obsess about it anyway.

Most of the letters I get about the subject are pathetic ("How can I make it bigger?" "How can I at least make it *look* bigger?"). The small number of people—size queens—who truly believe that bigger dicks mean better sex, have inflicted a terrible inferiority complex on gay men.

Nothing captures the poignancy, the pain of this, our magnificent cultural failure, like the letter I received from a twenty-five year-old. Read it. It will change the way you think and talk about dick size.

Otherwise, the letters I get on the purple-headed custard chucker are all over the map. Sadly, the inability to ejaculate in the presence of someone you love seems to be a common problem among gay men.

Sad because it reflects how uncomfortable some of us have become with having sex in the context of love. Gay men have more sex than anyone on the planet and yet in some ways we're the most inexperienced at it.

By trivializing sex, mechanizing it, "sizing" it, some of us have ended up removing it, permanently, from intimacy. Luckily, this is not the case for most gay men, who struggle with less tragic problems, like figuring out where their next ejaculation is going to land.

*   *   *

Hey, Woody!
Why are gay men so obsessed with penis size? I'm tired of going out on dates and having friends ask "how big was his bird?" I can just see my dates telling their friends how disappointed they were that they only got 6 inches when they reached into my pants. I don't know, maybe I'm just bitter that I'm not bigger. I think I'm pretty normal-sized, but then, I don't know what normal is. Do you?

—The normal hard

Dear Hard:
You know, the whole size obsession reminds me of a joke. Four Catholic ladies are having coffee together. The first one tells her friends, "My son is a priest. When he walks into a room, everyone says 'Father.'"

The second one chirps up, "My son is a bishop. Whenever he walks into a room, everyone says 'Your Grace.'"

The third Catholic lady says smugly, "My son is a cardinal. When he walks into a room, everyone says 'Your Eminence.'"

The fourth Catholic lady sips her coffee in silence. The first three ladies all ask, "Well?"

She replies, "My son is a 6' 2", hard-bodied stripper, and hung like a rhino. When he walks into a room, everyone says, *'Oh, my God.'*"

The point is . . . wait, I'm looking for it . . . oh, here it is, right where I left it. The point is that our obsession with size is a joke and we're the butt of it.

Here's the set-up: We act like the totality of sexual pleasure can be reduced to a hash mark on a ruler. Here's the punch line: It's not true.

Here's the proof: Ask yourself if the hottest sex you ever had involved a big dick. If you're honest, the answer is no. The answer is much more likely to have involved an electrifying chemistry with the other guy, because he kissed so well, because you were flat-out in love with him, because his smell had a pheromonish effect on you, because Fill In The Blank But It Probably Had Nothing To Do With The Size Of His Dick.

Don't get me wrong, size matters. Visually, but not sexually. When I think of the worst sex I've ever had, many of the sessions involved men with baseball bats between their legs.

Mutual desire, energy, love, lust, smell, sight, and a million other things in combination are more important than size. Alas, I know you're going to obsess about size no matter what I say. But if you're going to obsess do it with facts, not fear. And these are the facts: The largest study to date of "erect penile dimensions"—the Kinsey study—showed that the average erect dick size was 6.1 inches.

But the Kinsey study has a deal-breaking flaw: Kinsey's subjects measured *themselves. What was Kinsey thinking?* Asking men to measure their penis size in private and then report it truthfully? That kind of optimism should be bottled.

The most reliable study of penis size to date appears to be out of the University of California, San Francisco (where else?). In

1996, researchers let 80 men measure themselves with an observer present (don't ask, I'm just reporting it). And guess what? The average erect penis size dropped a *whole inch* from Kinsey's study, to 5.1 inches.

In other words, left to their own devices, men lie. Shocking isn't it? The study proved that lying about your dick-size is the most common male deception, second only to lying about your trick's dick size.

Here are some other stats from the groundbreaking study: Average erect girth, 4.8 inches. Average flaccid length, 3.5 inches, average flaccid girth, 3.8 inches.

There have only been three penis size studies that urologists consider reliable. The interesting thing is that each time a reliable study is done, it shows shorter and shorter erect penis sizes. Why? Because we're men. We lie, therefore we are.

Each successive study has had tighter and tighter controls to eliminate the, ahm, more creative mathematical interpretations of the ruler. Sadly, urologists are faced with the dilemma of men with normal-sized dicks wanting penile augmentation surgery because their sense of inadequacy is as big as the lies we tell ourselves.

Instead of fretting over how big we are, we should be concentrating on the real reasons that make sex with a man so great—the way he moves, the way he smells, the way he looks, the way he shtuups. And don't forget the greatest thing of all: The physical and emotional energy he brings out in you.

Hey, Woody!
I'm getting penis envy from hanging around the online chat rooms. Amazingly, the average dick size in these chat rooms is eight inches! Yes, eight inches! I know because people tell me so. Of course, they're measuring from the crack of their ass to the tip of their lies, but maybe I'm being a sore sport. My question: For those of us who want to know how big our dicks REALLY are, what's the best way of measuring them?

—Digging deep for one last inch

Dear Digger:

There are three great lies in gay life:

1. "I'm bisexual"
2. "I go to bars for the music"
3. "I have an eight inch dick"

You can't really prove the first two, but there's no hiding the third, unless you're online.

Penile size can be measured in a lot of ways. Obviously, the differences will impact the results. There are two widely recognized ways to measure the treasure. The most common is the "You Wish" method first popularized by America Online's chat rooms. It involves looking at your pinky and describing it as a thigh.

The more accurate method, preferred by urologists unconcerned with scoring potential, involves the following:

1. Using a paper tape measure, not a ruler
2. Measuring to the nearest half-centimeter, not the nearest half-foot
3. Measuring flaccid length as soon as you undress (room temperature and other factors will affect length and girth)
4. Boy, are you guys going to scream at this one: Forget about starting the measurement from where your balls meet your dick. The proper measurement starts at the junction of skin between your pubic hair area and the base of your dick. In other words, when you're erect, measure the side of the penis facing your stomach. I know. It sucks. But that's how all studies do it.

Actually, there's a much faster and easier way to measure your cock. You don't even need to get hard to do it. All you have to do is stretch your flaccid flogger and measure it from the penopubic region to the tip. Believe it or not, every major study shows a high correlation between erectile and flaccid-stretched length.

To measure girth, use your partner's mouth and . . . wait. No, that's later. Place the edge of the tape measure on your erectness right under the glans (you know, the edge of the "helmet"). When all is said and done, the majority of us will fall somewhere near 5.1 inches in length and 4.8 inches in girth.

Skip the weepy letters about how awful it is to have an average-sized dick. Studies show that men with larger than average penises do not report greater sexual satisfaction than men with average-sized dicks.

I know you didn't hear me so I'm going to say it again: Having a bigger dick doesn't mean you'll have a more satisfying sex life.

Hey, Woody!

I like it when guys play with my balls but one overly ambitious squeeze and it hurts like a mother. My dick may be sensitive but I'm never afraid of guys hurting it. I am afraid, though, of having my balls hurt. Why does sensitivity in my dick mean pleasure but in my balls it means pain?

—Scrotum-scratcher

Dear Scrotum-scratcher:

Why are our balls so sensitive? Survival of the species. Mother Nature made our testicles sensitive so we'd stand guard over her precious jewels. The more we guard, the more likely we're able to impregnate women. Some of us, anyway.

Of course, what nobody tells you is that Mother Nature is a post-op transsexual. What else could explain the fact that she made testicles the genetic equivalent of female ovaries? The same sack of cells that become testicles in men become ovaries in women. The testes actually rest inside the pelvis during fetal development and descend before birth.

Testicles are home to seminiferous tubules where sperm is produced. "Seminiferous" means to contain or convey semen. It's just another way of saying "My Boyfriend's Mouth," really.

The testes (another word for testicles) also rent out space to interstitial cells which produce a majority of your testosterone, which as you know, is the reason you're such a pig.

Testes is Latin for "to testify." Instead of placing their right hand on the Bible, the early Romans put their hand on their testicles when they testified in a court of law. We're just a couple of centuries late from hearing the judge say "Do you swear to tell the whole truth and nothing but the truth, so help your balls?"

Hey, Woody!
I'm in my mid-twenties, I'm good-looking and I know it. I work out five days a week and you could slice tomatoes on my stomach—my abs are that ripped. For the past two months I've been dating a great guy. He is all that and a bag of chips. He has just about anything you would want in a man. So what could possibly be wrong? Me, gym bunny, can't come when I'm having sex with this guy. I mean sometimes I can, but mostly I can't, even when he's fucking me. I've always had this problem but it gets worse when I really like a guy. And this guy I really like. Do you have any suggestions or helpful hints? I've tried different kinds of positions but nothing really helps. Oh, and one more thing. Is there any physical damage to having sex regularly but NOT coming?
                                    —Full of muscles and too much cum

Dear Full:
Mid-twenties and ripped abs, you say? Too bad I don't make house calls; I'd milk you like a cow.

First, the easy question. No, chronic avoidance of ejaculation will not harm you. Your spooge will come out anyway through nocturnal emissions. It will, however, make you temporarily less likely to fertilize an egg. But, just between us boys, unless we're talking about omelets who cares about eggs?

You're suffering from "retarded ejaculation." Well, that's what the doctors call it when they're awake and sober, which frankly, is happening less and less since the advent of managed care.

They also call it "ejaculatory incompetence." It's an inhibition of the ejaculatory reflex in the presence of a partner. About one to four percent of men suffer from it, according to the National Institute of Mental Health.

If you have any sexual dysfunction always check out the possibility there may be a medical condition causing it. You said you could come when you're jerking off alone, so congratulations, there's nothing medically wrong with you. You're just nuts.

Or maybe you're just on drugs. The kind that "retard" ejaculation. Anti-depressants are famous for keeping the baby from burping. So are other drugs like guanethidine, which lowers blood pressure.

If there's no medical or drug explanation, experts say the leading causes of retarded ejaculation are: 1) Strict religious backgrounds (can you spell "G-U-I-L-T?"); 2) Deeply-grooved masturbation patterns (you can only come if you're doing the one thing you've been doing for years); and 3) Traumatic events (being discovered while masturbating, finding out your lover is cheating, or worse, finding out he's NOT cheating).

If the problem is situational, a little mental re-framing can help. You can't "will" yourself into an ejaculation any more than you can will yourself to sleep or to sweat. So don't "try." The harder you try the more inhibited you'll become. The only way to master an involuntary reflex is to stop caring so much about it. If it's not that big a deal whether you ejaculate, you'll have more ejaculations.

Very Zen, isn't it?

And twisted, too. The only way you can get what you really want is by not wanting it? How fucked is that? But it's true. It's one of the key components in treating involuntary dysfunctions.

Your problem isn't situational though, it's chronic. And for that you need to get on the couch and figure out what issue you're dealing with. Therapy's success rate is very high, around 70–80 percent in 12–18 sessions if you go to a sex therapist. Don't go to a regular therapist.

And for God's sakes, don't go to the psychologist my editor goes to. Actually, he goes to a psycholofist, the kind that put their hands up your ass in search of an insight. Which explains a lot about my editor, come to think of it.

Hey, Woody!
I just saw some porn videos by this French company called Bel Ami—you know, the ones with that hot guy "Lucas." Can I just say three words? Oh. My. God. But I digress. The videos were filled with gorgeous but uncircumcised men. I've been with a lot of men, but never with an uncut one, so it was kind of shocking for me to see it. Still, I was really turned on by it. Now I'm dying to go home with an uncut guy, but I can't find anybody! Why is that? Also, if there's more skin on the penis does that mean there's more feeling in it?
—Feelin' gypped cuz I got clipped

Dear Gyp:
How do you get uncut guys? The same way you get uncut cocaine—you leave the country. About 85 percent of the world's male population is uncircumcised. Experts think only about 20 percent of American men are uncut (am I the only one wondering who takes the count, and where do you sign up to assist?).

Basically, if you want to swim with the hoods you're going to have to hang in their 'hoods. The 20 percent of Americans who are uncut are probably of Latino descent or from other cultures that don't have a strong tradition of cutting the man out of their boys.

As a culture, we believe that circumcised penises are more hygienic, even though there is no real supporting data. Some reports show circumcision lowers risks for infant urinary tract infections, penile cancer, and possibly-maybe-but-nobody's-sure, sexually transmitted diseases. But come on, infant urinary tract infections aren't very common and penile cancer is extremely rare.

We've turned circumcision into a fashion statement and disguised it as a medical need so we can feel good about it.

In fact, the American Academy of Pediatrics was so unimpressed with the clipping crowd that in 1975 it recommended that circumcision no longer be performed as a routine procedure because it wasn't medically necessary.

Most experts agree that the uncircumcised penis is more sexually sensitive. It makes sense if you think about it—the heads of most American dicks are constantly rubbing up against underwear (or, for some of you out in the bars, denim), while our compatriots around the world get to wear protective sausage sacks. Well, no wonder Latinos are so passionate! They're feeling so much more than we are. Too bad we can't paste our foreskins back on. I'd do it faster than you could say "prepuce."

Hey, Woody!
Several years ago a boyfriend squeezed the head of my cock just as I was about to ejaculate. He was trying to stop a premature ejaculation but I came anyway and it hurt like a motherfucker. Later on I developed what I think is Peyronie's disease—a bent erection. Plus, the head of my cock doesn't engorge as much as it used to. Medication given to me by a urologist helped very little. He said surgery is my best bet. Is it?

—Bent over

Dear Bent:
Peyronie's Disease (curvature of the penis) can develop from drama to the penis. Wait, that's not right. If that were true, my dick would look like a pretzel. I meant "trauma."

As in rough sex trauma, or in your case, shit-for-brains boyfriend trauma. Here's what most likely happened to you: When Mr. Stand Back I Know What I'm Doing squeezed your cock, the pressure from the ejaculation caused microscopic tears in the vascular pathway. As it healed, scar tissue formed and allowed plaque to build up, essentially calcifying the direction of your joystick.

Scar tissue pulls on one side of the tissue while expanding the other, creating the unseemly bend that marks Peyronie's disease. If it's a slight case, vitamin E taken orally might help. Forget the creams, they're like AOL chat room profiles—all hat and no cattle. Approximately 20 percent of the cases resolve spontaneously. If yours doesn't, surgery is the only effective way of straightening you out.

Surgery on your dick may sound scary, but think of it as an orgy: You're laying there with your thighs wide open and everybody around you wants a piece of you.

Hey, Woody!
Sometimes I go weeks without so much as beating off. When I finally break my "fast" I get an awful cramp-like feeling when I cum. It sort of feels like it's coming from the bottom of my ass. It goes away after a few minutes but I'm concerned.

—Getting off but getting worried

Dear Worried:
It's probably just a muscle cramp. The bulbocoxygeous muscles control ejaculation and are closely related to the genital and lower rectum muscles.

Which reminds me, are all scientists drunk when they name body parts?

Anyway, during ejaculation, these muscles pulse and contract like your eyes do at a college wrestling meet—you know, involuntarily. This helps propel semen out through the urethra.

The bulbocoxygeous muscles are likely to cramp up when their hibernation is suddenly and forcefully terminated. When you don't cum for a long time, your load would strain the fittest UPS delivery man, so what do you think it's doing to your "bulbo" muscles? Your question calls for the answer I love to give: "Have more sex."

Hey, Woody!
The good news is that I got us into the soccer play-offs by
blocking the opposing team's penalty kick. The bad news
is I blocked it with my crotch. I'm still limping from it. My
question: Why did my stomach hurt so much if it was my
balls that took the hit?

—Ballsy

Dear Ballsy:
The reason your stomach hurt so much is that the testes are connected to the abdomen by nerves and blood vessels. Testes form
in the abdominal cavity and then they descend into the scrotum
sack before birth.

Warning—tangent coming up: "Undescended" testicles are
fairly common in premature babies and occur in about 4 percent
of all full-term babies. If they can't "find" your testes (funny, my
boyfriend never has that problem), an abdominal ultrasound
may help figure out where the suckers went.

Okay—back from the tangent. Getting a soccer ball kicked
into your groin is no laughing matter. I'm wincing even as I type.
The recommendation: Ice packs for the first 24 hours, followed
by sitz baths, and then by prayer. A blow like that could result in
"testicular torsion," a serious emergency where the testicle becomes twisted in the scrotum and loses its blood supply. You've
got about two hours from the time it happens for a doc to relieve
the twisting or you can literally kiss your testicle goodbye.

Hey, Woody!
When I woke up from penis enlargement surgery, my penis
was way swollen and covered in a kind of maroonish pur-
ple color. Injecting fat into my dick was part of the proce-
dure and there were stitches all over the place. My
stomach was bandaged and so were my thighs where the
fat had been suctioned out (I didn't have enough fat in my
stomach so they took it from my legs).

Seven months later I'm still bruised from the liposuction and my dick hurts like hell. My new enlarged penis has a marble-like lump close to the head with two smaller bumps around the base. I'm headed for surgery again, to undo the mutilation. I don't have a question for you, what I have is a warning for all your readers and I can sum it up in one word: DON'T.

—Did and regretted it

Dear Did:

Oh, come on, you big crybaby. The 98 percent of you guys who suffer the anatomical abominations of penis enlargement surgery ruin it for the 2 percent who walk away satisfied.

I refuse to discourage people from experiencing crooked, lumpy, and deformed shafts, erections that point downward, raw nerves caught in scar tissue, and fluid that chronically collects around the testicles.

So what if every major medical association in this country considers penis augmentation to be experimental surgery? So what if the surgery is so controversial and yields such poor results that it's considered unacceptable by both plastic surgeons and urologists (unless you fall into the 2 percent of people identified as having a "micro-phallus")?

I say go for it. Don't let facts and common sense over-rule your vanity. I say plunk down $7,000 to $10,000 for penile augmentation surgery, especially if you have an averaged-sized dick. You wouldn't be alone. Most of the guys requesting the surgery are average-sized.

There is a cheaper, alternative form of penis enlargement, though. The procedure is simple: You put your penis on my desk, I whack it with a hammer, and it swells for about six months. It gives you the same results as the surgery at a fraction of the cost.

Dude, you needed help between the ears, not between your legs. Good luck. You're going to need it.

Hey, Woody!
Maybe it's my imagination but it seems guys with bigger
dicks have a tougher time achieving full erections than
guys with smaller dicks.

—Am I right or wrong?

Dear Wrong:
See my greeting for the answer. Most urologists don't report a
connection between big dicks and a rougher time getting a full
erection.

However, researchers believe it may be easier to treat erectile
dysfunction in men with shorter dicks. Because so many treatments rely on partially increasing blood flow to the penis, they
believe treatment for erectile dysfunction is more effective in
men with smaller dicks (because they require less blood to fill
them up).

My ex-boyfriend would have made a great treatment for erectile dysfunction. Small dicks, big dicks, it wouldn't matter. He understood the concept of blood flowing to the penis like no one
else. Too bad he doesn't come in pill form.

Hey, Woody!
I've gone on a date with this guy three times. We mash and
do everything but cum, because he won't let me (or him-
self). Something about "Let's wait." It's like dating a girl.
But my question is this: My testicles are sore after our
sessions. Why?

—All balled up

Dear Ball:
You, my friend, are experiencing blue-balls, or technically-speaking,
"prostatic congestion." It's caused by a build-up of semen in the
prostate and seminal vesicles, the two glands that produce most
of the semen your date refuses to unleash. Sperm can literally
build up, creating pressure and pain around the testicles.

Here's what happens: You're on the couch mashing with a

hottie but, for whatever reason, he doesn't want to give you what you deserve. Your sperm get trapped in the highway traffic jam because Mr. You Won't Respect Me In The Morning refuses to grant you an exit lane. When blood stays in the genitals for a long enough time, it can cause achiness (blue-balls).

You've got three options when it happens: Take an aspirin, a warm shower, or do the job yourself. Orgasm really does relieve "blue-balls."

Hey, Woody!
Sometimes I get a hard-on so hard it hurts and the problem is that it won't go away for hours. Should I be worried?
—Hurtin' when it's hard

Dear Hurtin':
Sounds to my experts like you may have a condition called priapism. It's a prolonged and painful erection that can last from several hours up to a few days. The blood flows into the penis, but it won't drain normally.

When the blood in the penis becomes stagnant it can acidify and lose oxygen—like your friends on the dance floor at 6 a.m. Without oxygen, the red blood cells become stiff—again like your friends—and even less able to squeeze their way out of the penis. Wait, that sounds more like MY friends.

Priapism can be caused by penile injections used to treat some forms of impotence. Some anti-depressants can cause it too. Another cause of priapism are certain medical conditions like anemia or leukemia. You MUST go see a doctor. Priapism can scar the penis if not treated early enough, and can lead to impotence.

Oh, and you'll love how they'll drain your dick—by sticking it with a big fat needle. If that's what you're up against, remember the words my father uttered when I was ten years old. He poured me a shot of whiskey and said "It's never too late to start drinking."

Hey, Woody!
I spent a lot of time in Europe and I got really turned on by uncircumcised penises. It's the norm over there. I love the sharp odor. I call it "dickincense."

In America, dicks smell just like any other body part. I'm going out with a European living in the U.S. and thank God I get a faceful of dickincense and myrrh when I unzip his fly. My question is, when does the distinctive odor turn offensive? Sometimes I go from being turned on to turned off because it smells a little different.

—Taking the time to smell the smegma

Dear Smeg:
Smegma and sweat combine like high and low pressure zones to produce the kind of wind that sets sails or droops mastheads, depending on your personal choice.

Smegma is a cheesy secretion found under the foreskin. It's also found under the Capitol Rotunda when Congress is in session. Smegma can act as a natural lube, though I suspect most Americans aren't ready for that visual. Smegma can be a friend, despite its off-putting name. Clinical studies show it has anti-bacterial and anti-viral properties.

Still, macaroni and cheese should be served on the dinner table, not in the bedroom, so pulling back the foreskin and washing away excess smegma is important. Hygienically, if excess smegma isn't washed away, it can turn to glue, preventing the foreskin from easily moving back and forth along the head of the penis.

If his penis perfume turns bad, it could be an infection. Yes, women aren't the only ones who can bake someone happy with a yeast infection. But you'll know if that's what it is—there's redness and abnormal pus. To prevent infection, uncircumcised men need to retract their foreskin and wash with soap and water every day. Sorry, boyfriend spit doesn't have the cleaning power to do the job.

Hey, Woody!
I'm constantly comparing my dick size to other guys and I
always feel like I'm smaller than average. Intellectually, I
know I'm at least average size (I've asked some of my
partners and they've all said I'm actually bigger than aver-
age), but why does it FEEL like I have a small dick? I'm
kind of obsessed about it. In the locker room I check other
guys out and they always look bigger than I do. I'm not a
size queen, I just want to feel okay about what I've got,
but I don't. Any words of wisdom?
—A lobster who feels like a shrimp

Dear Lobster:
Perception is everything. And perception is often colored by position. Like the position of your eyes when you look. Guys always look bigger than you do because you're looking down at
yours and straight on at theirs. When you look down at something it always looks shorter than if you look straight at it. If
you're going to go through the process of comparing yourself to
other guys, at least be fair to yourself. Look at your dick from the
same angle you look at others. Use a mirror.

You need to heal this obsession you have about being smaller
than other guys. First, get some facts to fight your fiction. Measure yourself with a cloth tape. Compare your pole to the polls:
The average length of a penis is 3.5 inches when it's flaccid and
5.1 inches when it's hard. No, that wasn't a typo. The average
length of a man's erect penis is 5.1. inches.

However, the average length of a man's imagination is eight
inches, and that's the problem. A while ago *Men's Fitness* did a
poll of over 5,000 men aged 29-32, asking them to guess the average size of a man's erect penis. Fifteen percent said seven
inches, four percent said eight inches and two percent said nine
inches.

It just goes to show you how clueless men are about size. And
just about any other aspect of sex. Especially straight men.
Men's Fitness reported how a sex expert went to a bar and asked

men to pinpoint a woman's clitoris on a diagram. The ninth guy got it right. Good thing the expert didn't ask gay guys to pinpoint a man's heart. He'd still be at the bar.

Anyway, make sure you're measuring correctly. I hate to dash your hopes on the rocks of reality, but forget about measuring from your balls to the tip of your cock. That's how tacos get confused with burritos. The only acceptable standard in sex research is to measure it from the base of the penis facing your stomach when you're lying down. Odd, how the word "lying" seems so appropriate in discussions about size, eh?

Hey, Woody!
I have seen many a schlong in my life—big ones, small ones, fat ones, skinny ones, hooded ones, bald ones—you name, it I've seen it. Curiously, they all had one thing in common: They were darker than the bodies they dangled from. Why doesn't the color of dicks match their owner's bodies?
                    —Wondering when I'm not slobbering

Dear Wondering:
Hey, what about the scrotum? It has a darker coloration too. But no, you didn't mention that, Mr. Penis-centric. As a journalist once asked a bunch of Nixon-obsessed historians, "Dick, Dick, Dick. Is that all you guys think about?"

Anyway, back to the question. The answer depends on Dick's condition (yours, not Nixon's. He's dead, you know). Is he saluting or lying in the hammock? If he's hard, his skin will look darker because anything engorged with blood is going to darken. Well, except vegetarians. They look pasty whether they're engorged or not.

Actually, dicks are generally darker than the bodies they hang from, whether they're hard or soft. At birth they start out the same color. But at puberty, Nature introduces Willie to a special friend—your hand.

As Mr. Nice To Meet You, Too, You Can Let Go Now will tell

anybody who'll listen, someone needs to teach you the difference between a handshake and a chokehold.

But I digress.

Genitals will darken with or without your insolent hands. It's part of the sexual maturation process. But being manhandled hastens the process. If we grabbed our faces the way we grab our dicks, the skin on our cheeks would look like a tar pit, too.

Hey, Woody!
Help me shoot farther, man! I want to explode like a rocket when I cum but I end up dripping like a leaky faucet instead. When I'm cumming I feel like my whole body is going to explode—like I'm going to shoot all over the room, so why does it just dribble out? I get jealous whenever I watch porn and see these guys painting walls from across the room. Is there any way to increase my "shooting" range?

—Dribbler

Dear Dribbler:
There's little you can do to increase the arc of your spark. Genetics plays the biggest factor. Only a lucky few are born with the ability to spray semen like a depressed teenager with an Uzi at a suburban high school.

There actually are two things you can do to increase the spread of your spray, but they're a hassle and take a lot of discipline. First, stop whacking off so much. The more ejaculate you "save," the more distance you'll earn. It's like a pressure valve—the more pressure, the harder you'll blow. But hell, who wants to reduce the frequency of coming just so you can shot-put the white stuff a few inches farther?

Orgasms happen via a spinal cord reflex that causes strong rhythmic contractions in the urogenital system. Your ejaculation isn't ruled by your hand, your partner's mouth, or your wild imagination. It's ruled by the urethra, the prostate, and the muscles at the base of the penis as they involuntarily contract.

You can't do anything to strengthen the urethra or the prostate other than having frequent orgasms (they're not kidding when they say "use it or lose it"). Wouldn't it be great if you could work out the urethra and the prostate at the gym? Imagine the lines at the machines. Or asking somebody for a spot.

The muscles at the base of the penis (pubococcygeous muscles, otherwise known as the PC muscles) can be strengthened through Kegel exercises. How do you figure out where the muscles are? Well, you know when you're peeing on your partner and he changes his mind and orders you to stop and you shut yourself off mid-stream? Those are the muscles.

Just contract and relax them in a series of sets. Hold them tight for 10 seconds and let them go. Vary them by doing "butterflies" (contracting and relaxing as fast as you can). Work up to hundreds of these a day. After a few months, you should notice stronger, more powerful orgasms and ejaculations. Yes, you read right, I said after a few MONTHS.

If it's any consolation, most of the porn personnel (sorry, I can't bring myself to call them "stars") can't shoot very far either. To get the money shot they want, directors will often use synthetic semen which is shot-squeezed from a small tube. The preferred substance is condensed milk.

I want to see Jeff Stryker, milk-mustached, hawking dairy products in magazines with a headline asking "Shot Milk?" Talk about new uses for an old product.

Hey, Woody!
A straight friend started poking his girlfriend right after a vasectomy. I told him he should wait cuz he could still get her pregnant. He said "Shut-up, you're gay, what do you know?"

I said let's bet and if I'm wrong, you blow me. Please tell me I'm right.

—Waiting to collect

Dear Waiting:
Drop your drawers and buy him some kneepads. A vasectomy cuts or blocks the vas deferens, the tube that carries sperm away from the testicles (and adds it to the liquid components of semen). But sperm already in the pipeline can still cause pregnancy. The ideal is to wait for 30 days or about ten ejaculations to flush out remaining sperm.

Even then, I wouldn't recommend poking his girlfriend without first going back to the doctor with a sample of ejaculatory fluid for a sperm count test. Until he knows for sure he's shooting blanks, he needs to use birth control.

About 500,000 vasectomies are performed annually. It's an outpatient procedure that takes 15 to 20 minutes. About the time it'll take him to give you a long, slobbery blow job.

Hey, Woody!
How do you check yourself for testicular cancer?
—Going nuts with fear

Dear Nuts:
Checking your balls should be a monthly routine. First, take a warm bath or shower to relax the scrotum and have it descend to its lowest level. Then roll each testicle between your fingers and press gently. It should be smooth and oval-shaped, like a hard-boiled egg.

You're looking for lumps or hard areas that don't seem to belong in the neighborhood. Interestingly, tumors are more likely to be found in the right testicle than the left. I swear, whether it's tumors or arrogance, the right always has more than the left.

Warning: Tangent approaching. If your boyfriend tries to cut your balls off for cheating and he only slices one of them on account of you're fast and easy and that's what got you into trouble in the first place, the good news is that one testicle is plenty to produce enough testosterone to get it up and cheat again. It doesn't take much for the nectar of the gods to do its job. Of course, your tricks might gross out. In that case, you can have a synthetic testicle inserted, much like the way artificial breasts are inserted into half the women in Hollywood.

Testicular cancer is the most common form of cancer for guys up to age 35. It's highly curable if, IF, you detect it early. If you're lump-free, celebrate and jerk yourself off. Hell, you're already down there, why waste the trip?

Hey, Woody!
When my partner was fucking me really hard his dick slipped out right before he was going to ram me. He ended up jamming it into my perineum instead. He screamed in pain and we haven't fucked since. He's blaming it on me, saying he's afraid I might "break his penis." How do I get back what I gotta have?

—Dick breaker

Dear Dick:
A penis can't "break" in the normal sense of the word because there is no bone in it. Well, at least the ones I've tried to break haven't.

What can break is one of the three tubes that hold the blood of an erection. But if this happened your partner would have acted like he read this column—he would have heard a popping sound and then he would've doubled over in pain. And when he looked up his dick would be severely bruised.

Your problem sounds more like a trust issue than a medical one. Talk to him about it and be everything I'm not: kind, patient, and sensitive. Have gentle oral and manual sex and work your way up to the slash-and-burn fucking.

Hey, Woody!
I can just look at a hot guy and—oh, dear—there go the buttons on my jeans. It's, totally involuntarily, like magic.

But I know there's a science to it, too. What exactly happens "down there" when I get the Man-hots?

—Just curious

Dear Just:

Well, you're right, it's not magic. Your manhood doesn't throb because elves spray trixie-dust on it. It throbs because the blood in your body decided it was time to play "pack the sausage."

The penis has a head and body (glans and shaft). And for once in male life, the head has more say than the body. That's because the head, or glans, has a higher concentration of nerve endings than the shaft.

The entire penis has a lot of nerve endings that make it sensitive to touch, pressure, and temperature. The glans has a coronal ridge separating it from the shaft (the outer edge of the "helmet").

On the underside of the penis (the side your trick sees when he kneels in front of you) there's a small triangular region where a thin strip of skin called the frenulum attaches to the glans. Both the coronal ridge and the frenulum are highly sensitive. Slurp there and he's yours for the night.

The shaft of the penis is made up of three cylinders of soft, spongy tissue, which contain a lot of small blood vessels. What you think of as Man-Meat Magic is actually the blood vessels of the spongy tissues filling with blood and swelling up. That's the science. The art is finding a port that will dock your swollen ship and let you unload the precious cargo.

The transition from a soft (flaccid) penis to a harder, stiffer penis is called getting an erection. In my house it's simply known as "Dinner."

Hey, Woody!
Latex is a pillar-killer. I generally have no problem catching and holding a lumber-yard worth of wood, but when I put on a condom, the loss of sensation and something psychological about it, brings me down to about 3 out of 5 stars on the bone-meter.

This is usually not a big deal since most guys, once I've gotten them nice and relaxed, can easily accommodate me. Once I get going, we're right back on terra-firma regardless of the rubber.

But recently I've been seeing this gorgeous guy who's just . . . well . . . really tight, no matter how relaxed he is. This would be a blessing if we could get going with the horizontal hula, but my rubber-covered "semi" just ain't stiff enough to part the curtains, and losing the latex ain't an option.

We've tried lots of things to relax him more, and keep me hard, and nothing works. Of course, the mental part gets a little worse with each failed attempt. Any suggestions? I don't think I can do "cock rings" . . . I think they look silly and the idea seems kind of unhealthy.

—Too soft to boff

Dear Softie:

First, you need to know that a lot of men experience what you're going through. You ain't the first witch to yell *"Help me, I'm melting."*

Don't run from cock rings till you try them. There's absolutely nothing unhealthy about it. They come in three of my favorite flavors—rubber, leather and metal. Cock rings fasten around the base of the penis and testicles to keep the pillar from peeling. It works by trapping the blood in the penis. Go for the adjustable straps, that way you can adjust to your size. The metal rings can be hard to pull off, so don't get them unless you want to stand in the middle of the emergency room trying to explain why you can't get rid of your hard-on.

There is also a multi-ringed toy called the Gates of Hell, but something tells me you're not ready for it.

If you're dead set against the ring, I have three suggestions:

1. Relax, nobody performs well under self-induced pressure. It's okay not to fuck every time you're with him. Do everything but that, the next few times you see him.

2. Introduce him to a boy toy, like Peter the Penetrator. A dildo, or artificial penis, is usually made of stiff flesh-colored latex and runs about 6 to 9 inches in total length. Pant, pant. They also make them smaller, for beginners. I can't think of a better way of loosening him up.
3. Viagra. But I have to qualify this because there's a danger you'll end up using Viagra as a crotch-crutch. I think you should use it a two or three times as a way to reverse the mental spiral you're in about not getting it up. Once you've gained your confidence (and he a wider stretch), stop taking the Viagra and swim without the water wings. But talk to the doc first. About 10 percent of men taking Viagra report side effects like headaches, dizziness, facial flushing, indigestion, and visual disturbance. You know, like when you listen to Jerry Falwell. Do not use Viagra with nitrate medications, and forget the entire recommendation if you have even the hint of a heart condition.

Hey, Woody!
I'm 38 and I jerk off every day without fail. Sometimes twice a day. Is this normal for my age? Also, will jerking off that much increase my chances of getting prostate cancer since I'm over-using the gland?
—Worried I'll break something

Dear Worried:
Once a day for your age is higher than average but within the normal range. Better to use it too much than not enough. "Use it or lose it" isn't just an excuse for your hands to migrate south, it's the official tested and studied conclusion of sex experts. The less you use your sexual plumbing, the more problems you're going to have pumping the well later on.

As far as too much ejaculation causing prostate cancer, that sounds like something a catholic priest would say. What is true is that the prostate is a little temperamental about how much ejaculatory fluid to produce. Any dramatic increase or decrease in the frequency of ejaculation irritates it, which sometimes leads to prostatitis, or inflammation of the prostate. Like any factory, it likes a schedule.

Hey, Woody!
Why do I have this line all the way down my penis and over my testicles?

—**Linear man**

Dear Linear:
It means if you don't keep your hands where they belong your dick is going to crack open in half like a coconut. Well, that's what my priest told me when I was twelve, anyway.

Actually, it's like a "seam" on the underside of the penis. It forms when the fetus is in the uterus. In women, the seam becomes the inner lips of their vagina. In men, the seam encloses the urethra along the length of the penis.

Hey, Woody!
My scrotum seems to ride high against my body, hardly ever lowering like most guys. Should I worry?

—**Worried about my boys**

Dear Worried:
The scrotum is the sack that holds the testicles. It has a muscle affected by temperature. When it's warm, the muscle pulls out a lawn chair and starts sunning itself, making the scrotum and testicles hang lower. Cold makes it fold the lawn chair up and bring the boys in for some hot chocolate. There is a condition that prevents testicles from descending into the scrotum.

Check it out by feeling your testicles (with your own hands, thank you) inside your scrotum. There's a reason we call them nuts—they should feel like peanuts in their shells. If you can't feel them or you're confused, get an appointment with a urologist and ask him if you're nuts. Or whether you have any in your scrotum.

Hey, Woody!
You've talked about the length and girth of our prized puppies but you've never talked about the angle of the dangle. I've slept with guys who hard up in all kinds of angles—some like a rocket, some like a boomerang and others like the Tower of Pisa. Is there an average angle?
                              —Working all the angles

Dear Angler:
According to the experts the best way to measure the trajectory of your hard-on (mine's always aiming "mouthward"), is to stand with your back against the wall. Then get yourself hard. Better yet, get somebody else to get you hard. If the head of your dick points directly in front of you, you've hardened at 90 degrees. 180 degrees means the head of your dick points to the ceiling. The average? 106 degrees.

Hey, Woody!
I keep hearing about exercising your "penis muscles." Hell, I thought I was doing that every time I entered my partner. What am I missing?
                              —Too busy playing to exercise

Dear Busy:
Just as every team exercises before playing the game, every member should exercise before playing the field. If you really want to get good at sex you have to master the domain between your legs.

Strictly speaking, your penis isn't a muscle, so you can't exercise it. You can take it for a swim in the tunnel of love or make it do push-ups and pull-ups with your hands, but it's not the same thing. It's the muscles *around* your penis that need exercising. Namely, the pubococcygeal—"PC"—muscles, which are located in the lower pelvis and form a horizontal sling between your legs.

Did someone say "sling"? Yes, but not the kind that makes you scream "Mount me, Hercules, I am your mare!" This sling is filled with muscles crucial to putting the flex back in sex. Experts agree that regularly exercising your PC muscles (also called Kegels) can increase the strength of your erection, give you more control of your ejaculations, and deliver more powerful orgasms. Daily exercising gives you more contractions when you ejaculate. And who doesn't want that?

Finding your PC muscles is easy. Next time you're taking a piss, start and stop the flow of urine. The muscles you use to stop pissing are your PC muscles.

The basic exercises are the "Flutter" (tighten and let go quickly) and the "Pinch and Hold" (tighten and don't let go till you count to 15). You need to work up to a couple of hundred reps a day for a few weeks before you notice the effects.

To get the best of your Kegel exercises, don't do them all while sitting or standing. Try Kegeling while lying on your back or side, or while squatting. Different positions help give your PC muscles better tone. Try doing "Kegels" when you're hard, too. Squeezing the PC muscles after you've pitched your pup tent makes your penis jerk up. Have your partner hold a finger about an inch above your penis and flex hard enough to touch it 10 times in a row. Or go for the bonus round by placing your partner's *mouth* an inch away. Now *that's* what I call home fitness training.

Of course, my favorite Kegel exercise is what I call "Lift and Separate." Enter your partner, flex, and watch him separate. Your partner can do it, too. It'll feel like your penis is getting massaged. Sticking to an exercise regimen will help you stick it to your partner but good. Now hit the floor and give me a hundred Kegels.

Hey, Woody!
I've been thinking of getting a penile augmentation proce-
dure to give me a bigger cock. Only thing is, it scares me to
go under the knife. What if they cut the wrong thing? Still,
I feel as if making myself bigger is the only way to com-
pete with all the pretty boys. Should I do it?

—Uncut

Dear Uncut:
When are we gay men going to learn that what's between our
ears has more to do with sexual satisfaction than what's between our legs? We're like Republicans who make a living flog-
ging the welfare system even though it represents maybe 3
percent of the gross national product. Penis size represents even
less than that of our gross sexual pleasure but that's the only
thing we pay attention to.

That's not to say that big cocks aren't a turn-on; they are. But
so what if you're not big? The hottest sex rarely involves size. It's
about how someone touches you, looks at you, feels to you; it's
how they woo you, how they shtuup you, how they kiss you; how
they move in bed, how they move on you; how they move the
earth. If you think having a bigger dick gives you a better sex life,
forget it. Research shows no difference in reported sexual satisfaction between men who have sockeye salmons swimming
against the current of their jeans and men who have tadpoles
lapping up their boxers. According to men with big dicks, men
with big dicks are no more sexually satisfied than men with
small or medium-sized dicks.

The emphasis on size in the gay community is overwhelming.
It's like a run-a-away eighteen-wheeler careening down an icy
hill. It slams everything off the road, especially the people who
try to slow it down. We insist that "bigger is better" and snidely
brush off the possibility that cock size isn't important.

There is profound misery in the gay community about "measuring up." And the irony is that some of the bigger specimens
among us are the loudest complainers. "During routine physicals

I've seen some of the biggest penises in captivity," one of my medical advisors told me. "And it's pitiful because these guys are convinced they're small."

What's even more pitiful is what urologists say: Most of the men seeking penile augmentation have normal-sized dicks. Urologists also report that many men don't care about their erections getting bigger, they just want to attract more attention in the locker room (there's actually a procedure for making your flaccid penis bigger without impacting the size of your erect penis).

So do I think penile augmentation is desirable for you? Yes, if you're one of the 2.5 percent of the male population who has a "micro penis" (believe it or not, that's the clinical term). But even then, urologists report you'll actually have less sensation than you do now. And it's not uncommon for a tectonic shift—having the additional fat and skin slide over to one side. Hmmm, *that's* attractive.

As for the other 97.5 percent of the population I have a different piece of advice: Get your head out of your ass. There are better things to put up there.

Hey, Woody!
I notice my penis has a prominent vein that I haven't noticed on other guys. Is this something I should worry about?

—Striped and worried

Dear Striped:
Visible veins on the penis aren't unusual. The valves in your testicles may be hiccuping involuntarily. Try scaring them by getting a stud to sneak up behind you and grab them while he yells "Gotcha!" If that doesn't work, send him to my house and quit being so selfish.

Either way, you don't have much to worry about. Prominent veins rarely interfere with hot sex. They're just abnormally dilated. If the valves in the veins are defective, blood can pool, distending the vessel walls. The condition is pretty harmless. For most, it's a cosmetic annoyance. If it really bothers you, your doctor can remove it.

Hey, Woody!
Is it true that a man's erect penis size can be predicted by dividing his shoe size in half?

—Just wondering

Dear Wondering:
No, but you can predict my average letter-writer's IQ by locating the page number this column appears and dividing it in half.

What, are you kidding me with that shit? There is no research validating any correlation between penis size and *Fill In The Blank*. Bigger hands? Bigger gloves. Bigger noses? Bigger boogers. Now go home and come up with an interesting question.

Hey, Woody!
My salmon is sagging. It used to point toward the ceiling when it got hard, now it droops at a ninety-degree angle. Is this normal as you grow older or should I be worried?

—Party-drooper

Dear Party-drooper:
Getting older sucks. Women get sagging tits, men get droopy dicks, and drag queens get tapes that skip.

Here's why dicks hit bricks: As you age less blood rushes into the penis because the arteries narrow. Then the suspending ligaments decide to loosen up. Both work together to lower the angle of your dangle.

There are a couple of things you can do to help Willie reach for the sky: First, lose weight. Excess fat along the stomach and base of the penis interferes with the upward angle. Second, squeeze the muscles that angle the penis upward (the muscles that stop urination). Do it hundreds of times a day.

Yes, you heard me, HUNDREDS of times a day. Do I stutter? Third, get hotter guys. Or better porn. An 80-year-old can have the angle of an 18 year-old if he's stimulated enough.

Hey, Woody!
Is there anything I can do to make my dick bigger? I'm in my early thirties. Will it grow bigger as I get older?

—Here's hoping

Dear Hoping:
For the bazillionth time, there is nothing you can do to make your penis bigger. Well, other than sleeping with my boyfriend. He ALWAYS makes my penis bigger.

But I digress. The penis stops growing by the time you reach your early 20s. Sorry, you're S.O.L., pal. Like the rest of us.

The good news is that having a bigger dick wouldn't make you more sexually satisfied anyway. Studies show that guys with above-average-sized dicks don't score any higher in sexual satisfaction than guys with average-sized dicks. Of course, they probably score more, period. But that's a study of a different size.

Hey, Woody!
I've had a bent penis most of my life. I don't know if it's my imagination, but it seems like it's got its left turn blinker on more and more these days. I don't have any discomfort during sex, but I don't like the way it looks or where it's heading. How can I "straighten" myself out?

—Curvy

Dear Curvy:
You may have Peyronie's disease. It's a condition that causes plaque buildup alongside the erectile tissue. Flossing won't help—this is a different kind of plaque.

As it hardens the plaque makes you less flexible and arcs your erection like an Esther Williams side-flip. It occurs in about one percent of men. Congratulations, you may already be a winner.

There are treatments, but there's no strong evidence that anything other than surgery works. You should see a urologist or at least get more information about it. Try the American Foundation for Urologic Disease at (800) 828-7866.

Hey, Woody!
In the annals of stupid penis tricks I have one I'm trying to get rid of. Whenever I drive in my car, I get an erection. I can't just whack off in the middle of stop-and-go traffic. First, why is this happening, and second, how can I stop it?
—Traffic-stopper

Dear Traffic-stopper:
Men get hard in the oddest places. Some even get hard in vaginas.

Urologists say you're suffering from "Road Erection." It's similar to Road Rage. They both leave you spent, but for entirely different reasons. Road erections come from the vibrations your car makes because you're too cheap to buy a Lexus. Car vibrations set off blood into the penis. Sitting puts pressure on the veins, effectively trapping the blood inside, helping you-know-who stand at attention. Plus, if you're like the rest of us, you're thinking about sex every other time you blink anyway.

If you're tired of car-pooling with willie, try a doughnut-style seat cushion like the ones hemorrhoid sufferers use. It'll help keep pressure off the veins and your attention on the road.

Hey, Woody!
The other day I was about to, you know, "Enter the Dragon" when suddenly I went limp. I've never had this problem before. Luckily, it hasn't happened again, but the fear of it repeating is almost worse than it actually happening.

Can you say some words to put me at ease? Or, rather, at hard?

—**Expecting the worst**

Dear Expecting:

They say the watched pot never boils. Same thing with your dick. Forget about it, man. At some point in his life every man will look down at his crotch and glare at the laziness of his penis. How could it just sit there, lounging around when there's so much work to do? Easy. You're a man, not a machine. Shit happens, and it happens a lot more often than you think.

"Situational impotence" happens to everyone. Did I spell that last word right? E-V-E-R-Y-O-N-E. And if it hasn't happened to you yet, wait, your card will be drawn.

You can't will yourself into an erection just like you can't will yourself to sleep. A guaranteed way of keeping yourself awake at night is to constantly ask yourself "Am I asleep yet?" A guaranteed way of repeating situational impotence is to constantly ask yourself "Is this the time I'm gonna go soft?"

The only way to get out of the obsessive loop you're in is to take the sting out of occasional impotence. If it's okay—and not some unbearable hell—to occasionally lose your erection, you won't feel so pressured. So sit yourself down, close your eyes, put your hand on your heart and say "It's perfectly okay to occasionally lose my erection. It's true I don't like it, but it's also true that it means nothing."

If you truly "get it," that occasionally losing your erection is meaningless, then your body and mind won't have to stand sentry, scanning for the possibility of disaster. And if that doesn't work, I'll let you have my boyfriend for a night. He can suck a softball through 30 feet of garden hose. If he can't get you up, no one can.

Hey, Woody!
I'm uncircumsized, and I have an unusually long foreskin. When I have an erection the foreskin still covers the head.

I've got to pull it back with my hand when I'm beating off or fucking somebody. I'm thinking of snipping it. I'm in my late 20s—it scares me to snip anything in that area. Do you think I should have a circumsicion?

—Snip and Tuck

Dear Snippy:
I say it's time to carve the turkey. It's not that I think being circumcised is better—it's that I don't think you should live with anything that gets in the way of sexual pleasure. Boyfriends are the only exception to this rule.

In 1871 the *New York Medical Journal* published a piece by a doctor who contended that a long foreskin was a cause of masturbation. At the time, masturbation was considered unhealthy (and I agree. I feel healthier when someone blows me). Anyway that idiot doctor advocated circumcision as a way to stop guys from masturbating. I say it's time to lighten your load, but if you have reservations about it, go to a urologist—he can alleviate your concerns and explain the procedure in detail.

Hey, Woody!
What are you crazy? Advising "Snip and Tuck" to get a circumcision is like recommending a frontal lobotomy for Monday morning blues! The average man loses 10,000 nerve endings from circumcision and all the nerve transmissions traveling through what once was the foreskin. Once he's cut, the head of his dick is going to rub up against his underwear until his glans' skin thickens, toughens and gets desensitized. To quote one of the many adults who were misled or involuntarily circumcised, "I once had a sex organ, now I have a stub." In a hundred years, circumcision will shock and disgust people and remind them of the leeches and "humors" of medieval medical practice.

—Go snip yourself

Hey, Woody!
How DARE you tell anybody it's okay to get their skin clipped?!! They're going to hate it in the future, man! You have no business giving that kind of advice.

—Boilin' mad

Dear Foreskin Fetishists:
Looks like I hit an uncircumcised nerve with my latest advice. You guys were too busy grabbing your pitchforks and looking for my address to notice the letter-writer's dilemma: His foreskin was so long it covered his head completely even when he was hard. How'd you like to fuck with the head of your dick covered with a protective layer of skin?

Hmmm. Actually, that sounds suspiciously like wearing a rubber. So imagine wearing two rubbers before entering the highway. Talk about giving your dick a flat tire. . . .

So, my advice to Snip and Tuck stands—with one qualifier: Visit a urologist and ask about plastic surgery techniques that could shorten but not eliminate the foreskin. It may be possible but Snip needs to be examined first. If it can be done, I say go for it. I'm for anything that'll maximize pleasure.

Hey, Woody!
Is it true that black men make our hammers look like nails? People are always talking about it like it were fact.
—Wondering and slobbering

Dear Wondering:
In my personal experience, the answer is no, black men don't have bigger dicks than white men or Latinos, etc. But anecdote, schmanecdote, I checked the literature, and lo and behold if it didn't confirm my experience. I quote from a penis size study published in *Contemporary Urology* (I call it "Today's Dick"):

"Variations in penile size between races have not been documented in any peer-reviewed literature."

Hey, Woody!
After I ejaculate, I feel this kind of ache deep in my geni-
tals. It goes away after a few minutes, but I'm worried that
something awful's going on. Please tell me it's a sign my
dick is gonna grow another three inches. Seriously, should
I be worried?

—Pain après pleasure

Dear Pain:
Better to put up with achy balls than chatty post-coital tricks. At
least your pain has the good sense to go away after a few minutes.

It could be a couple of things, but because you didn't mention
blood in the semen, painful urination, cloudy urine, discharge,
swelling, or an alarming attraction to rainbow flags, it's probably
nothing to worry about.

My advisory panel thinks it's most likely a perception of pain
and relief, the kind you get after a hard workout at the gym when
your muscles can get tired and achy. In other words, you're nuts.

If it truly is a medical condition causing the pain, it's most
likely a prostate infection, which can easily be solved with antibiotics. If you suspect rainbow flags might be involved, then the
problem is much more serious and will require surgery to sew in
a sense of good taste, the kind Martha Stewart tried to graft into
Kmart, which of course rejected it like a bad organ transplant.

Hey, Woody!
Every time I take a shower at the gym I get real embar-
rassed because my pup doesn't measure up. When I'm
erect, I'm actually pretty normal-sized, but when I'm not,
it's pretty small. Why does my penis shrink to a cigar stub
when I need to impress the most?

—Small in the stall

Dear Small:

Tell you what. The best way to grow your penis is to get into a gay chat room on America Online. Everyone there is eight inches. Just ask them.

You can't tell how big someone really is by seeing their flaccid penis in the locker room. A recent study at the University of California at San Francisco confirmed what Masters & Johnson told us decades ago: There is no correlation . . . let me repeat that . . . there is no correlation between flaccid penis size and erect penis size. If your penis is unusually large when its flaccid, it does not mean it will be unusually large when it's erect. The reverse is also true. You're a "grower, not a shower."

Hey, Woody!
I'm dating a certain Mr. Tripod. I love his huge dick but then when I touch myself—and I'm pretty big—it feels like I have a tiny penis. All of a sudden I feel "less than." It's getting in the way of making myself cum when we jerk off together. How can I get over this?

                    —Large in an even larger world

Dear Large:

First, I never give advice about big dicks unless I see them first. It wouldn't be right. So send me a jpeg on email. Until then, I have a question. *What the hell are you doing playing with yourself when you need three hands to manage Mr. Tripod?*

Since you didn't mention oral or anal sex, I'm assuming that jerking off is the only thing you feel comfortable doing. If that's the case, fine. Then keep your hands to yourself and let him jerk you off to orgasm. It's so much more fun that way.

Hey, Woody!
Is it true you can do exercises to improve your sex life? I go to the gym but I can't say it's done much for my sex life. Is this a fad thing or does it really work?

                    —Willin' to train

Dear Will:

It's true, exercising something called your PC muscles will improve your ability to have hot monkey love.

PC stands for pubococcygeous, the muscles you use to stop and restart the flow of urine. It's at the heart of the ancient Taoist training in the art of making love. It involves strengthening the PC muscles that form the pelvic floor between your legs by contracting and releasing them in a series of exercises.

These muscles surround the urethra and control everything that passes through it—urine, semen, and in some gay men, hair gel. One exercise is to contract the PC muscles and keep them tightened for a count of ten, then relax. Another is to contract and relax the PC muscles as quickly as possible.

You start by doing ten of these types of exercises a day and work up to 100. Sex researchers say a steady regimen of these exercises can give you greater staying power, a greater number of orgasms and firmer erections.

Try the classic *Taoist Secrets of Love: Cultivating Male Sexual Energy*—it's chock full of the exercises. In America, these "secrets" are called Kegel exercises. They should be done with legs slightly apart (but not with your ankles soldered to your ears, like so many of my friends do).

The cool thing about the "Kegels" is that you can do them anywhere—driving, walking, watching TV, doing dishes, or baking K. No one will ever know. About the exercises I mean, not the K. Don't expect overnight success. This ain't Viagra. It takes six to eight weeks of daily exercising before you see results.

Hey, Woody!
I'm thinking of using an ejaculation control cream like Mandelay but I'm worried about my partner. Will the cream rub off and cause a loss of sensation for him as well?
—Hung but numb

Dear Hung:

Of COURSE it's going to rub off and cause your partner a loss of sensation, you idiot. And on top of that, he may be allergic to its active ingredient—benzocaine, the topical anesthetic used to treat canker sores.

I can just see you now, "Oh, look honey, this'll numb your ass so you won't feel anything and then afterwards I can take you to the ER." What a guy.

Most sex therapists do not recommend ejaculation delay creams. There are lots of exercises you can do to get control. We've covered them before and we'll do it again later. Meantime, lose the creams and find some info on the net.

Hey, Woody!

I LOVE your column but I live far from the city so I can't pick it up very often. Do you email your responses? Cuz if you do, please tell me what I can do about guys losing their minds over my uncut dick. I'm from Brazil where everyone is uncut, so I don't understand why so many guys are turned off by it. I know it's different from what they're used to, but can it make that much difference? I've actually had guys, when they go down on me, go "eeeewwww" and come back up. Any suggestions for handling this?

—A halibut without the cut

Dear Halibut:

No, I don't email my answers, especially when the requests come without shirtless pictures.

Besides, I hate uncut dicks.

KIDDING, I'm kidding. I love all dicks. Well, except the ones hanging from chicks.

Listen, when you're dealing with the shallow and superficial (did anyone say "gay"?), you need to re-think your poaching strategies. If you know that something about you has the potential for turning Mr. Sunflower into Mr. Sunburn, don't wait till you're in bed for them to find out.

Whether you have a small dick, an uncut dick, HIV, or worse, a penchant for singing Broadway musicals when you first get out of bed, you need to let your partner know about it. It's only right. Who wants to hear that shit so early in the morning?

I'm a great believer in making bedrooms a shame-free zone. So, tell guys you're uncut before you go home with them. Don't say it with pride or shame, don't say it with confidence or meekness, just say it. And the funnier, the better. For instance: "Hey, man, before we go home together there are three things you need to know about us Brazilians:"

1. We can suck the rind off a watermelon without slicing into it.
2. We can make gringos sing two octaves higher in bed.
3. We have beautiful uncut dicks.

And then go for the close: "Me? I got two out of the three. Wanna help me work on the third?"

Hey, Woody!
My flaccid dick is quite small, and is terrible advertising for my hard dick, which is nicely average, but a tad skinny. My flaccid dick's size provoked incredible teasing and emotional abuse in summer camp starting in the swimming pool changing room at age five—"Look, he doesn't have a penis, is he a girl?" And then it resurfaced again at ages eleven through my first year of college with equally brutal comments. I remember one guy, he was so abusive, he used to yell out "Your dick is so tiny, it could fit through the top of a Coke bottle."

Despite years of therapy, these experiences have left indelible wounds. To have them reinforced in the gay locker rooms, on nude beaches, etc., has been a really disappointing aspect to being out and seeking sexual fulfillment. People who seem interested in me clothed, seem to dismiss me when they see my small flaccid dick. Nude, I'm usually dismissed. Little do they know how content they'd be with my erect dick.

I've also had sexual partners spontaneously gasp in disappointment when they first see me naked (if I'm not immediately erect) or, after I ejaculate, when they see how small my dick becomes after I cum. A few overly honest friends or tricks have commented on this, and said that this was a reason they couldn't continue with me as a sexual partner, though they wanted to be friends.

One close non-sexual friend, who I would love to be sexual with, recently told me that he can only get aroused by big dicks. He said he heard from an old boyfriend of mine that I had a small dick. And then, with embarrassed sensitivity and honesty, this close non-sexual friend said he'd otherwise be interested in dating me, but he couldn't be sexual with me or consider a relationship because of my dick size. He apologized profusely, but said he knew himself too well. I have been friends with this man for several years. He is very sensitive and self-aware, educated, professional, popular, charming, mature, and good looking. It's disappointing, anger inducing, and hard to accept that he could be so limited. And yet the prevalence of small dick size as chatter and comment in the gay community makes me feel I can't condemn him; or pathologize him.

Woody, do you have any suggestions for how to improve my chances with men? I long for an emotionally and sexually intimate relationship. I know there are other factors than flaccid penis size in the establishment of attraction. And there must be some men out there who don't place such a premium on penis size. Also, any suggestions on how to be more at ease in situations where clothing is optional? I like hot tubs and nude beaches a lot, but the subtle and not so subtle snubs and smirks make me want to avoid these pleasurable aspects to being alive.

—Not that small

Dear Not:

Your letter reminds me of something a friend once told me: The difference between men and pigs is that pigs don't turn into men when they drink.

You think straight society is judgmental and hostile? Welcome to the loving and accepting brotherhood of gay men. Your letter perfectly captured the cruelty and emotional brutality gay men struggle against in their own community.

The good news is that it's possible to meet good-looking guys who don't care about penis size, guys who know that a man can't be reduced to the sum of his parts, no matter how small those parts may be. And I'm going to show you how to find them.

First, handle your dick size the way positive men handle their HIV status—by telling people before you end up in bed with them. The comparison of size obsession to AIDS is more appropriate than you think. They're both infections. One attacks the body, the other the mind. One is transmitted through needles and sex, the other by gossip and cruelty. You can never tell who has it by looking at them and both result in severely limiting the range of sexual options. So it seems appropriate to use what we've learned about HIV to combat the effects of size obsession, a dysfunction marked by recurring hallucinations that size is the only thing that matters in sex.

For HIV positive men, a funny thing happened on the way to disclosure. What started as an ethical obligation to inform potential sex partners, ended up being an empowering way to overcome the shame society placed on their condition.

Here's how disclosure would work for you: You're at a bar at the end of the evening or at your door at the end of a date. The Fuck Me Meter is banging to the right. It's decision time. You lean in and whisper, "I can't wait to get you into bed. I have a smaller-than-average dick but I know how to use it. Do you want to come in?"

Don't announce your dick size as a matter of pride but as a matter of fact. If someone is going to have a negative, shaming reaction, let them have it outside your door or in the bar. Make your home and your bedroom a shame-free zone. No one comes in there without knowing what to expect. It preserves your dignity, screens out the size-obsessed, and dramatically improves your chances of a good roll in the hay.

Some guys, maybe most, will turn into Frosty the Snowman, tapping their wristwatches and wondering, loudly, where the time went. But there'll be others, like me, who will say "Cool. What are you cooking us for breakfast?"

Gay society has shame on sale and it's flying off the shelves. Like any popular product, it's hard to resist, especially when the price is so right. But I say let someone else have it. Treat your grocery cart as if it were full and move to the next aisle.

Gay men love imprisonment. As soon as we break out of society's closet we build one for ourselves. We're like housebroken dogs trained in the crate. Even after we have the run of the house, we'd still rather sleep in the crate.

Don't let your past experiences stop you from pursuing a rich and satisfying sex life. You deserve it and I promise you it's out there. You get it by rising above the swirling cruelty to build an enlightened life. Like you did when you first came out.

Hey, Woody!
Can you do me a big favor? Could you please provide my email address to the guy who wrote to you about having a small dick? That letter broke my heart. I have a big dick that I used to always brag about, but it never brought home good guys. Although I like the sight of a big one, I have never thought it was important for my boyfriend to have a big penis. I love sweet, tender, compassionate men . . . dick size means almost nothing. I wish that guy were here right now . . . I would love to send him a note.

Hey, Woody!
After reading the letter written by Not That Small, I felt so bad for him I wanted to cry. Please tell him not every-

one is a size queen. I can honestly say that the best sexual experience I have ever had was with a man whose dick was way below average size. I live in New Orleans, also known as the Big Easy—and for good reason, too—where casual sex is king and a big dick is a requirement. It never ceases to amaze me how people can judge a man's character by the size of his dick. Tell him not to give up looking for that special someone as there ARE those like me who are out there looking for an all-around great guy, where size is not a requirement. As for the good friend who was not interested in a relationship with you because he heard about your dick size . . . damn, man, you need to pick better friends.

Hey, Woody!
Just wanted to drop a note to say I really admired and appreciated your handling of the small dick issue. Although I LOVE being a gay man, I hate how shallow, condescending, and just plain mean-spirited our community can be sometimes. I hope this guy realizes that not all gay men are like this, that there are guys like me who know that a smaller wrench doesn't mean you can't fix the machine.

Dear Everyone Who Responded But There Isn't Enough Space To Print You:
Thanks for the heart-felt sentiments. It's time to move on. I'd say "to bigger and better things" but the wording is unfortunate, so I won't say it.

Chapter 2

Safe Sex Doesn't Mean a Padded Headboard

Every gay man has to make peace between his medical and emotional health. We're living out a profound dilemma and it all comes down to this: Life isn't worth living without sex, but sex isn't worth dying over. Every gay man lives in relationship to this suffocating contradiction.

How do we steer through the enormous forces that play into our sexuality? How do we stay safe, not just from HIV but from every sexual harm, when biological drives, emotional hunger and physical longing combine to overpower logical thought? The letters I get on this subject fairly ache with the pain of this struggle. Every new HIV infection is a gong that vibrates through the gay community, reminding us of our awful dilemma.

Unfortunately, we can't seem to turn to safe sex experts for guidance. Yes, they're bright, educated and well informed. But have you ever noticed how unhelpful they are? They all sound like Charlie Brown's teacher. Talk to one. Ten bucks, you end up more confused than when you started.

Most of my letters express massive confusion and exasperation about safe sex. I'm right there with them. I remember talking to a safe sex counselor after receiving my HIV test results. I couldn't get a simple answer without him clear-cutting acres of the English language to build prefaces, qualifiers, disqualifiers, caveats and conditions.

The disconnect between safe sex experts and us civilians

comes down to this: We want wisdom; they give data. We want advice; they give information. We want answers; they give theories.

So in my column, for better or for worse, I give advice, not just information. The truth is, there is no way of keeping yourself absolutely safe except by locking yourself in the bedroom with an extensive porn collection. But the dialogue in these videos is so bad you'll fling the door open in no time.

The most interesting questions about safe sex aren't necessarily the medical ones, but the ones that give us glimpses of the painfully real dilemmas we find ourselves in. Like the guy who was furious that his trick told him he was HIV positive *after* he went down on him. Or the guy seeking support for his "viral-centrism." He's positive and won't even consider dating someone negative because "I don't want the emotional turmoil of wondering what their next HIV test will show."

It's questions like these that'll make you keep turning the pages over like a congressman in heat.

* * *

Hey, Woody!
I love your column, man. All my friends read it cuz it doesn't have that preachy tone we hate. I want to ask you something I'm afraid to ask anyone else because I know they'll bite my head off. Here it is: What's so bad about getting HIV? I mean, everyone I know who has it looks great. They get to take steroids and testosterone, and this is no shit, man, they look better than I do, and I'm negative.

Even the ads, especially the ads, make it look like HIV is something worth getting. Add in that hardly anyone is dying of it anymore and I come back to my question: What's so bad about getting HIV?

I just came out. I'm 18 and I guess I just don't see that much of a downside to it, especially given the upside (doing whatever the hell I want without a rubber). Let's face it, AIDS is a manageable condition, like diabetes, which my sister has. Yes, it's a pain in the ass for her, but she's

gotten used to it. And that's what I mean about HIV. Is managing it that big a deal? Yes, it may be a pain in the butt but look at the rewards—complete sexual freedom.
—Wondering and wandering

Dear Wondering:
You know why all those HIV+ guys look great? Because the only HIV+ guys you see look great.

Capiche?

In other words, the poz guys that are doing the circuit, the parties, the gym, are the ones capable of doing it, or looking good enough to do it.

What you don't see are the guys that look like hell and feel like shit. And here's where you have to have some faith in me: There are a lot more of those guys than the guys you're seeing.
A lot more.

What you don't see are the guys who've developed disfiguring fat deposits on their necks and stomachs.

What you don't see are the guys constantly going to the doctor, experimenting with new cocktails because this one gave them too much diarrhea or that one gave them too many headaches.

Once you get on meds (assuming you have a job with plenty of health insurance), being on them is like going to a Pride march. Odds are high you're going to experience nausea, dizziness, respiratory congestion or unexplained rashes.

Even the ones lucky enough not to experience any side effects to their meds have to contend with the psychological aspects of living with HIV.

Ask a poz guy how many times he's been rejected by a negative guy who was too afraid to go home with him.

Ask a poz guy how many thirsty people will pause when they offer them a sip of their water.

Ask them how many of those thirsty people will actually sip from their bottle.

Ask a poz guy how many novels he sacrificed reading, how many sports he sacrificed playing, how many movies he sacrificed seeing so he could be conversant in more personally relevant issues like lipodystrophy, peripheral neurologic symptoms, gamma interferon, pneumocystis pneumonia, osteonecrosis, neuropathy, and fatal and non-fatal pancreatis.

You mentioned steroids and testosterone. Dude, the reason they're on testosterone is because HIV caused their libidos to slump like sexual hope in a crowd of ugly people. The reason they're on steroids is because HIV caused their muscle mass to shrink like my dick on crystal meth.

Nothing's completely free. As Allen Ginsberg said, "Even birds are chained to the sky." It boils down to this: What are you willing to give up for this supposedly complete sexual freedom? A lot? A little?

There's no right answer, but do yourself a favor—a BIG favor—and ponder the question.

Hey, Woody!
I grew up masturbating with Vaseline and I still like to use it, even for fucking. If I'm careful that it doesn't rip the condom, is there any harm in using it?
—The smell makes me hard

Dear Smell:
You might not know the condom has ripped until it's too late, and make no mistake about it, it will rip. Stick with water-soluble lubes. "Water-soluble" is a fancy way of saying the lube washes away easily with water. Either that, or it means you can get herpes from drinking tap water. I forget.

Vaseline isn't water-soluble. It's a petroleum jelly. It'll stick to you like that 18 year old you plugged just to say you did him but now he won't leave you alone.

I'm just kidding. About his age, I mean. He was seventeen.

Anyway, forget Vaseline. You might as well put the condoms in a blender and hit the puree button. Besides, there's another reason not to use Vaseline: It promotes infection.

Why? Because it's hard to wash off with soap and water. And that means whatever gets trapped in the Vaseline, like infection-causing bacteria, stays way past its welcome. You know, like your last late-night mistake. You want to get rid of the little buggers as fast as you can or they'll make your life miserable.

If you really insist on using Vaseline, then use it with condoms made out of polyurethane, which doesn't degrade when it comes in contact with oil. Many people claim polyurethane condoms transmit sensation better. The problem is choice. There are only two condoms made of polyurethane—the Avanti male condom and the Reality female condom.

Hey, Woody!
Even though I'm negative I like to sleep with positive guys (I swear they're better in bed). Most of the time I'm really careful but every once in a while my heels just seem to fill with helium and next thing I know I'm getting packed for a trip to heaven. And sometimes it's a rubberless trip, if you know what I mean. One of my poz tricks said I could just pop a few AZT pills and use them like a "morning after" prophylactic. Do you agree with that? Would it help me avoid infection?

—Positive or negative, it's beef

Dear Beef:
I agree with his premise but not the promise. Studies have shown that going on medication right after exposure is an effective way to avoid HIV infection, but popping a few AZT pills like they were Flintstones vitamins won't do it.

First, most doctors would put you on a cocktail, not just AZT alone. Second, you need to be on the cocktail within twenty-four hours, preferably twelve. Third, you have to be on that shit for three months. And I say shit because that's probably how you'll feel after taking those mother fuckers.

Depending on the cocktail, there's a great probability that you'll suffer from the same side effect of attending the Chicago Womyn's Music Festival: nausea, vomiting, dizziness, diarrhea, headaches, unexplained rashes, respiratory congestion, and more.

The medical consensus is that if you know you've just had unsafe sex with an HIV infected person, you should go on post-exposure prophylaxis (PEP). For years, the CDC has been recommending PEP for health-care workers and researchers accidentally exposed to HIV (like when they stick themselves with a contaminated needle).

But don't be an idiot. PEP should be used for one-time, accidental exposures. Using PEP as a way to continually have unsafe sex isn't just stupidity; it's stupidity on stilts.

Hey, Woody!
I saw this really hot guy across the bar and I swear my zipper started moving down by itself. He was tall, with the kind of long, sinewy, athletic muscles I pop off to in my fantasies. But then we met. What an asshole! He had all the social skills of a drunken farmhand. Everything inside me said "don't do it, don't take him home, you'll regret it." But the fuse was lit and once again the demon below my belt took over.

Anyway, we're in bed and I'm thinking, "If I can just get this guy to shut up I could really get into this," cuz Woody, this guy's body was just fucking beautiful. Well, needless to say, he was horrible in bed—graceless with no sense of give and take, no sense of timing, no rhythm, nothing. We're flopping around and suddenly he sits on my hard cock without a rubber. When I said "Dude, I got a rubber right here," he lifts his ass off me, blows me, and then, get this—he FRENCH KISSES me.

I just about had a stroke. My cock was in his ass without a rubber, picking up God only knows what kind of germs, then he sucks it, and then he kisses me. All I could think about was what kind of horrible disease I'm going to get from this jerk. Why do I keep going home with guys that are physically attractive but socially repulsive? And could I have prevented getting a disease if I had jumped out of bed and brushed my teeth or gargled?
—Sorry it ever happened

Dear Sorry:

Why do you sleep with guys you know you'll regret? Because men are pigs and you like bacon.

Dealing with good-looking assholes is like dealing with drugs or alcohol: When you have enough bad experiences, you'll eventually know when to say "thanks but no thanks."

You just haven't had enough bad experiences. Like the mark of a good partier, the mark of a highly evolved sexual being is to know when to say no.

Memorizing Woody's Theory of Sexual Relativity will help. Remember, Einstein proved that space and time aren't viewed as separate, independent entities, but rather that they form a four-dimensional continuum.

It's the same thing with desire and disgust. They aren't separate, independent entities. They form a braided dimensional continuum known as WHID ("What Have I Done?").

Here's my theory in question form: *Ripped abs divided by your prey's assholiness multiplied by your level of horniness equals what degree of morning-after disgust?*

It's the ability to work this formula out in your head before you leave the bar that will make the morning after worth the night before.

As for the disease you're likely to catch, I predict you'll be dead in three months. Your only hope is to tithe half your earnings to my ministry. No, wait, that's not right. Damn, I gotta stop writing these columns when Pat Robertson's on.

Your biggest fear should be Hepatitis A, which is spread by putting something in your mouth that's been contaminated with the stool of a person with the virus. It's a lovely disease, really, what with the jaundice, fatigue, abdominal pain, loss of appetite, intermittent nausea, diarrhea and surly sex advisors using you as Exhibit A for getting vaccinated.

Jumping out of bed and gargling may have helped, but it all depends on how far the guy's tongue went into your mouth and whether you swallowed before you had a chance to gargle.

If you really fear he exposed you to Hepatitis you can get the

IgG shot. It's a painful motherfucker but if you get it within 48 hours, it's an effective post-exposure protection.

If you're gay and you haven't been vaccinated for Hepatitis A, then stop being gay. It's an easy series of two shots and it doesn't hurt. Remember, a dose of insurance gives sexual reassurance.

Hey, Woody!
I never know which condoms to buy. They all make the same claims. Got any suggestions?
—Snapped to attention

Dear Snapped:
There are all kinds of hats for all kind of heads. Whatever you choose, keep in mind a couple of things:

1. Squeeze the condom away from the edge of the foil wrap so you don't tear it.
2. Put lube on your dick or on the inside of the condom.
3. Always yell "Incoming!" before entering your partner.
4. Feel the shaft of his cock as it slides in and out of you to make sure it's still on.
5. Get out while you're hard. After you come pull out before you go soft, so the condom doesn't leak semen into him.
6. Don't throw it in the toilet. Condoms can block pipes. Throw it in the garbage or out the door, along with your trick.

Now, as far as the type of condoms, the only way to figure out what's best is to try them on yourself. Here are a few suggestions:

Too Big?

Dream on. But if you really are one of the 6 percent of men who require a bigger than average condom, then Trojan Magnum XL is your best bet. How do you tell if you need a bigger condom?

Slide a toilet-paper tube over your erection. If it slides down to the base of your penis you don't need an extra-large condom. If it doesn't, you need my phone number.

Cum Too Soon?

Try Trojan Extended Pleasure. It's coated with benzocaine, which dulls the nerves in your dick temporarily. Be sure to put it on correctly. The benzocaine is on the inside of the condom. Wear it inside out and you'll dull the nerves of your partner's ass. There's nothing worse than getting stuck with a dull ass in bed, so be careful.

Needle-Dick?

Try Contempo Exotica Snugger Fit. It's 6 percent narrower than regular condoms, making it the narrowest rubber in the market. FYI: Condom sizes are based on slurp, not length.

No, wait. My computer keys got stuck. I meant GIRTH.

Too Dry?

Paradise Super-Sensitive with Astroglide might do the trick you brought home. It's the only condom that comes pre-oiled with a good lube.

Partner Too Frigid?

Try the Inspiral and see if he doesn't spiral out of control. That is, if he doesn't laugh himself off the bed first. Inspiral is shaped like a soft-serve ice-cream cone. Take a lick at it and see what you think.

Fingers Too Wet?

Don't you hate it when you're ready to enter his mangina, only your fingers are too lubed up to open the condom's foil packet? And pretty soon your trick is drumming his finger on your thighs because you're spending more time entering the package than you'll ever spend entering him and by the time you tear it open with your mouth and open the fucker you look down and your hard-on is gone? You know that feeling?

Well, I'll have to take your word for it because that shit's never happened to me.

Anyway, LifeStyles Discs come in sealed plastic containers, like the pats of butter they serve in those tacky diners my ex-boyfriend used to take me to when he was feeling generous and wanted to splurge on me, that cheap fucking bastard, now where was I?

Oh, yeah. Just strip away the top and get to the bottom. It's the very best in "Peel and Bang" condoms.

Room Too Dark?

Try Global Protection's Night Light, the first government-approved glow-in-the-dark condom. Put the package (the condom, not your dick) near a lamp and the condom will glow for 15 minutes after the lights go out.

Too Selfish?

Try the GOP condom, the Republican Party's first contraceptive. It's made to protect pricks and give the wearer a sense of security when they're fucking somebody over.

Hey, Woody!
I'm tired of my friends giving me attitude for being "viral-centric." I'm HIV positive and for the last ten years I've had negative lovers, and I'm tired of it. I don't want the emotional turmoil of wondering what their next HIV test will show. I don't want to be pitied, worried about, fretted over, or hear "I hope when we (insert sex act here) that it was safe enough. . . ."
I want a man who has an idea what I'm feeling without

getting overly dramatic. I want less anxiety in the bedroom. I want my lover to lean over me after sex and say hungrily, "Excuse me, are you going to eat that?"

So when I'm cruising, I always disclose my status right up front, before anybody starts fantasizing about wedding platters. If the object of my affection is negative, I find a way to gracefully exit the situation. My friends find this mortifying. I don't see why—negative guys have been rejecting positive men for years.

Every one of us has our preferences. Blondes, tall men, muscles, the right job, the right car, the right ethnic background. I just want the right blood type. Woody, tell my shortsighted friends to lighten up, will ya?

—Gimme poz, please

Dear Gimme:

Sorry, I'm with your friends. Your reaction may be understandable but it's unacceptable if we're going to consider ourselves a community that cares for each other.

You've poignantly described the aching circumstances of being positive. It's exhausting to be "on-guard" about your status 24/7.

Some of my poz friends have had guys react so badly to their HIV disclosure they've been left in the middle of the street with no way home, breathing in the exhaust fumes of four-wheeled rejections.

So yes, who could blame you for walling yourself off from that kind of cruelty? But I say tear the wall down. The last thing our community needs is another thing that divides us. We're already divided between black and white, old and young, male and female, gym buff and cream puff. And now you're advocating that we be divided by another category: Blood type.

No thanks.

Consider how diminished we all are when we capitulate to the fear within us and the cruelty around us; when we contract in the face of pain; when we make our world smaller and smaller and our choices narrower and narrower, all in response to the fear of hurting or being hurt.

Besides, there's a difference between preference and prejudice. To say you prefer other poz men is one thing. To flatly dismiss a whole group of people, regardless of their individual worth is the textbook definition of prejudice. It's like saying you wouldn't date Jewish guys no matter how much you liked them because, well, they're *Jewish*.

Personally, I think your confident, macho pose of being "viral-centric" is a psychological reaction to the pain you've suffered. You've decided the best way to defend yourself is to go on the offensive: Reject before being rejected.

If you're going to hold fast to your position, at least be aware you've built another misguided fantasy: That poz on poz sex is safe. Whether you sleep with positive or negative men, a compromised immune system makes it much easier to contract other STDs like gonorrhea, syphilis, and if you're a Log Cabin Republican, hoof-in-mouth disease.

Also, it's possible you could re-infect yourself with a stronger strain of the virus than the one you currently have, a strain that may not respond well to your current meds. Though this is the medical consensus I would be remiss if I didn't qualify it by saying it's a consensus theory in search of evidence to back it up. Ultimately, you're in charge of what risks to take, but at least be aware of what they are.

Hey, Woody!
A funny thing happened on my way to the online orgy— like, frequent stops to the sexually transmitted disease clinics. Is it my imagination or do chat room fuck buddies carry more STDs?
—Afraid I already know the answer

Dear Afraid:
Be afraid, very afraid. New research by the Centers for Disease Control shows that men who rely on meeting people for sex on-

line have a much higher risk of contracting STDs than guys who cruise offline.

The study, published in the *Journal of the American Medical Association,* showed online cruisers had more exposure to HIV-positive partners and reported more previous STDs. The study also showed that online cruisers had up to ten times the number of tricks than offline cruisers.

In other words, the news isn't all bad.

The study was limited to about 900 people who sought HIV testing at a Denver public health clinic, but common sense tells you it's projectable to the rest of the country.

And speaking of common sense, it's something you should use when cruising online. Knowing that guys online are much likelier to be walking petri dishes shouldn't stop you from hooking up with them. Just be more careful—meet them somewhere neutral (face it, if they just come over, you're as likely to bang them out of convenience, as out of desire) and be pickier.

If you're going to get a STD, for chrissakes, get it from a "10" not a "2."

Hey, Woody!
I don't think I'm alone when I say I was SHOCKED at the latest HIV studies from the Centers for Disease Control showing that 8 percent of all HIV transmissions occurred through oral sex. Anal sex has never been my thing anyway, but going down on a guy—I can't give that up. I always saw blow jobs as a safe harbor but now they're saying the harbor is mined. I'm so frustrated and angry by all this safe sex shit that I just want to say "fuck it, I'm going to do whatever the hell I want." But then I come to my senses and I think . . . well, that's just it, Woody, what should I think?

—Dazed and confused

Dear Dazed:

Every cage was rattled when the CDC announced their "8 percent" conclusion, including mine. The announcement was like an after-shock after the big AIDS earthquake—it was nowhere near as dangerous as the first one, but it produced just as much fear.

The first thing to remember is that the CDC didn't say that 8 percent of the time you blow someone you're going to get infected. It said, of the people who contracted HIV, 8 percent got it from oral sex. There's a huge difference. One tells you the odds of contracting HIV from oral sex, the other tells you how prevalent oral sex transmission is within HIV infected people.

The truth is no one knows what the chances are of contracting HIV from any sex act, let alone oral sex. It's a little like the risk women run of getting pregnant when they don't use birth control. Do they get pregnant every time they have unprotected sex? Of course not. Will they get pregnant eventually? Of course. What are the odds? No one knows.

As one of the brighter minds in the AIDS fight reminded me, the "8 percent" study made no reference to how the subjects in question had the oral sex that resulted in HIV infection. Did they swallow cum? Did they brush or floss before they had sex? Were they unknowingly suffering from gum disease like gingivitis, which promotes transmission? Did they have small cuts or bruises in their mouths? And most importantly, how big were the dicks they were sucking?

Wait. How did that get in there? Never mind. The point is we always knew oral sex carried some potential for transmission but most of us thought the numbers would be in the ones and twos, not eights. Actually, they probably still are, because again, the CDC did NOT say that 8 percent of the time you blow someone you'll get infected. It said, of the people who got infected, 8 percent of the transmission route was through oral sex.

Everyone needs to design their own risk table tying together the three greatest factors in deciding what to do in bed: The known level of risk, the heat level of your sexual prey, and of course, the level of your own stupidity. Needless to say, this last factor is probably the swing vote in the HIV transmission election.

My advice is to make like the wind and blow. And forget rubbers. As my AIDS braniac said, "It's as ridiculous to fuck without a condom as it is to suck with one." Just make sure your mouth isn't an environment conducive to transmission. Before you go down on Mr. He's-bursting-out-of-his-pants-and-it's-all-for-me, remember the rules: Don't brush, don't floss, don't swallow, don't have any cuts, don't have any gum diseases.

There's always an idiot running around wondering if his hand will burn if he sticks it in an oven set on BROIL. This is the guy that says "I have a small tear in my lower lip and a dash of gingivitis, but what the hell, he's hot so I'll let him cum in my mouth." If you're that person, do me a favor and stop reading this column. You're going to bring down the intelligence average on the next readership study. Then I'll have a surly editor negotiating my rate down by pointing out what idiots I have for readers.

Hey, Woody!
I was really disappointed by your comments on the CDC's study showing 8 percent of people infected with HIV got it from oral sex. You advised people to keep having oral sex anyway. You're in a position of authority—you shouldn't be advising anyone to do something risky. How would you feel if someone got infected from doing something because "Woody said it was okay"? I think you owe your readers an apology.

—Steamed

Dear Steamed:
Get your eyes checked, Cha-Cha. Last time I looked, this was an ADVICE column. If you want mealy-mouthed, hand-wringing platitudes about safe sex, talk to any AIDS expert—they'll be more than glad to make you more confused than you started out.

I stand (or kneel—depends on my mood) by my previous advice: As long as you haven't brushed, flossed, have gum disease, cuts, or bruises in or around your mouth, I think you should bob for bananas all day long.

I never said there wasn't any risk to it. I said the risk is so small, the longing for sex so great, that if you're going to engage in unprotected sex, this is what you should probably be doing.

Everyone in AIDS-related services is scared to death to give advice. That's why you hear the kind of circular bullshit coming out of AIDS organizations that make everyone just want to throw their hands up (and legs) and say, the hell with it.

AIDS educators are so frightened about giving advice all they do is give information. But guess what? Information, like a small dick, can only penetrate so far.

Sometimes you need to add a little length and girth to get guys to light up like a solar event. Nothing adds a little tungsten to the darkness of safe sex discussions like advice.

Here's a clue to all AIDS-educators: Get off your "sex-isn't-that-important-you-should-just-want-to-be-held" pose. Come talk to us where we live—in our shorts. For most men, straight or gay, sex is the organizing principle of life.

You can drape yourself in the mantle of information, but until you start giving advice all you're going to do is confuse people, shut them down, and lose them to REALLY unsafe sex, like condom-less fucking, because the information you're giving out is too complicated to sort out.

As for you, Mr. Steamed, I will not apologize. I only say I'm sorry when I've done something wrong, like forgetting my boyfriend's name, which I unfortunately tend to do when we're in bed. I don't recommend repeating that mistake if you can help it. Talk about having safe sex—when you're ordered out of the room it's the only kind you can have.

Hey, Woody!
What's the deal with Nonoxynol-9? I've been using it along with condoms and now I keep hearing they may not be so good at preventing AIDS.
                                        —Playing it too safe?

Dear Playing:

Nonoxynol-9 helps protect you from getting pregnant (can you spell i-r-r-e-l-e-v-a-n-t?) but also from catching STDs if a condom breaks or leaks.

The problem is that Nonoxynol-9 often causes skin rashes and sores, which can let in viruses like HIM. Wait. I was thinking about my ex-boyfriend. I meant HIV.

A recent four-year study presented at the International AIDS Conference in South Africa showed Nonoxynol-9 actually promotes HIV transmission. More studies are needed, but many researchers are calling for a complete ban of "N-9."

This is one detergent you don't want your friends telling you "you're soaking in it." Dump it—you're better off without it.

Hey, Woody!
So I wake up one day after a night of total debauchery to find myself in an empty bed with a sore ass, dirty condoms and what looked like tread marks on my throat. I freaked! Not about my ass (been there, done that), but my neck! It was practically covered with red, splotchy bruises. Woody, what are they and how do I get rid of them?!

—Necking gone awry

Dear Necking:

You woke up with a sore ass, a used condom, an empty bed and no recollection of what happened? Man, you are class with a capital K.

Even in the dictionary, fun comes AFTER control. Perhaps you should crack one open and see. While you're there, look up "idiot," and see if it doesn't say "See mirror."

Would you let someone drive your car if the brakes weren't working? Then why let someone drive you when yours aren't? You need to wheel yourself in to the nearest brake shop for a re-alignment. It'll only cost about $100 an hour.

As for the bruises on your throat . . . what, did you sleep

through high school? They're hickeys, whorina. They're made when guys suck your neck through slightly parted teeth, rupturing small blood vessels under the skin. Blood seeps into the surrounding tissues, causing those yummy-looking blotches.

To reduce the size of a hickey apply cold packs every 15 minutes for the first two hours. Well, that's for conscious people. For the unconscious who wake up with a sore ass and amnesia, it's probably too late for ice. Try therapy. And maybe a topical vitamin K (make sure it's a cream containing phytonadione). You need a turtleneck and a good swift kick in the ass. Hold still, I'm lacing up.

Hey, Woody!
Trying to figure what you can and can't do in bed without risking HIV drives me crazy. Sometimes I just want to say "FUCK THIS SHIT, I'M GONNA DO WHATEVER THE HELL I WANT." But then I panic about getting it.

I don't care what those freaks say about "The Gift," I do NOT want to get HIV, but at the same time, I wanna live life. I know all about using condoms to fuck, but what about oral sex? Can you give me some no-nonsense advice?

—Horny but worried

Dear Horny:
Trying to get a straight answer from doctors or AIDS workers about HIV is like trying to get straight answers from politician about taxes.

The way the medical profession answers questions about HIV risks makes you feel sorry you asked. When I talk to my doctor, I have a few simple questions, none of which he can answer without planting acres and acres of qualifiers, conditions and circumstances. Sometimes I just want to slap him and say "Doc! Snap out of it! Should I or should I not blow hot guys? Yes or no?!"

The truth is, when most of us ask the HIV professionals, we

don't really want facts. We want advice. And advice is the one thing they won't give. But I will. There are two basic questions anyone afflicted with man-mania has about oral sex:

1) Can I get HIV from RECEIVING oral sex?

The Medical Facts: Risk of infection is extremely low. If all you're doing is receiving, you're only being exposed to saliva, which has very little concentration of HIV. The chances of getting HIV through saliva are remote, unless the person has visible blood in his mouth.

Woody's Advice: If you're stupid enough to let somebody who's coughing up blood go down on you, then you owe it to the rest of us to get sick and die. That way you'll open up some parking spaces at Starbucks for the rest of us who want to stay awake for life. To everyone else, I say let your pants fall to your ankles. It's time for your partners to play "Hide the Salami."

2) Can I get HIV from GIVING oral sex?

The Medical Facts: There is a risk of infection since preejaculate and semen can get into your mouth. The more of these body fluids you're exposed to, the greater the risk of infection. If you have any open sores, cuts, abrasions, or gum disease, the virus can get into your bloodstream. There have been reported cases of HIV infection through giving oral sex.

Woody's Advice: I say go out and buy a good pair of kneepads. Yes, there have been reported cases of HIV infection through giving head, but, Christ, if you look hard enough and long enough in the medical literature, you'll find just about anything in medicine is possible, regardless of the disease. The sexual essence of a man is his dick. If you can't taste it, kiss it, lick it and bathe it with your mouth, then what's the fuckin' point? Just because there've been reported cases doesn't mean it's a high-risk activity.

The overwhelming majority of HIV infections occur from anal sex, not oral sex. Just don't be stupid about it. Don't brush your teeth right before sex and check your mouth for any cuts or openings before you stick any groove tubes in there. Wipe off any pre-cum and let yourself go, man. Life is full of low-risk activities. You don't stop yourself from participating in them just because there are recorded cases of injury and death. By that measure, you shouldn't ride roller-coasters.

Hey, Woody!
Explain something to me. I understand why "bottoms" are at high risk for HIV if they don't use condoms, but why are "tops"? If I don't have any sores or cuts on my penis, and the virus can only be transmitted through blood, there's no route of entry is there? What am I missing?
                                                      —Tops in my class

Dear Tops:
As you enter a mangina, the opening to your penis gets stretched wide, allowing fecal matter, bacteria and other wonderful things to enter and irritate the lining of the urethra.

We're talking major irritation. Like when the ugly one in the three-way keeps getting in the way. *That* kind of irritation. The kind that damages even the strongest layer of patience or mucous membranes.

Blood can get in your penis, too, even though it's not visible to the eye. Everyone's got hemorrhoids and almost 75 percent of us will have trouble with them at some point in our lives. Meaning, they'll swell, itch, burst and bleed. You know, like dot.com careers. You could be fucking a guy who's bleeding internally and you wouldn't know it because it's microscopic.

As you thrust, the head of your dick opens, allowing matter and specks of blood into the urethra. As you back out to thrust again, the urethra closes, pushing down the "material" that just entered farther down the shaft, scraping and scratching it. Lovely thought, isn't it?

That's why it's so important to pee right after sex. The acid in the urine helps kill bacteria and basically hoses out everything that's in the urethra. In fact, whenever you have sex be sure to drink a big glass of water beforehand, so you'll piss like a racehorse afterwards. You might even want to do it on the ugly one, the one that keeps getting in the way. Urine baths have a way of making even the most annoying tricks hoof it in a hurry.

Hey, Woody!
I get these red itchy rashes in my groin area. Like my tricks, they come and go. Is this some low-level STD? Do I have to go to a doctor and embarrass myself, or is it treatable with over-the-counter medications?
—Scratching in the wrong place

Dear Scratching:
Sounds like you've got tinea cruris, which means your dick is going to fall off in 15 minutes.

Oh, wait, I got that confused with a fantasy I have for my good-for-nothing ex-boyfriend. Tinea cruris is actually jock itch. You can get rid of it with any over-the-counter anti-fungal cream. If it doesn't go away with regular use, you've got to see a doctor. You can prevent the jock from itching by:

1. Using a hair dryer to dry your crotch after a shower. The rashes are caused by yeast or fungus that thrive in moist environments.
2. Drying your feet last. Fungal infections on the feet can be transmitted to the groin area.
3. Wash your bowels often. No, wait, that's not right. Dammit, I've got to switch medical advisors. The ones with medical degrees from the Dominican Republic are so hard to understand. I meant "towels."

Hey, Woody!
Any updates on men using the "female condom" for anal sex? I know you talked about it a while back, but I was wondering if we have the green light to use it. Do we?
—Just wondering

Dear Just:

Unlike regular condoms, the female condom is worn by the receiving partner rather than the active partner.

You insert it into the anus and bang away. But there's a bing in the bang. Over half the men in the study reported problems. Some said it irritated them (the condom, not their partners. Although there's probably a study on that too). Others said it "bunched up" on them. Others said the texture sucked, and yet others, said it made too much noise (it squeaks like an old chair).

One of the biggest complaints is the "ring" that holds the condom in place. There are two hoops you have to jump through—your partner's and the condom's, making the effort closer to a circus act than a sex act.

I say forget the female condom. Studies have only been done on their comfort. There are still no studies done on how well it prevents HIV transmission. And I don't know about you, but that's the only reason I wear a condom.

Hey, Woody!

If all these drugs are making HIV undetectable in blood tests, then why can't I bareback safely with an HIV positive guy? I don't get it. If it's undetectable, then it's not there, right? And if it's not there, why should I use a rubber?

—Detect THIS

Dear THIS:

Undetectable doesn't mean non-existent.

Let's say you and Mr. He Wants Me But He Doesn't Know It are leaning against the bar. He turns his back on you and you slip some GHB in his drink because you've been watching too much *Queer As Folk*, where conscience is portrayed as emotional baggage.

The bartender, who doesn't give a shit what people do to each other as long as it doesn't cut into his tips, immediately comes over, grabs the drink and conducts an on-the-spot test. But the test only measures the active ingredient in GHB to .005 mgs per liter, and you put in .004. The bartender leaves you alone. Does this mean your hatefulness was non-existent? Or undetectable?

Same thing with HIV. The hatefulness of this virus can only be measured up to a certain threshold. If it dips below this threshold, we know it's still there, it's just that our instruments aren't sensitive enough to pick it up.

What AIDS experts will not say publicly (because they're allergic to speaking clearly) is that having sex with an HIV-infected man with undetectable levels of HIV in his blood is safer than having sex with one who has detectable levels.

So yes, it's safer. But is it safe? Hardly. For one, HIV strains left in the wake of an onslaught of powerful drug combinations are often drug-resistant. This means that some people with undetectable viruses in their blood risk passing on HIV strains that can't be treated with current drugs.

Don't assume that just because someone's on a cocktail therapy, that they automatically have undetectable levels of HIV in their blood. Studies show that 45-50% of cocktail-chuggers have undetectable levels. It could rise to as high as 85% but only if patients take the drugs as prescribed. A good many don't.

Listen, my editor pays me according to the number of acceptably stupid people I attract to this column. If you still want to bareback after what I just said, then stop reading this column, babe, you're costing me money.

Hey, Woody!
Okay, everybody knows you're not supposed to brush or floss your teeth before sex because it'll create minor tears and cuts which raises the risk of HIV infection and the chance to pad the pockets of those blood-sucking drug companies. I've heard it ad nauseum. What I haven't heard is a discussion on timing. Do experts recommend not brushing one hour, two hours, four hours, a week, a month before you lay tongue upon the wonderment? And what if

you brushed your teeth moderately? Does that make any difference? Come on, Wood-man, tell us. Nobody wants to have sex with a mouth that smells like a meat packing plant. How do you work the timing?

—Bad-boy breath

Dear Bad-boy:

This is where all the experts get wormy on us. "There is no real way to tell," said one of my brighter medical advisors (I rely on stupid ones too, but only for the stupid questions).

There is no such thing as saying "I'm safe as long I've brushed my teeth three hours before I suck someone off." The closer the time between brushing and sucking the more risk you take on. How's that for a definitive answer? I know, it's hard to swallow, but hey, you shouldn't be swallowing in the first place. Spitting is much safer.

Brushing and flossing cause minor tears and cuts. When you brush you remove layers of cells in the gums. The good news is that your mouth heals very quickly from the cell-zapping. A tongue burn, for instance, takes only 24 hours to heal (a tongue lashing, on the other hand, can last for weeks. Ask some of my letter-writers).

That's because the mouthal area re-generates cells faster than amoebae at a protozoan all-you-can-eat buffet. And no "mouthal" isn't a real word; I made it up.

The inside of a mouth heals quickly, but who the hell's going to take the chance an hour or two before dick and destiny get together? Not me. I do what my advisors tell me: Fuck the brush, suck the wash. This is no time to be butch—it's time to swish. Listerine, Scope, urine, whatever's gonna get you laid faster—swish it around and gargle.

If I long for toothpaste, I use my index finger to spread it around. As for moderate brushing, yes it reduces the risk. But here's the problem: What's "moderate"? And who's going to volunteer to find out? I say stick to mouthwash if he's going to stick it in you.

Hey, Woody!
**A friend of mine told me you can get STDs just from touch-
ing. Touching! Say it isn't so, Woody!**

—**Please, God, no.**

Dear Please:
Sorry, dude. Gonorrhea, syphilis, and herpes don't require penetration or ejaculation to spread. You can catch them just by touching.

The only disease spread by skin-to-skin contact worth catching is osteopornosis, a degenerate disease caused by watching
too much porn. It's fun to get and easily cured with an inexpen-
sive cum shot.

Hey, Woody!
**As I waited for my fuck buddy to show up I accidentally
cut my finger. It was a pretty superficial cut, but it did
bleed. I put a couple of Band-Aids on it and hoped for the
best.**

**When he came all over his chest, I got caught up in the
moment and swiped the semen off his chest and used it to
jack off.**

**After I came I realized I had the cut on my finger and
jumped out of bed and washed it off with soap and water.
My hands were full of Wet Light, the lube. Would that have
helped keep the semen out of the cut? The Band-Aid was
fairly secure and I didn't feel any stinging sensation
(which is another question—would I have felt a stinging
sensation if cum had gotten into the cut?). Woody, tell me
what I want to hear—that I'll be okay, that I won't catch
HIV. My buddy says he's negative, but I'm obsessing. What
if he's lying?**

—**Help me**

Dear Help:

You're asking a question with no answer. You might as well ask why men are pigs. Who knows?

If your cut was fresh (i.e., still bleeding), the virus could get through the Band-Aid if there was enough cum to soak through. The epithelium (the most superficial layer of skin) needs several hours to build an adequate protective layer to keep HIV out of the bloodstream.

Although there is salt in semen, there might not be enough to cause stinging. There's only one way to tell, according to one of my unindicted medical advisors (they're a dying breed, you know): Get someone's cum on your cut. Funny, how he didn't want anybody but me trying it out, the bastard.

Oh, and Wet won't stop the virus. It just means instead of walking into your bloodstream, the virus will roller-blade into it.

Hey, Woody!

I'm negative and I sleep with guys who are positive all the time. I don't give a shit about somebody's sero-status, if I'm hungry for their body I'm going to chow down. What I want to know is if there are times when poz guys are more contagious than other times. I'm safe about our sex so spare me the lectures.

—Positively charged

Dear Charged:

First, I don't lecture. I pistol-whip. Ask my ex-boyfriends. They can tell you the difference.

Your positive partners are more contagious when:

1. They first get infected. Most will experience a flu-like illness (chills, body aches, etc.).
2. They catch an unrelated illness. Like a cold or strep throat. The immune system can weaken and cause viral loads to rise.

3. They take medications that fail. Or if they don't take any medications.

4. They hear George W. Bush speak. Okay, it's not viral, but believe me, it's a load, and it rises in your throat.

Hey, Woody!
My friends and I were having an argument about condoms—how to use them, how long to keep them, even how to open them. Can you give us the Wood-burning scoop?
—**Wrapped too tightly**

Dear Wrapped:
Let's go through the whole process—from buying them to putting them on: First, always sulk around the display shelves, complaining loudly that they're out of the extra large sizes—*again.*

Second, pick the latex condoms—they offer the most protection. Natural membrane condoms, like lambskin, are porous and aren't as effective in keeping sexually transmitted diseases from skimming across your rubber moat.

When you get home, store them in a cool, dry place or they might get damaged. And by the way, don't keep condoms more than five years. If they're laced with spermicide, the shelf life is three years. Of course, if you're waiting that long to use them, just put a big "L" on your forehead so everyone'll know what a Loser you are. And for God's sake, don't carry them in your wallet—it's the most common way condoms get damaged.

Okay, so now you're winging, you're swinging, you're dancing to his groove thing. Your crotch is snap-crackle-popping like milk on Rice Krispies. It's time to dip in for a spoonful. You grab the latex love thing and you tear the package down the middle to show him the beast within.

Wrong.

Tear a condom like that and you'll do just that—tear it. Always open a condom by carefully tearing across the top from left to right (or vice versa).

Once you're ready to play poker to his wood-burning fire-place, make sure you lather up with a water-based lubricant. It's a good idea to lather the slather everywhere—on your hardness before you unfurl the flag over it and then the flag itself once it's on.

Never use Vaseline or other oil-based lubricants like petroleum jelly, mineral oil, or cold cream. It'll rip the condom.

Oh, and one last tip before you take a dip—leave some space between your head and the end of the rubber as a reservoir for the semen to collect. Don't want any cum karma coming back at ya.

Hey, Woody!
Is it safe to have sex in a hot tub or a pool? Wouldn't the chemicals kill the HIV virus?

—Swimmin' in it

Dear Swimmin':
You can use silicone-based lubes on condoms for underwater sex (water-based lubes will wash off), but the real risk is that water containing chemicals, salt, or bacteria can be forced into the rectum during sex causing the same reaction I get from reading stupid letters: Irritation.

And you know what that means. My wrath, and an opening for HIV to get in. Frankly, I don't know which is worse.

Hey, Woody!
Can you spread canker sores through kissing? It's bad enough I have them, I don't want to give them to my boyfriend.

—Blistering for an answer

Dear Blistering:
Canker sores are tiny, crater-like lesions. They're small, oval, with a gray center and a surrounding red, inflamed halo. Like the

kind you find sitting in the pews of fundamentalist churches every Sunday.

Canker sores aren't caused by viruses, so they're not contagious. They go away by themselves in just a few days. If only religious sores would, too.

The sores are ordinarily parked inside your mouth, under your tongue or inside your cheeks. They're pretty common. About 20 percent of the population has it on any given day.

No, you can't get canker sores from kissing or oral sex. But are you sure they're canker sores? That's the risk. They could be herpes or cold sores which *are* contagious. Go to a doctor and find out.

Hey, Woody!
I was on a ski vacation, standing outside the bedroom of one of my friends just chatting and sucking on a lollipop. I had the lollipop in my hand when another friend walked by, put it in his mouth for a few sucks and put it back in my hand. I was so deep in conversation I was only vaguely aware he had done it. I finished the lollipop and suddenly I realized what he had done and FREAKED OUT. The guy is HIV positive. Am I going to catch it?
—Sucking on the wrong thing

Dear Sucking:
What is this, 1984? No, you're not in any danger. There is not a single recorded case at the Centers for Disease Control of seroconversion from the exchange of saliva. You have a better chance of catching a cold or flu than HIV.

Make no mistake; your friend is a slob. Taking a lollipop out of your hand without asking, slathering it with mouth juices, and handing it back is a punishable act of grossness, if you ask me. I'm all for people sucking on what I hold in my hand, but only when I order them to do it.

Hey, Woody!
I have a really embarrassing problem. I'll get all hot and
hard, ready to enter my partner but then I start fumbling
with the condom, get all self-conscious, and well, it's hard
to put on and I start losing it, and then I just kinda say
screw it, let's just jerk off. What am I doing wrong?
          —Where the rubber meets the road less traveled

Dear Rubber-Road:
If I had a dime for every hard-on that shriveled through my
condom-wrapped fingers, I could pay the Clinton Legal Defense
Fund out of petty cash.

There are two ways to overcome the "sensation cessation"
caused by clumsy hands. The first involves practicing while
you're alone. Just keep doing it till you get the hang of it.

Method number two is by far the most effective in my opinion. I call the technique "delegating dick duty." Simply put, it's
your partner's job to put it on. I first learned it from a great lay
who got tired of hearing the announcers yell "fumble!" every
time I scrambled for yardage.

Basically, when we're getting ready to rumble he takes the
condom out and does the honors. He puts it on a lot faster than I
can. Here's what he does: Instead of laying the condom on my
head and forcing the thing to unroll down, he takes his two index
fingers and sort of lifts and separates the condom as he rolls it
down the shaft. This stretches out the condom without getting
my skin caught in it.

Thank God for impatient, but clever bottoms. Now go find
one.

Hey, Woody!
Did you hear about the HIV prevention educator in San
Francisco who told the *New York Times* he visits the back
room of the Powerhouse, a bar on Folsom Street and has
unprotected sex with men he doesn't know? The "educa-

tor" says he's HIV positive and admits that he doesn't always practice what he preaches at work. The *Times* said his "lapses do not draw the concern and censure from his peers that they might have even a few years ago."

Here's where it gets interesting: Dan Savage, the grand dame of sex advice, called the HIV educator a "barebacking piece of shit" and said he should be fired from his job. Like you, he takes a lot of pot shots and he spared nothing, noting that AIDS organizations aren't exactly staffed with Mensa members, and that the reason they hire so many stupid prevention educators is because they're so fucking stupid themselves.

So, Woody, since you remind me so much of Dan Savage, I thought it might be interesting to do a side by side comparison of my two favorite sex advisors. Do you agree or disagree with Dan?

—Breathing hard for your answer

Dear Breathing:

Thanks for comparing me to the master of sex advice. A lot of people say that if it weren't for my pathetic sense of humor or my complete lack of insight, they wouldn't be able to tell the columns apart.

The bastards.

There's no need for me to join Savage in tearing the HIV "educator" a new asshole, and not just because he'd just use it as an opportunity to get barebacked by two guys at the same time, but because Savage did such a good job of eviscerating him.

Can Dan dish or what?

Still, while I share Dan's outrage I don't agree with his answer. Firing somebody over personal conduct outside the job is unfair and immoral. Ask James Dale, the former Boy Scout troop leader. Or, for that matter, any gay man in the military.

It's entirely possible that the educator was practicing what he preached. Many AIDS organizations have adopted a "Harm Reduction" strategy after initial studies showed that incremental approaches resulted in better adherence to safe sex practices than the traditional "all or nothing" strategies.

If you can get guys who never use a rubber to use it, say, 40% of the time, you've dramatically reduced the chances of infection. And once you get them to 40% it's easier to get them to 60% and beyond.

I have always said that condoms aren't the answer; they're the question. A question that has different answers for different people in different situations.

Instead of giving people an unequivocal answer (100% safe sex 100% of the time) we should be giving them a thoughtful question: "Should I use a condom with this particular guy in this specific setting for this particular act?"

Here's why I believe in the Harm Reduction approach: I can't think of a basic human drive that can be managed with an on/off switch. Every attempt society has made to control people's drives through a right/wrong, yes/no, black/white approach has met with miserable failure. Exhibit A: Diets. Exhibit B: Prohibition. Exhibit C: The war on drugs. Shall I go on?

Sex is no different. It's impossible to expect total adherence to safety when sex is so riddled with emotional longing, psychological need, and physical hunger.

Having said all that, I'd give the educator two options, and I'd do it with a clothespin on my nose so I wouldn't have to breathe in the stink of his stupidity: 1) Resign. 2) Move to an administrative post that has nothing to do with education.

If all we do is trash this guy (which he admittedly deserves), we'll miss an opportunity to use his stupidity as a "teachable moment." Meaning, what kind of helpful discussions can we generate from his idiocy that will encourage people to practice safer sex?

Hey, Woody!
Settle a bet. Can you get herpes without having sex?
                                        —Please say no

Dear Please:

You lose. There are two types of viruses: Herpes simplex virus 1 (HSV-1) and herpes simplex virus 2 (HSV-2). HSV-1 infects the oral cavity ("mouth" to us civilians) and is not sexually transmitted. Not true with HSV-2.

The word herpes comes from the Greek word "herpein," which means "to creep." Not as in "to creep out," which it will certainly do when you see it, but as in the advancing pattern of the skin lesions.

HSV-1 is far more common than HSV-2. It often infects children by the time they're five years old. In some regions, 90% of people test positively for oral herpes.

The Centers for Disease Control estimates that 45 million Americans are infected with genital herpes and its prevalence has increased by 30% since 1976. Now that's creepy.

Infection usually occurs around the genital area two to eight days after exposure. You'll probably get flu-like symptoms, fever, nerve pain, itching, lower abdominal pain, and urinary difficulties. Tricks will note your forward genital fashion sense. "Where'd you get those creeping blisters?" they'll ask. "They're quite fetching on you." If you end up in bed with someone and notice blisters anywhere except his palms, run don't walk. Skin lesions are out this year. Don't be a Fashion Don't.

Hey, Woody!

Settle something for me. My friends don't agree with my reaction to taking this guy home. We're in bed, the clothes come off, and next thing you know he's bobbing for apples. The road to ecstasy makes a U-turn when he goes down on me for a few minutes and then tells me he's HIV positive! He asks me if that's a problem and I sort of stutter, cuz I can't believe he decides to tell me AFTER he blows me.

My friends think I'm over-reacting because they say receiving oral sex is low on the risk scale. But I say the guy was wrong for not telling me BEFORE we had ANY kind of sex. He named himself judge and jury, deciding for me

what was acceptable risk. I think I should be the one to decide what's acceptable risk for me, not him. By telling me after the fact, this guy got what he wanted—my big, beautiful dick in his mouth, and still got to come off noble by disclosing his status. Woody, am I wrong for being upset?

—Hung jury

Dear Hung:

You're both wrong. I agree with you that he should have disclosed his status before any sexual activity. But you weren't exactly an innocent bystander in the matter.

If you are HIV positive you have the obligation to disclose your status before you slip off your clothes. You do not have the right to decide for your partner what's acceptable risk. What's acceptable to you may not be acceptable to him.

And don't give me that bullshit about "Well, if he goes home with me and doesn't ask my status, then he obviously doesn't care or already assumes I'm HIV, so he's okay with it." How convenient. It isn't often you get to put people at risk for their lives and feel honorable about doing it.

A lot of poz guys feel their responsibility to disclose is absolved if their trick doesn't ask. Wrong. YOU DO NOT HAVE THE RIGHT TO MAKE A DECISION ABOUT RISK FOR ANOTHER PERSON.

I understand how tough it can be to volunteer disclosure. Sometimes the loneliness, the shame, the intense need to connect physically with another man, prevents one from doing the right thing.

Shame and rejection aren't just ghosts haunting positive men. They're real and they're excruciatingly painful. The reluctance to tell is understandable, but the failure to do so is inexcusable.

Building dignity and self-respect is more important than getting off with a trick. What you may lose in the physical short-term by disclosing, you will gain in the emotional long run.

By not disclosing your HIV status you're perpetuating the idea that there's something wrong with you, that you're damaged goods. You are not damaged goods; you are worthy of great sex. The fact that you may get rejected is a statement of the rejecter's worth, not yours.

I am negative, and disclosure has never stopped me from taking a guy home. Well, once, but only because he disclosed his membership with the Log Cabin Republicans.

So enough about your trick, let's talk about you, you preening, self-absorbed fruitcake. Not once in your letter did you cop to being responsible for your own sexual safety.

Why didn't you ask him about his status before he boarded your bed? I'll tell you why. Because by not asking—that is, not knowing—you got to have unsafe sex and feel protected from the consequences.

Plausible denial ain't just a president's mantra, boy. It's a transmission route.

Wake up and smell the lube. You shouldn't be doing anything with an HIV Unknown that you wouldn't do with an HIV Positive. Your trick ruined your fantasy and made you come face to face with your own irresponsibility, and you're pissed off about it. Spare me your victim pose; if you had asked him in the first place you wouldn't have been moaning in the mornin'.

Hey, Woody!
I had laser skin resurfacing to reduce fine facial lines and wrinkles (hey, a girl's gotta do what she's gotta do). Well, when I did, I got a severe outbreak of herpes. I've had herpes for a long time but I hadn't had an outbreak in years. Is it just coincidence that it happened after the laser surgery? And what do I do to keep it under control?
—No wrinkles but lots of sores

Dear No wrinkles:
There's no question that the laser surgery reactivated the outbreak.

More than 60,000 laser skin-resurfacing procedures are done

each year, according to the American Society of Plastic and Re-constructive Surgeons. It's almost become standard procedure for doctors to recommend that anyone with a history of herpes put the Norton Anti-virus CD into their hard-drive to prevent the bomb icon from exploding across their screens.

Of course, I'm talking about antibiotics (usually twice a day for seven days). Recently, a seminal study showed that a course of antibiotics before laser "peels" greatly reduced or even elimi-nated outbreaks of facial herpes.

Which reminds me, why do seminal studies never include semen? It's not fair.

Anyway, what's all this got to do with sex, since facial herpes is associated with cold sores, not—ahem—bed sores? Well, here's a little-known fact: Because more people are having oral sex, it's harder to separate type 1, the oral-facial herpes, from type 2, which is primarily genital.

So if you're going to do a laser "peel" and you have herpes, take antibiotics before the procedure.

As far as the outbreaks from the laser, you treat them the way you treat any herpes outbreak: You take medicine (usually acy-clovir—Zovirax—), reduce stress with yoga or meditation, and if you have a particularly annoying boss, sleep with him.

The lesions should be kept dry and clean (corn starch is your best bet, believe it or not). It's important not to touch the sores and to wash your hands frequently. Fingernails should be scrubbed daily (the virus loves to hide under there). Sores won't heal as quickly if you restrict air circulation, so don't wear tight-fitting clothes. If that doesn't prove herpes is an anti-gay virus, I don't know what does.

Hey, Woody!
I bought one of those at-home HIV test kits 'cause I don't want anybody knowing my business. But now I'm a little nervous about it. How reliable are they?
—Tested but worried

Dear Tested:
You should be worried. The Federal Trade Commission recently evaluated five poke-yourself-at-home-kits and tested their ability to detect HIV in a positive blood sample. All five said the HIV positive blood was negative. Appropriately, the FTC bared its fangs at the five companies. One of them, Medimax, Inc., recently settled out of court and agreed to stop selling their kit.

Faulty HIV kits are no laughing matter. People with a false sense of security can delay treatment that could save their lives. There's only one home testing kit that has FDA approval: Home Access Express HIV-1 Test System. You send a blood sample to a lab by mail, then call a toll-free number for results. If you don't have this kit, then throw away what you've got and get it.

Hey, Woody!
I didn't have time to change the sheets before my parents arrived for a weekend visit. I slept on the couch and gave them my bed. I'm afraid that's not all I gave them. After they left I realized I had pubic lice. Could they have caught the lice sleeping in my sheets? Please, oh God, PLEASE tell me I don't have to warn them.

—The bad son

Dear Bad:
Let me get this straight. You gave *your mother* a sexually transmitted disease? YOUR MOTHER?

If I were St. Peter standing at the pearly gates with a clip board and saw *"Gave his own mother the crabs"* next to your name, I'd slap a "Special Delivery" tag on your ass and send you crashing through the clouds into hell.

Now, what was your question?

Did your parents catch it? Maybe. It all depends on the timing. When did you contract the lice? How far had they spread by the time of your parent's visit? Had the lice been transferred to the sheets?

You *must* tell them about it. Here's why: If your parents got the crabs they might not say anything to you and instead suspect each other of adultery. It's enough that you gave them an STD; don't give them a divorce too. You made your lice-infested bed, you lay in it.

You need a good conversation starter to sort of ease into the difficult subject. Invite them over for dinner and prepare a big plate of fresh stone crabs. When your mom says, "Son, pass me the crabs," you can say you already did.

Hey, Woody!
Is it safe to use the spit of other guys as lube for mastur-bation? If the guy has HIV and he spits up a bucketful of saliva, am I in danger if I use it to pound my pud?
—A handful

Dear Handful:
Wait, let me get this straight. You ask guys to spit up pails of saliva so you can beat off with it? What is this, Sick Week at the Sex Advice Corral?

Actually, it sounds hot. It doesn't fall under safe sex, but it's pretty low on the risk meter. The virus is present in saliva but at very low levels. In fact, the risk of using the saliva of an HIV positive man to masturbate with is much lower than the risk of having oral sex with that same man.

Hey, Woody!
I can never come when I'm wearing a condom. They don't provide enough stimulation—I feel like I'm encased in, uh, rubber. What can I do?
—Latex hater

Dear Latex hater:
Try using a water-based lube on the outside and inside of the condom. It'll reduce friction and increase the warm, slurpy feelings that'll help you heave-ho.

You might also want to try the new polyurethane condoms. They're made with a thin type of plastic allowing greater sensation. But most interestingly, they conduct heat. And you know what that means to our heat-seeking moisture missiles. It makes them scream "Mama!"

Hey, Woody!
Can you get genital herpes if you're just receiving oral sex (as opposed to kissing them) from someone with a sore in his mouth?

—**Don't want him to stop**

Dear Don't:
Yes, it's possible. A herpes sore begins with a tingling or painful group of tiny fluid-filled sacs. When they pop, they release a clear liquid and form painful ulcers. Fever, headaches, and tiredness are common symptoms of the first herpes breakout. Herpes virus Type 1 usually causes a sore on the mouth, while Type 2 causes genital sores.

Type 1 is most commonly spread by oral sex. Interestingly, herpes simplex can also be contracted through the skin anywhere on the body. It's common to find it around the fingernails at the nail bed, for example.

If you see your partner has sores anywhere on his body, treat it as a blinking neon "DANGER" sign and head for the door.

Hey, Woody!
I've got a great suggestion for the tops who can't keep it hard when they have a condom on. Take a cue from the hets, man—let the women be in charge of contraception. When I take it like a woman I use the Reality Condom. It's designed to be inserted into the vagina so the men don't have to screw with anything.

—**Never been happier**

Dear Never:

You're an idiot. First of all your contention that "receiving" makes a guy like a woman is the worst kind of sexual stereotype, the kind that prevents people from enjoying the full range of their pleasure ports.

When a man is entered by another man, it doesn't make him a woman. Just like when a lesbian enters another lesbian (with a strap-on), it doesn't make her a man. Giving and receiving is neither male nor female, they're just different ways of enjoying sex.

Now where was I? Your stupidity took me off-track. Oh yeah, the "female condom." I have not talked with any MDs who were familiar with the Reality Condom's effectiveness in preventing HIV infection in male-to-male sex. These condoms are designed to fit the shape of vaginas. Last time I looked, vaginas and rectums didn't have the same shape. Until there is some data on it's ability to stop male-to-male HIV transmission, I do not recommend anyone using it.

The female condom was invented in the 1980's by a Danish doctor. The FDA approved it in 1993 and the Female Health Company of Chicago, the sole maker of the product, sells it under the name Reality for about $2.25. They're selling at 700,000 units a year, pitiful compared to male condoms. According to Planned Parenthood, women hate the way it looks (it's a ghastly-looking thing—a guaranteed boner-buster to anyone who looks at it). And besides, they complain, it squeaks. Just what you want to hear when you're getting fucked.

Interestingly, the female condom is a huge hit in Africa. Men say it feels stimulating and appreciate the fact that foreplay doesn't have to stop to put it on. As for you, I say take the Reality out of your ass and put some in your head.

Hey, Woody!
The other day I was at a pool party and I know for a fact that half the people in the pool were HIV positive. It scared the hell out of me. Can you get HIV from a swimming pool?
—Afraid to dive in

Dear Afraid:
You can't get HIV from a swimming pool. Or from a mosquito bite or sitting on a toilet. Technically, yes, there can be virus in a pool or on a toilet, but it's so minute there's no way to transmit it. Gawd, I hope you're a mute. I'd hate to hear what you've been telling your friends.

Chapter 3

Cruising: How to Stalk Your Prey

When you're single you live under two organizing principles:

1. Trying to meet new guys.
2. Pretending you're not trying to meet new guys.

That's why you hear bullshit like "I go to gay bars for the music," or "I don't care if I meet someone, I'm just here to have fun."

Right. And I go to the baths to get wet.

Cruising is an art form with difficult rules. Worse, the rules change depending on the players, the venues, and the circumstances. Cruise too hard you scare them off; cruise too little you won't get off.

We all know people who can walk into a bar and leave with the best-looking guy in ten minutes. It takes me twenty but only because there's a time-delay in the drugs I slip into their drinks.

Assuming you want the guy to walk out on his own and not slung over your shoulder, you shouldn't listen to me. You should listen to my friend Tony.

Tony's no great looker. I mean, he's above average looking but the guys he snags, they're not above-average looking. They're WAY above above-average looking. So above, you get a nose-bleed just looking at them.

"How do you do it?" I once asked him. "Watch," he said, as we walked into a bar. He didn't just walk in like he owned the place;

he walked in like he paid cash at the closing. And then he walked around with a genuinely warm smile, like he couldn't wait to buy you a drink.

Contrary to what porn videos and *Queer As Folk* will have you believe, confidence and approachability, not contempt and inaccessibility, is what'll get you plowed more often than a snowy Minnesota highway.

I bring this up because, as you'll see, I get so many sad-sack letters from guys who've pretty much given up the idea of meeting Mr. Right, Mr. Right Now, or even Mr. Oh You'll Do.

My advice is to listen to Tony. Do the unthinkable in a roomful of good-looking men: Smile and be friendly.

* * *

Hey, Woody!
I'm not even close to getting laid as much as I want to, and I've been thinking maybe I'm just not that hot. I can't ask people I know, cuz, well, they wouldn't be family or friends if they didn't lie, right? So how do I find out what my real fuckability quotient is? How do I get an unbiased opinion of what I look like?

—Wanting to know

Dear Wanting:
Your friends won't critique your physical appearance? Mine won't shut up about it.

Are you sure you're gay? Being heterosexual isn't just an unnatural attraction to women, you know. It's also the total absence of male friends yapping at your fashion sense.

"How Fuckable Am I?" is the gay version of "What's the Meaning of Life?" Straight people think Rodin's famous sculpture, "The Thinker," symbolized man's contemplation of his nature. Please. He wasn't thinking, "Who am I?" He was thinking, "Would I do me if I saw me walking down the street?"

Rodin didn't have the Internet to find out, but you do. Try a site called "Am I Hot Or Am I Not?" It's a virtual beauty pageant that posts your picture and invites sadists like me to vote on your attractiveness by clicking on a scale from one to ten.

I thought this column had cornered the market on exploiting people's insecurities for profit, but this site takes it to a new level. If you have faith that people are telling the truth it will either make your day or make your therapist rich. Try it at: *www. amihotornot.com.*

The second way is to post your pictures on America Online. Build one of their idiot-proof web pages, put some pictures up on it, and direct traffic to it by entering one of their chat rooms and posting your website on your profile. Be direct. Tell people you want them to rank you on your physical attributes. I'd ask the following questions:

"If you were in bed with me . . ."

1. Would you tell anyone afterwards?
2. How important would the dimmer switch be to you?
3. Would you insist that I be face up or down on the pillow as you fucked me?

Hey, Woody!
There was this really cute German boy across the aisle on an international flight I was on. We start talking and he does that cute, blonde smile thing that made me want to hijack the plane to the moon.

We traded American and German CD's on our Walkmans. He held my gaze, smiled, and practically beamed at me every time we talked. At this point I'm pretty sure he's gay, especially when I realized that almost all of the music he had were dance tracks. When he asked me if I liked Cher I thought it was only a matter of time before I joined the mile high club. Besides, he was drinking wine. Don't Germans drink beer?

So I gave him a pen and paper and asked him to translate four words into German: 1) Are, 2) Beautiful, 3) You,

and 4) Very. When he handed me back the pad I rearranged the German words into a sentence that said, "You are very beautiful" and handed it to him.

Well, Woody, that was the end of that. He sort of gave me this frozen smile and he just kind of withdrew for the rest of the flight. He wasn't gay. How could I have been so wrong? I have his email address and I was thinking of apologizing to him. Do you think I should?

—Airsick over America

Dear Airsick:

Anybody's gaydar would've gone off with all the cues you picked up. Still, anybody who's gone to Europe can tell you that straight people over there have a pronounced gay sensibility—they love dance music (it's about all they play in Berlin), holding your gaze, smiling, and God help us, listening to Cher. I'm sorry, but that woman's singing makes me howl like a dog hearing a siren.

Anyway, it's not unusual for European straight men to kiss each other hello and goodbye. Didn't you see the Russian gymnasts greet each other at the last Olympics when they came off the floor? They were "high-fiving" each other with their lips.

And forget about the apology. What the hell for? You didn't do anything wrong. If a woman came on to him and he wasn't interested, would she feel the need to apologize? Fuck that shit.

It's total homophobic crap to believe there's something wrong with a gay man hitting on a straight man. Herr Blonde should have felt complimented, not insulted. He could have simply said, "Thanks, I'm flattered but I'm also straight. Now, here, listen to the latest cut from Germany's most popular band, The Auschwitz Boys. It's called 'Cooking with Gas.'"

Hey, Woody!

Forgive me while I barf in your soup. The bulk of your response to the German international flight incident was rabidly gay, but that was okay. It's what makes your column amusing. But then you went into the Nazi past, like any homophobic American xenophobe would. According to the letter, the German guy seemed to be in his 20s. Auschwitz happened over 50 years ago. This is pure crap, associating him with what his ancestors did; ignoring the millions of Germans who were not Nazi and whose grandparents weren't either. You live in the South, from what I gather. How would you like it if a German said "Here, listen to the latest cut from the American South's most popular band, The Burning Crosses. It's called "Stringing Them High."

Think before you speak next time, Woody. Bigotry doesn't become your column.

—Horny but unbigoted

Dear Horny:

You know you're right. I need to apologize. For not typing the Auschwitz line in ALL CAPS, you humorless, hand wringing, schoolmarm.

If you hadn't noticed, Nancy Drew, I'm not writing a column for the *Ladies Home Journal*. This is Cock Central where we Greet the Meat with all the subtlety of a brick through a windshield.

I wrote that line because a) being half Jewish and all gay, I have the right to say whatever the fuck I want about the descendants of a generation who tried to exterminate my people, and b) because nothing gives me more joy than annoying the likes of you.

Plus, it was a really funny line, don't you think?

You would have had a point if I were attacking the victims, but you, you moron, you actually believe that the descendants of perpetrators shouldn't be made fun of. What a load of mustard gas. If you can't make fun of people who descended from a generation that tried to subjugate the whole fucking planet, who can you make fun of?

Besides, the German guy deserved it: He didn't put out for one of my readers.

This column works because readers get accurate medical facts and the satisfaction of seeing people like you get offended.

As long as I get my facts right and you get your dander up, this column is going to be around for a long time. So, please, I know you're angry, but keep reading. Without you I'm nothing.

Hey, Woody!
I'm a cop, and I get more respect for being gay from straight co-workers than gay acquaintances. Why are gay men so suspicious of gay cops? I guess part of it is that I work for the DEA (Drug Enforcement Agency) and though I've never done a bust in a gay bar, all the bartenders know who I am and spread it around.

Sometimes when I walk in, the place parts like the Red Sea. People who don't know I'm a cop hit on me, but when they find out, they disappear without a trace. When I go out to the bars, I don't go to case the joint, I go to party and have a good time. Guys will sneak me their phone numbers, want to meet me afterward (always with my uniform on, too), but they don't want to talk to me in public. Can you help us gay cops? Any suggestions for making our hunting a little happier?

—Cop no attitude

Dear Cop:
Well, this isn't exactly sex advice you're asking for, but I was so taken with the visual (guys circling like vultures, then scurrying like rats) I figured what the hell.

First thing is, you need to find new bars. I believe in skiing downhill, not up. If that's not possible, then make friends with the bartenders. Get to the bars a little earlier and chat them up when they're not so busy. Disarm them (with your charm, not your gun) and let them see you're there for the beef, not the arrest.

And be sure to leave big fat tips. Reduce their fear and they'll reduce the gossip. They'll never really trust you, but remember, you're aiming for peace not love.

Third, and most important, Duhmaster General, don't tell people what you do for a living while you're in the bar. Christ, I hope you're smarter in your stakeouts than you are in your cruising.

I'd be nervous too if I met a cop in a bar. Aside from the drugs, any intelligent person who's been drinking thinks about the possibility of a DUI. Meeting a cop in a bar would blow anyone's anxiety off the chart. And as you know, nobody's there to blow anxiety. Unless that's his stage name.

I suspect you're flirting with a little victimhood here. If you know saying you're a cop is going to freak people out, why do you tell them? So you can whine about how guys reject you? Tell them when you get home.

Anybody who reads this column regularly knows I don't believe in lying—unless it helps you get laid. Honesty is not the best policy in bars. That's why the lights are so low.

Hey, Woody!
I have a couple of friends who just can't seem to stop talking about how good they are in bed. I mean, it's one thing to talk about what you like in the sack, but to be bragging about what a great lover you are . . . it just doesn't seem right. I'm wondering what your take is on bed-braggers. Are they that good or are they hiding something?
—Tired of bragging rights

Dear Tired:
Your friends remind me of the old saying, "Those who can't do, teach. Those who can't teach, teach phys-ed."

In other words, your friends suck in bed. And science backs me up, too. A recent study in the *Journal of Personality and Social Psychology* showed that people who scored poorly in logic and grammar tests tended to think they did well.

Translation: Idiots don't know they're idiots, so they brag about how smart they are. It's sort of like their incompetence robs them of the ability to see their incompetence. The Cornell scientists believe that the skills you need to perform well are the same skills you need to *determine* whether you performed well.

The Cornell tests didn't measure "bedroom competence" (otherwise I'm sure they would have wanted me in the control group), but the lead scientist went on record saying he believed the same thing happens to bedroom braggers. The next time your friends start bragging, show them this column. That'll pucker their mouths shut faster than a vagina.

Hey, Woody!
I met this guy in an America Online chat room. His pictures were so hot I had to towel off my computer. An hour later, he opens his door and in a historic first for AOL, he was actually as hot as his picture. He's got porn playing in the living room and within minutes we're sucking face (and other extremities). During the instant messaging he said he wanted me to ride him like a lawn mower. And after all that kissing and sucking I was ready to cut some grass. He lays down on his living room floor, getting ready for his close-up, when suddenly I notice he's starting to lose his hard-on.

Then he says he has a conference call he needs to prepare for and says I've gotta leave. Huh? Next thing I knew I was out the door with blue balls Louis Vouitton could have used as a luggage set. What happened? My feelings are really hurt.

Everything was going great and then bam! I mean why would a guy say I'm hot, go down on me, then want me to fuck him and then give me the bum's rush before we even got started?

—Hurt . . . and not a little horny

Dear Hurt:
I have to admit, this one's for the books. Usually they throw you out AFTER you fuck them, not before.

Man, what a kick in the ass. Fourth and one at the end zone and you got pushed back.

I know it hurts, but suck it up, man. You weren't on a date, you were on a fuck. Well, almost.

He's allowed to change his mind, even if it's at the most inconvenient moment. You cannot know what was going on in his mind. Maybe he had a boyfriend who was coming home soon, maybe he's recently out and panicked at the last minute. Or maybe you just didn't turn him on that much. Sexual desire in the gay spectrum includes "hot enough to blow, but not enough to fuck."

I've said this before and I'll say it again: You never know how a man feels about you, even when he's got your dick in his mouth.

Whatever the case is, I promise you he didn't pull his pants back up because of a "conference call." If he had, he would have asked for your phone number, kissed you at the door, and promised to call. He didn't.

Hey, Woody!
I have a question for you. I am sick and tired of the creeps at my gym that come not to work out, but to cruise the locker room. I suppose everyone grabs a quick peek every now and then, but I'm tired of these old, overweight men who high-tail it to the steam room every time they see some in-shape guy trying to take a shower in peace.

Here's my issue with it, Woody. Shouldn't there be a cruising etiquette that says don't cruise someone after it's clear they're not interested?

And don't cruise someone if they're clearly out of your league. You may think it sounds harsh, but these trolls have the same standard of attractiveness I do, and I'm young, hard, and good-looking. They should be cruising their own level of beauty, but you never see them cruising each other!

—Workout bunny

Dear Bunny:

Apparently steam rooms are a great way to build self-esteem. How else do you explain the phenomenon of fat ugly men believing that the men who won't look at them when they're clothed will pop a boner when they see them nude?

I've pretty much given up on gay steam rooms. Once, I was reading a newspaper and practically had people turning the pages for me.

It's not that I think you shouldn't cruise, it's just that there are appropriate styles of cruising for every venue. You cruise differently in a bathhouse than in a bar, don't you? And you cruise differently in a bar than at a birthday party. Every discriminating horn-dog needs to respect the dynamics of the space they're in.

The wet area is a public facility with a specific purpose. You don't have the right to make somebody uncomfortable just because your love log needs lodging. Here are the four Cruising Commandments that should hang in every wet area:

1. If your target isn't looking back, stop looking.
2. If your prey gives monosyllabic answers to essay questions, shut up.
3. If you're much older, fatter, and uglier than the guy you're cruising and he's not paying attention, you need to stop. Say to yourself, "I'm much older, fatter, and uglier than the guy I'm cruising and he's not paying attention. I need to stop."
4. If you're old, fat, and ugly, you can only cruise other old, fat, and ugly men.

Hey, Woody!
I take strong exception to your recent Cruising Commandments. Let us not forget that our gay society has many people who find older men quite sexy.

I am a 48 year old man, a bit of a bear, and yet I still make a large percentage of my income as a call boy, with a

large percentage of repeat clientele, not all of whom are my age or older, thank you very much.

I especially disagree with Commandment no. 4 which you state as "If you're much older, fatter, and uglier than the guy you're cruising and he's not paying attention, you need to stop. Say to yourself "I'm much older, fatter, and uglier than the guy I'm cruising and he's not paying attention. I need to stop."

Basically, you're recommending that people damage themselves psychologically just because they don't appeal to some little rude snit. Your response should've been "Don't insult your own dignity by pursuing someone who is not interested in you."

—A semi-bear who takes long showers

Dear Semi:
You don't really make a good point, you make a good comma. What you say is true, comma, AND there are jerks out there that deserve everything I've said. I know plenty of dignified older men, handsome, maybe a little bit plump, who cruise in locker rooms but know when to stop.

In my last column I was referring to the people *who just don't get it*. My point isn't that young hard-bodies have the right to invade your personal space in a sauna but older flabbies don't. My point is that NOBODY has that right. Most of the jerks who do it happen to be old, fat, and ugly, and they need to be called on it.

So let me repeat my baiting credo for the cruising-impaired: You do not have the right to make people uncomfortable in public spaces just because you want to free willie. I stand by my answer—if your subtle cruising attempt fails, shut up and look at the opposite wall.

Hey, Woody!
You missed the boat on the Cruising Commandments. I doubt that "work-out bunny" follows his own advice to

"fat, ugly men" (that they should stop cruising when they don't get a response). I know WB pretty well, and he probably doesn't quite live up to that standard.

—Cruised & Bruised by WBs

Hey, Woody!
Define "old, fat, and ugly." I have no doubt that to some people you probably fit into one of these categories. Don't you think you're adding to the age-ism, weight-ism, and beauty-elitism when you say old, fat, ugly men can only cruise other old, fat, ugly men in the showers? Some younger guys are attracted to older guys. Besides, what's old? 30? 40? And what's fat? Love handles? And what's ugly? Big noses? What if you're into big noses? Speaking of noses, you oughta blow that piece of advice right out of your schnozz.

—Dick Tionary

Hey, Woody!
You are old, fat, and ugly—between your ears. I take great offense at your Cruising Commandments. I am neither old nor fat, nor ugly but I still think your advice sucked.

—Sick ovu

Dear Cruised Dick, and Sick:
For the record, I do not believe that the older shouldn't look at the younger, nor the thicker at the thinner or the less attractive at the more attractive. Most people have been the target of assholes that won't stop cruising even when your smoke signals spelling out "GO AWAY" coat the state with volcanic ash. In my experience, those assholes tend to be older, heavier, and less attractive. But you're right—you can be young, pretty, and still be an asshole. Thanks for pointing it out.

Hey, Woody!
A straight married couple has glommed on to me and we do the whole scene: drugs, circuit parties, gay bars. The guy is hot. I mean, like sacrifice-your-career-to-smell-his-dirty-shorts hot.

He's very affectionate with me, even kisses me hello. On the mouth. His wife (who's also hot) encourages it. One night we were dancing at a gay bar wired on ecstasy and his wife kisses him, then me, and then says, "Okay, now you two kiss." We did and I couldn't believe it.

But that's as far as it's really gone. Then one night his wife goes out of town and the husband calls me, wants to go out. So we dropped some E and went to a gay bar. When we came home he asked if he could crash at my place. I said sure, you can sleep in the spare bedroom. He's like, "do you mind if we sleep in the same bed?"

Did I mind? That's like asking do I mind if a Greek god feeds me grapes. So I figure okay, it's going to happen tonight. Well, I get in the shower and when I come out he's in my bed. Snoring.

We slept, even cuddled a little in the morning and then he went back to his wife. I don't get it, Woody. Why's he doing this? He's driving me crazy. Should I talk to him? Do you think he's secretly gay?
> —Looking for a Bi-lateral agreement

Dear Bi-lateral:
Talk about sending mixed signals. I can't pick him up on my AM or FM dial.

There are two possibilities here, none of which are going to get you in his pants, so I guess you can stop reading.

The first is that he's one repressed motherfucker and he can't give himself permission to express his homo tendencies. He's giving all the outward appearances of being open and liberal but deep down he won't allow himself the likes of you. The most he'll do is get worshipped at gay bars, which of course makes him suspect in my eyes. Spending more time in front of the mirror than under a guy is just a long way of spelling "FAG."

The second possibility, and the one I think is more likely, is that he's not gay. He's expressing himself exactly the way he feels comfortable.

I'm often affectionate with women. A kiss here, a cuddle there, but I don't want to have sex with them. Does that make me repressed?

Why is it that if a gay man flirts with a straight woman nobody considers him a repressed hetero, but if a straight man flirts with a gay man he's considered a repressed homo?

It reminds me of a great joke they tell in Montana:

You hunt all your life; nobody ever calls you a hunter.

You live in the woods all your life; nobody ever calls you a woodsman.

But you suck one cock, and they ALWAYS call you a cocksucker.

Hey, Woody!
A lot of people attack NBC's TV show "Will & Grace" for not showing Will in any sexual or romantic situations. They think it's unrealistic that a good-looking gay guy wouldn't be dick-hopping all over town. Well, I've got news for them; there are plenty of Wills out there in real life. I know, because I'm one of them.

Like Will (and by the way, I've been told I actually look like him), I wasn't just burned in my last relationship, I was incinerated. It's been two years since I had sex. I do masturbate (gosh, maybe they should at least show Will doing that, huh?), but I just can't get myself out there in the dating scene. I'm too scared and I just can't handle it, even though I'm dying to have another relationship (or just sex). What's your advice for Wills like me?

—The real Will

Dear Will:

I'd tell you what I tell everyone: Drink.

Never underestimate alcohol's thigh-splitting properties. I usually prescribe martinis to Frigid Friedas like you.

As Dorothy Parker once said, "I try to only drink one martini. With one I fall under a spell, with two I fall under the table, and with three I fall under the host."

I recommend you drink four.

I also recommend you take a good look at what kind of energy you're projecting. You can usually tell by your circumstances.

If you're alone all the time, it's because you project a *"Leave me alone"* energy. If you're constantly drawing in assholes that piss all over you, it's because you unconsciously have a blinking light above you that only assholes can see. And it reads *"Last Restroom Before Highway."*

I know you'd rather hear all that bullshit about "issues" you have to work out before you're ready to take a chance, but you know what? I don't sell cosmetics on this aisle. Try the next one over. I'm selling rebuilt engines.

I know it's tough to hear, but the reason you're not dating or having sex isn't because you're so wounded. It's because you unconsciously push people away.

You can revolutionize your sexual life by asking yourself this simple question: What are you unaware of about the way you come across, that if you became aware of and changed, you would draw the kind of people you want into your life?

This is a painful question because you have to be raw honest with yourself. Engage your friends. Ask them. What do you project? I promise you this: You have no idea what a lousy rotten energy you put out. How do I know? Because if you put out good, vibrant energy, you wouldn't be writing me. You'd be up to your dick in dick.

I know you're in pain, but if you wait for the pain to go away before you act you'll find out the true meaning of eternity. Take my advice. Don't wait to work out your "issues." Learn to project what you want to draw in and you will draw it in.

If you don't want to listen to me, listen to "Jack." Here's what he said to "Will" in a recent episode: *"I am telling you, you're gonna blink and you'll be 80 and alone in a caftan with a lap full of catnip saying, 'Here kitty, kitty.' It's time to put the sex back in homosexual, Will."*

Hey, Woody!
There's a guy . . . ok, there's more than just one—there's always a guy I'm attracted to at the gym but there's this unspoken rule—the etiquette of disregard—look or even ignore and definitely don't touch—while getting one's daily vanity pump in at the gym. Without stalking him or following him into the bathroom to try and catch a glimpse of his goods before he leaves, what's the proper way to approach him—or do I leave it alone and hope that chance and/or fate bring us together?

I read your missive about letting your fingers do the walking when at a circuit party, but I'm loathe to try this advice at the gym (even though if you turn down the lights, add water and stir it's almost a circuit party). Or perhaps I'm just looking for love in all the wrong places? What's a shy guy to do?

—Too shy to shy, hush hush eye to eye . . .

Dear Eye-shy:
You're not imagining this "etiquette of disregard" in gay gyms. It's very real, and typical of the gay "M.O." (as in Missed Opportunity).

What a waste. There we are, packed half-naked in a room, and we ignore each other like we weren't even there. It should be easier to pick up men in a gay gym than any other place save the bathhouses. But it isn't.

There's a certain level of dishonesty going on at gay gyms. We pretend we're not interested in order to preserve a sense of superiority or mystery. It's one thing to be subtle (who wants to work out where there's slobber on the floor? It'd ruin your Nikes), it's another thing to ignore people completely.

You're right about not letting your fingers do the walking. I believe in getting as much sex as possible but not at the cost of your dignity, his personal space, or my ability to work out without feeling like I'm in a bad porn flick. Which reminds me, is it redundant to use the word "bad" in front of "porn flick"?

You'd think eye contact at a gay gym would be so pervasive they'd install a Murine® counter in the corner. But wait for eye contact to make your move, and it'll be time to shave again.

My advice is to do the unthinkable around a pack of beautiful men—smile and be friendly. Ask Mr. Attitude-is-Better-Than-Sex if he'll spot you, then strike up a conversation. Or say something kind or funny about his shirt. You'd be surprised how many men put on the "I Can't Be Bothered" façade because they think that's the way you're supposed to be at a gym (and for good reason— everyone else is doing it).

Often, when they run into somebody warm, kind, and fun, they can drop the ice mask. And hopefully, their underwear too. But take it outside, I've got sit-ups to do.

Hey, Woody!
The other day I told an African-American friend I was in the mood for black cock. That shot him into space, ranting and raving about my supposed racism. "We are not a dish for white men to order out of a menu when they get a yen for something exotic" were his exact words. Is it racist to cruise black men because they're good in bed? He seems to think so.

—A faux racist?

Dear Faux:
First we had women equating sexual attraction with objectification and now we have African-American men equating it with racism. What a load of pomade.

Elevating sexual attraction to other manifestations of racism like lynchings, slavery, Jim Crow, and housing discrimination is an insult to all the decent, innocent black folks who came before and will live long after your friend. The charge stretches the concept of absurdity to its breaking point.

If you were cruising black men for a sick psycho-plantation role-play of a slave raping his white owner, he'd have a point. If in the middle of it you yelled out "Fuck me, nigger," he'd have an even bigger one.

But wanting a roll in the hay with a black stud doesn't qualify as bigotry to me. If you're racist for "being in the mood for black cock" then I'm the Grand Wizard of the Ku Klux Klan. I'm *always* in the mood for the black stick.

Even if you said you want to fuck black men but you don't want to date them, the charges don't stick. Personally, I don't like the company of circuit boys but I consider it sport to fuck them. They're good lays. So what if I don't want to date them?

I love sleeping with black men precisely because they're different than me. They smell different, they taste different, they feel different. To say that white men should only be with black men when they can see past the color of their skin is a total crock of shit. If black men didn't taste, smell and feel different they'd be, well, WHITE. And God knows there's too many of those people around.

My advice to you: Spice up your sex life but don't stop at black men. Point your pistol to Asians, Latinos, Hindus, anybody that will broaden your sexual palette.

My advice to your friend: Hmmm. I was going to say "Lighten Up" but he's so uptight he'd probably think I was asking him to turn white.

Hey, Woody!
I LOVE your column! It's the high point of reading the paper. Your letters are entertaining and your answers are irreverent yet informative, at the same time. You do a great job. Just thought you should know.

—A fan

Hey, Woody!
I've read your column for the last time. You're the most
negative person I've ever read. What kind of sex advisor
ridicules the people he's trying to help? Your articles just
get worse and worse. You suck.

—A foe

Dear Fan & Foe:
You guys remind me of two tricks I once had. The first thought I
was the best lay he ever had; the other thought I must've just
come out because, as a nosy friend gleefully relayed to me,
"Nobody could be that bad in bed."

That was a long time ago and I'm happy to report there's a lot
more "best" than "worst" votes out there. And the good Lord
willing, there'll be plenty of more ballots to count in the future.

Your "I love you/I hate you" mail reminded me how critical
feedback is to great sex. So instead of answering questions, I'm
going to pose them. And here's the first one: How do them that
you've done talk about thee?

Translation for the lube-impaired: Are you any good in bed?

I'm not talking about how pretty you are, or whether your abs
are so cut you can slice tomatoes on them, or whether your purple-
headed custard chucker is so big people faint at the sight of it.
I'm talking about whether you're any good in the sack.

Of course, you're the last person you should ask. You'll lie like
a rug on wooden slats. And it's next to impossible to ask the one
you're with. Whispering "How was I?" after sex is a guaranteed
post-coital buzz-kill.

So if you can't ask yourself because you'll lie, and you can't
ask your partner because he'll lie, how can you tell how good
you are? Well, imagine this: What if Woody conducted a survey
of the guys you've slept with?

If I polled the last hundred people who pulled your pole and
asked them to rate you, what would your average score be?
Would the survey show you can make men hear colors in bed? Or
would it say you just lay there like a piece of wilted lettuce?

I remember once overhearing someone I had sex with talking about our exploits. It wasn't my looks that turned him on (he described me as "good-looking but no Brad Pitt or anything"), or my body ("he's defined and muscular but he doesn't really stand out in the gym"), or my dick ("he's bigger than average but he's no Jeff Stryker").

Ouch, ouch and ouch, if you get my drift. The point (other than the need to fuck more diplomatic partners) is that what impressed my friend wasn't me, but how I made him feel. He'd been with lots of better-looking, bigger-dicked guys, but, damn if any of them left him begging for more like I did.

Though I could have done without the passive-aggressive body-slams, overhearing my friend talk about what I was like in bed gave me the opportunity to glimpse the Golden Rule of Getting More—"Do Unto Others So They'll Say Unto Others 'Get Onto Him.'"

In other words, if you want more and better sex, impress your sexual quarry. Pay attention to what he wants and deliver it like a pizza—on time and piping hot. Not only will you have a great time, it will get you laid more often than the traditional seduction strategies—alcohol and lying. Although I must say, there's a lot to be said for both of these time-tested methods.

If you want to be a better lover, next time you're about to shtuup some hottie, ask yourself this: "What do I want this guy saying in Woody's survey after I'm done with him?"

Hey, Woody!
When I was in my 20's, I liked guys in their 20's. When I was in my 30's, I liked guys in their 20's. And now that I'm in my 40's, guess what I like?

I can still pick up younger guys and get away with it because I look young, I lie about my age and, most importantly, I go to bars with bad lighting. Don't laugh; it works.

But here's the thing, Woody. I don't want to be in my 50's and 60's and still go after the twenty-somethings. It

just seems like a dead end. Besides, I think my conscience is catching up with my cruising.

What can I do to shift my desire to older guys? Do you think it's possible to change the object of your sexual desires? Or am I doomed to be a lecherous old man?

—Afraid of the future

Dear Afraid:

I feel your pain. I like younger guys, too. In fact, my last boyfriend called me a pedophile. "Oh, yeah?" I snapped. "That's a mighty big word for a 12 year old!"

You have to be firm with boyfriends or they'll walk all over you.

Look, at least you're not going after teenagers. And for the record, neither am I. My last boyfriend was 12 years old *emotionally*. Physically, he was much older.

Sixteen, I think.

Anyway, you are not experiencing anything most guys in their forties don't. Straight or gay, by the way. When was the last time you saw a straight guy pant when Madeleine Albright walked by?

Personally, I don't think you can stop being attracted to whom you're attracted to. If that were so, a lot of us would just "choose" to be straight. If you didn't get to vote on what gender you're attracted to, what makes you think you get to vote on which kinds of people within that gender you're attracted to?

Besides, why should you give up sex with twenty-somethings if all it takes is telling them something they want to hear?

Listen, truth and sobriety are overrated when it comes to dick. I say lie until lying doesn't work anymore. And believe me, you'll know when it stops working because you'll blurt out laughing before the twenty-something does.

I have a friend who constantly lies about his age when he's cruising. He calls it *"Foreploy,"* misrepresenting himself for the purpose of obtaining sex.

He's also got an interesting way of doing it. He tells his potential tricks he's 32 even though he's 42. That way all he has to do is subtract 10 from his year of birth, saving him the agony of doing the math when he's drunk. Better to look old for 32 than young for 42, he says.

Flawless logic, if you ask me.

Still, the problem with lying is its bankrupt premise—that there's something wrong with being 40+. There isn't. That's why the long-term answer is to be honest about your age. There are lots of twenty-somethings that want forty-somethings. Draw them to you with the qualities they seek: confidence, honesty, experience, and courage.

Men over 40 are beautiful; they're just not beautiful in the way men under 40 are. For example, their abs may not be as tight, but they're way better in bed. And more importantly, they pick up the dinner check. What's not to like?

Just because you're attracted to twenty-somethings doesn't mean you can't learn to be attracted to men in their 40s. You don't have to give up one for the other. Be attracted to both; you'll get more BANG for your buck.

Cultivate a desire for men your own age. Pay attention to what you find attractive in them and build from there. It's possible to attach desire to a man's character, not just to his body.

Hey, Woody!
I'm curious what you, a sex advisor, think about the sex-drenched *Queer As Folk*.

—It's Showtime, baby

Dear Showtime:
Watching QAF is like cruising a hot but really stupid guy who wants dinner before he'll put out. Is the agony of the dinner worth the sex? Is the agony of QAF's lame dialogue and cardboard characters worth the $10 a month? It's the same question. There is no real answer.

The sex scenes in QAF are stunning. Certainly the best I've ever seen on television. Gawd, if only porn could have the production values, the camera angles, the editing, the rhythm that leaves you panting as much as QAF does.

HOWEVER.

Like the hot but stupid guy you want to fuck but not talk to, QAF is the stupid show you want to see but not hear.

How could a show about gay people have dreadful dialogue, one-dimensional characters and plot lines so thin you could floss with them? Please. We are much more interesting than that.

And don't get me started about Brian, the Head Whore of the series. He's the least believable character on the show. Not because of all the sex he has, but because of the way he has it.

Somebody convinced Showtime that contempt is an aphrodisiac for gay men. Bullshit. We all have friends who can walk in a bar and leave with the best looking guy within ten minutes. But by showering contempt on them like Brian does? I don't think so. When was the last time you went home with a guy who looked at you the way a neat-freak looks at a stain?

Brian hates sex and he hates the people he has it with even more. Compare him to Samantha of *Sex and the City*. Like Brian, she too has an odometer on her bed, but look at the difference. She loves sex, adores men, and revels in her promiscuity. Samantha is a role model, a true inspiration for the whore in everyone. Brian shows sex as a contemptible duty. Samantha reminds us it's a joyous privilege.

It pains me to say this, because I really admire Showtime for having the guts to produce the show, but here's the thought that usually crosses my mind the few times I've watched it: "I'm missing the 10 p.m. news for *this?*"

Hey, Woody!
You know what I really hate? Running into guys I've had sex with, who I don't want to have sex with again. They always want to stop and talk and then I have to wiggle my way out of why I didn't call and do I want to have a repeat performance.

Now, I don't actually say this but I'm always like, "If I wanted you again I would have called; now please move, you're blocking my view of that really cute guy in the corner."

What exactly is the politics of greeting a trick you don't want anymore and getting him to move along?

—Only once, baby

Dear Once:

You're the kind of person people stand in line to hate. I'd be at the front of it, too, brass knuckles and all.

How dare you treat people like they were a piece of meat? Who do you think you are—ME? I've got the patent for treating men like a T-bone. Keep that shit up and I'll slap you with a copyright infringement suit.

To answer your question, what you should say depends on the asshole quotient of the trick. If I ran into you, for instance, I'd probably greet you with something like "Good to see you! You sure are a parasite for sore eyes."

However, as arrogant as you are, you do bring up a good point. What's the protocol when you run into someone who wants to continue seeing you when all you wanted was a one night stand?

Most of us attended the Greet 'em, Meat 'em, and Street 'em school of seduction and graduated with honors. Unfortunately, the school needs to add some advanced courses on courtesy and respect.

Don't assume that running into a trick who chats you up necessarily wants an encore performance. Maybe they see the potential of being friends. Although why anybody would want to be friends with the likes of you is a mystery.

Most of us have the experience of having good friends who started out as tricks. Don't rob yourself of a potential friendship just because you don't want to have sex with him again. If he's unmistakably looking for a second session, change the subject gracefully by simply saying, "You know, I had a great time with you the other night, but I'd prefer to be friends."

This is the right thing to do for three reasons: 1) You owe him the honor and respect of a decent conversation, 2) You might get a great friendship out of it, and 3) He might lead you to your next victim.

Hey, Woody!
I've met this guy at the gym. In real estate terms he's ocean-front property. The problem is, I think he may be straight. His easy smile and constant eye contact make my battle bulge in a war I'm not sure I can win. I've thought of just making a pass at him and let the chips fall where they may (hopefully, around his ankles). Do you think I should?
                                            —Kent standit anymore

Dear Kent:
No, I don't think you should. You wouldn't appreciate it if a woman made an overt pass at you, so why visit the indignity on him? Straight or gay, I do not believe in making a pass at anyone unless you're pretty sure the feeling's mutual.

A romantic overture should feel like a delight, not a mugging. By all means, find out if he's willing to do Stupid Penis Tricks with you, but do it with style. Escalate your attentions; buy him a little gift and see how he reacts. And remember, never underestimate the power of liquor to sand rough wood.

Hey, Woody!
This boorish trick came by on a Sunday afternoon. What a clod. He was dressed and headed for the door before the cum had even begun to coagulate on the sheets. I mean, hold me for God's sakes! He was up and standing right away, and I'm like, please, relax on the bed, let me get you a warm towel, you know? And besides, you're dripping on the hardwoods. So my question is, how do you get a trick

to just stay put long enough to have some post-coital snuggling? I don't want to marry the guy, I just want to be held.

—Touch & Go

Dear Touch:

I'm right there with you, babe. There's something so delicious about holding a man after sex, to feel smothered by his body as your mind gently drifts and your body descends into a blissful peace and calm. There's nothing worse than a guy who comes and goes.

There's really nothing you can do if he's just a ship passing in the night. There's a period right after orgasm when a lot of guys like you and I feel vulnerable and want the warmth and intimacy you only get from cuddling after sex. But you don't discuss vulnerabilities with tricks. The most you can do is what you did—invite him to stay for a pretzeled snooze.

If he doesn't accept the invitation you need to be a champ and honor his decision without trying to talk him out of it. Remember, one does not talk to tricks. One moans, groans, points and spreads. Heavy discussions about intimate needs? Try brunch with straight girlfriends.

Hey, Woody!
I was at a bar the other night and met this really great guy. We were doing the eye thing, the ten-laps-around-the-bar thing, and finally we met. As the bewitching hour came I asked him if he'd like to go home with me. "It depends," he said. "Are you a top or a bottom?"

Now, Woody, I'm kind of a modest guy. I was floored, speechless. I actually started stuttering. "Well?" he pressed me. I finally said, "Why does it matter?" and he said, "Because I feel like fucking tonight and if you don't want to get fucked, there's no point in going home together."

I ended up not going home with him because I was so insulted. My question: Was I wrong for insisting on a little

class? This whole top/bottom classification is lost on me. Should I just give in to it and label myself like everyone else does?

—Defiant

Dear Defiant:

I think asking a guy if he's a top or a bottom is a pretty tacky thing to do, and it reveals the shallow, superficial take most gay men have about sex.

Sex flows from the energy between two people. Sometimes that energy translates into fucking, getting fucked, blown, getting blown, getting a hand-job, giving a hand-job, or none of the above or all of the above, some of the time, none of the time or all of the time—depending on the situation, the players, and the conditions.

To diminish the glorious and limitless possibilities of sex down to two cold and calculating categories—top and bottom—is one of the great embarrassments of gay culture we are inexplicably proud of.

The drive to categorization is a very male thing, and particularly a very GAY male thing. We live in a culture that insists, no, REVERES, the idea of living out of an artificially-constructed identity. Gay, Lesbian, Bisexual, Transgendered, Questioning, everyone must have labels and those labels must be used by everyone.

Labels are helpful to oppressed people who are invisible to each other. They help build bridges between people who thought they were the only ones "like that." But the helpful labels almost always turn to psychic prisons, preventing you from experiencing that which lies beyond the bars you've constructed for yourself. And it also limits people from experiencing you as more than the prisoner within those bars.

I've actually heard one self-described "top" say how attracted he was to another self-described top, but that he'd rather go home alone than have a fuckless night. What kind of bullshit is that?

So I don't agree with this whole top/bottom dichotomy. It di-

minishes us, it doesn't serve us, and it perpetuates the narrow—
Goddammit, is it narrow—belief that penetration is the only acceptable sexual act.

As for whether you over-reacted by not going home with him.
I don't know. How cute was he?

Hey, Woody!
The letter from "Defiant" cracked me up. He was "insulted"
because the guy who wanted to take him home asked if he
were a top or a bottom. As a 43-year-old gay male bottom,
I know what I enjoy and what I don't enjoy sexually.

In my twenty-three years of having gay sex, by now I
know what works for me, and have had enough unsatisfac-
tory sexual experiences to avoid those that I know will
not work out. You say that labels are bad, but they're not
always bad. Sometimes you know what you are and are not
ashamed of it.

What made me laugh out loud at the guy's letter was
him asking you if he was "wrong for insisting on a little
class?" Ha! Here's a man picking up a total stranger in a
bar, planning on having sex with him, which would mean
exchanging spit, sucking each other's dicks, sticking dicks
in assholes, and he WANTS A LITTLE CLASS? Lordy, if
just talking about the type of sex the two might have is
"insulting" to him, then what would the actual sex be like?
"Defiant" needs to loosen his pigtails a little.

—A muscle bottom and proud of it

Dear Proud of it:
I don't disagree that "Defiant" needs to lighten up a little, but I'm
more on his side than not. Here's why: 1) There's a totalitarian
expectation in gay culture that you should label yourself; 2)
There's a growing and mistaken tendency to believe that penetration is the only sex act worth performing; and 3) There's a
ubiquitous but unstated belief that the thrill of discovery has no
place in a sexual encounter.

If you believe in labels, if you believe in reducing the glorious expanse of sex into one limited act—penetration, if you don't believe that part of the wonder of sex is discovering your partner's body and his preferences, then be my guest, man, label yourself and ask other people for their labels.

But that is such a limited view of sex. And worse, such a mechanical, assembly line, approach to it. If that's what you want, go for it, but don't expect me to endorse it.

Hey, Woody!
My friends and I were sitting around one day talking about the greatest pickup lines we ever used. One friend was out of town playing pool with a hottie. They were both going for the eight ball, when my friend said, "Let's make this interesting. Whoever loses . . . pays for room service when we get back to my hotel room."

One time I saw this guy standing alone against the wall. I asked him what he was up to and he said, "Nothing." So I said, "Why don't you come home with me and we'll do nothing together?" It worked! My question: What's the greatest line you ever used?

—Picked up and over

Dear Picked:
I was sitting in a bar when some hot stud plops down on the seat next to me and says, "God, I'm so thirsty I could lick the sweat off a cow's balls!"

I turned and said, "Mooooo!"

He about split his jeans laughing, which of course saved me the trouble later on. This was a perfect example of an immutable law in the art of seduction: Make a guy laugh and you're halfway up his leg.

The first step in a manhunt is lulling your prey into a false sense of security. Don't ever come up to a guy you haven't met and say, "I want to take you home and fuck your brains out." It may be honest but it's also a guaranteed way to turn him off.

Unless he's the owner of a gay bar. But that's a whore of a different color.

The home/fuck/brains thing is a worthy pursuit but one that needs a certain polish in its delivery. A good line is like a well-aimed blow-dart. It pierces the subconscious to release attitude-blockers, which fade the gay male pretense of being at the bar because the music's so good.

Good-natured laughter is the best way to cut through the fear and anxiety of meeting guys that turn you on. Remember, a dab of lubrication gives you a stab at penetration. If the guy is already interested, you don't need to come up with something clever because you're getting laid no matter what drops out of your mouth, unless it's a purse. If that's the case, we can only hope your prey is in the mood for some girl in his boy.

The truth is, if someone's interested in you it doesn't really matter what you say to him as long as you're not being an asshole. Reserve your best pickup lines for the real challenges—guys who haven't shown interest yet.

A guy may not be interested in you at first glance, but if you make him laugh, feel at ease, have a good time, he'll see you in a different light. And in bar light, this can only be a good thing.

Chapter 4

Kink: Putting the "Fuck" Back in "Fucked Up"

I have curly hair. To me, being kinky means having sex on a humid day without washing it.

I put the "ill" in vanilla and I make no apologies for it. Along with most of my readers, I pretty much gross out at some of the letters I get. Like the one about peeing in your partner's rectum after you've fucked him.

Yuck.

The kink crowd tends to send me the most venomous letters. I don't know what their problem is. I'm constantly encouraging people with sick urges to hook up so they can gross each other out.

I believe in total sexual freedom. You get the freedom to do whatever the hell you want; I get the freedom to make fun of whatever the hell you're doing.

The kink crowd is weird. They think sticking a fist up their ass is progressive but sticking a sense of humor down their pants is repressive. I don't get it.

They do make one good point, though: Who's to say what's kinky? Whose definitions are we going to use? Besides, those definitions keep changing. It wasn't long ago that blow jobs were considered kinky. Today, they're considered a tad more exotic than kissing.

So how can I give advice on something I know nothing about? Easy. The same way I write about the other issue I know nothing

121

about—the medical aspect of sex. I rely on experts, I do the research, I apply common sense.

The Super Fudge Nutty Bar Chunky Monkey Phish Food crowd tends to write slightly different questions than the plain old vanilla types. They usually involve asking how to undo the damage caused by their kinkiness.

Like, for instance, getting a large Coca Cola bottle stuck up your ass with no way of getting it out except surgery through your stomach. Or those fetching tire marks on your underwear from the rectum's inability to retain its elasticity after years of fisting. Or cantaloupe-size nipples from upping the tit-work ante to calf castration devices.

Here's my message to the BDSM "community" (Bondage, Discipline, Sado-masochism): If you people are going to weird out in bed, at least heed the creed: Be safe, be sane, be consensual, and consider the risks.

God, I love calling BDSM guys "You People." Drives them nuts.

* * *

Hey, Woody!
One day I came home early and snuck upstairs hoping to catch my boyfriend beating off to Internet porn (he's a freak about it). I tiptoe in but he hears me before I reached the computer screen and he goes berserk, yelling and screaming at me to leave the room.

That's when I realize he's trying to block me from seeing the screen. Suddenly a chill runs through me, and I tell him to move away from the computer. He refuses. I figure it's kiddy porn and I go nuts, pushing him aside so I could see.

Well, Woody, nothing could have prepared me for what was on the screen. It wasn't kiddy porn he was beating off to. It was pictures of Chris Farley's corpse, the fat comic from *Saturday Night Live* who died of a drug overdose. They were police shots of his bloated, purple body.

I hit the back button on the browser and there were

pictures of charred burn victims and men covered in
bloody gun shot wounds.

I walked out and haven't talked to my boyfriend since.
Please don't print the site, since I don't want to give them
any publicity. But would you look at how repulsive it is so
you understand my problem?

What should I do, Woody? He's sick and I refuse to talk
to him (what could he possibly say to get me back?). Yet I
miss him. Help me.

—Broken-up by the web

Dear Broken-up:

First, let me state the obvious: Your boyfriend needs the couch
like the democrats need a spine—urgently.

Your boyfriend has a fetish, and a ghoulish one at that. I went
to the site. Sorry, but I'm printing it—it's been all over the news
anyway. It's www.rotten.com.

There are only four words to describe the site: HOLY MOTHER
OF GOD. It is without doubt, the darkest, deepest, most sordid
site on the web. I mean, other than heterosexual porn sites. Talk
about gross!

Rotten.com states that it wants to "present viewers with a
truly unpleasant experience." And they do. Two hundred thousand people visit the site every day to click on macabre head-
lines like "A gallery of severed hands and whatnot."

Your fear is understandable. What if his fantasies progressed?
What if he started sneaking into morgues and beating off to *real*
dead people? And what if he started fucking them? And what if
the next step after that was to kill people so he can fuck them before their skin goes cold?

Experts believe there's *very* little chance of that happening
but you'd have to be a fool not to consider it. It's reasonable to
be scared about this.

But know this: The majority of people with socially unacceptable fantasies do not act them out. Either because it's physically
impossible (like fantasizing about fucking Ricky Martin. The line

to his bedroom's too long—you'd never get in) or because the fantasizer himself doesn't want it to become a reality. Being raped, for example, is a recurring fantasy that most people don't want to actually experience.

And finally, most people don't act out unacceptable fantasies because the consequences are too severe—jail, death, having to cook breakfast for the guy you put in a coma the night before, and so on.

The real question is how well the relationship was going before your discovery. Was sex good? Were you getting along? Was your emotional connection strong?

I suspect it was. And in that case, his fantasies didn't create problems in your relationship. Your discovery of them did. A fetish, no matter how ghoulish, is not considered a problem unless it becomes a problem. Capiche?

Your boyfriend isn't a horrible person for having horrible fantasies. He's deserving of compassion. I hope you can find it within you to help him get help.

Hey, Woody!
I liked your answer to the guy who jerks off to the horrible pictures on www.rotten.com—that his fantasies are horrible, but that he probably isn't.

You recommended "the couch." Yes, but which couch? Most therapists aren't prepared, emotionally or conceptually, to help such a person.

He should hunt for those few who are "kink-aware" and who already serve "safe, sane, and consensual" SM players (who may indeed enjoy fantasies and porn which are unsafe, insane, non-consensual). And also he should read up on his fetish, and related ones. Know thyself—even when the insight makes you want to puke.

Self-knowledge can be the first step in "harm reduction." The self-aware sadist can seek safe means of expression; but the so-called normal population contains too

many people who have never dared to recognize their hidden sadistic tendencies, and thus may fail to limit or control violence when an opportunity arises. Likewise, a non-aware submissive or masochist may wonder why he repeatedly chooses partners who will beat him. Tell him to try websites including the Black Book (blackbooks.com); sex educator Dr. Carol Queen (carolqueen.com); Society of Janus (soj.org); Greenery Press (greenerypress.com); Black Rose (br.org), and Deviant Desires (deviantdesires.com).

—Been there, done him

Dear Been:

Great letter. Filled with useful information except for one thing—looking for "kink aware" therapists. What a crock of shit.

I swear to God, you BDSM people drive me nuts. You're constantly cloaking yourself in the high-priest garments of the anointed and croaking on and on about how special and different you are.

"Only *specialists* can help us," you cry out in that special brand of arrogant self-pity you've perfected, "because we're so *unusual.*"

Let me tell you something—you're about as unusual as a hard-on in a Falcon video.

I called the lead psychologist in my panel of advisors to see if he could handle the "specialness" of a patient who beats off to pictures of corpses on the Internet. I caught him at lunch with several of his therapist friends. Not a "kink-aware" specialist in the bunch. He put the phone to his chest and yelled out, "Hey, Woody wants to know if we're emotionally and professionally capable of handling patients with disgusting fantasies and behaviors." The table exploded with laughter.

There isn't a thing you could tell a good therapist that would shock them. They're trained to handle startling deviations in human behavior. And they do it by creating a safe space for saying things, by being non-judgmental and accepting.

You know, like I do. You pompous, over-wrought drama queen.

Hey, Woody!
My boyfriend has gotten into catheters so much he can
now bury his pinky down his shaft. Am I dating a maso-
chist? Do you think this type of "Extreme Sex" is danger-
ous?

—**Rethinking him**

Dear Rethinking:
You have a boyfriend who gets off by sticking a soft plastic tube
into his dick until it reaches his bladder? What's there to re-
think? He's a shiver looking for a spine to run up.

And he found one: Me. I'll never understand freaks like him.
I'm all for pushing the flap of your sexual envelope, but not if it
means you have to throw the envelope away after you're done.
You can become such an excitement junkie you literally run the
risk of killing yourself for an orgasm.

Your boyfriend doesn't sound masochistic, though. Masochists aim for pain; your boyfriend aims for a sexual high.

You rarely see masochists go so far as to kill themselves, even
accidentally. But it's not that unusual to see "Extreme Sex" en-
thusiasts die. Exhibit A: "Autoerotic asphyxiation." This is where
you suffocate yourself while masturbating and the race is on to
see who gets to the finish line first—your semen or your life.

There's only one acceptable excuse for death by erotic asphyxiation, and that's when you give someone head for half an hour,
they come, turn over and fall asleep without returning the favor.

There isn't a jury in the world that would convict you.

Your boyfriend runs a high risk of urinary tract infection if
he's not especially careful of disinfecting everything before he
starts—the tube, his hands, the urethral opening (which should
be cleansed not just with soap and water but with betadine).

Stretching the urethra, by the way, isn't a big deal. Within reason, there aren't serious complications.

He also runs the risk of blood infections (septicemia), urethral injury, skin breakdown, bladder stones, blood in the urine
(hematuria), and bladder cancer.

Jesus, whatever happened to a simple blow job?

Hey, Woody!
A friend "came out" to me but I'm so repulsed by his se-
cret I don't know if I can remain friends with him. He's not
gay; he's sexually obsessed with amputees.
   And it's worse than you think, Woody. He constantly
cruises websites showing amputees in bathing suits. He
doesn't just obsess about having sex with them; he wants
to become one. He wants to sever his right leg at mid-
thigh!
   Wait, there's more. When I came out to him he was the
only one of my straight friends who didn't abandon me. He
didn't get sick, call me weird or try to push me off on a
shrink, and so now he's asking why I'm doing that to him.
   So, Woody, am I being a hypocrite? When I came out of
the closet he embraced me. When he came out I rejected
him. Who's right? What should I do?
                                    —Don't know what to feel

Dear Don't:
It's questions like these that make me think "Why can't I get normal questions like Dan Savage?"
   First of all, let's get something straight. Disclosing a fetish is
not the same thing as disclosing an orientation. Last time I
looked, Kinsey's spectrum of sexuality wasn't "Heterosexual,
Homosexual, Bisexual, Ampusexual."
   It's preposterous to suggest that severing body parts in order
to fulfill a sexual fantasy is equivalent to a man wanting a deep
emotional and sexual connection to another man.
   So tell your amp freak he's full of shit. The only similarities
between your disclosures are that they're both socially unacceptable and run the risk of alienating friends and family.
   We are not attracted to other men because they're gay. We're
attracted to them because they're men. Your freak friend isn't attracted to women; he's attracted to their disability. That's different. And may I add, *grotesquely* different.
   Another difference is that gay men are attracted to each
other. Most amputees *loathe* "amp-lovers." Put a bunch of gay

men on either side of a room, ring the starting bell and see what happens: We'll meet in the middle, mingle, cruise, swap recipes, phone numbers, and maybe even hook up.

Put amp-lovers on one side of the room and amputees on the other and see what happens when the bell rings. The amputees would stampede out of the room as fast as possible. Most would probably saw their remaining limb off to get away. Most amputees are horrified, do you hear me, HORRIFIED by amp-lovers.

Compare that to gay men. We're only horrified when guys wear white before Memorial Day.

There's nothing you can do to prevent your friend from severing a limb. Fortunately, there aren't too many doctors willing to surgically remove a body part to satisfy a fetish.

Maybe he'll settle for what other "amp devotees" do: Pretend. It's not unusual to see them act like actual amputees. They walk on crutches, roll around in wheelchairs, or tuck an arm in their shirts.

Or he could, like some freak-leak amp-lovers, attend disability conventions and chase amputees with flashing cameras like paparazzi at the Oscars.

It's a tragedy that people born with major disabilities or people who go through the trauma of losing limbs have to deal with assholes like your friend. It isn't enough to deal with phantom pain, body image issues, society's attitudes, and the emotional nightmare of the healing process. Now they have to deal with being lusted after, not for who they are, but for the body parts they don't have.

Here's your role in this mess: As disgusting as your friend's fetish is, his obsession doesn't define him anymore that your orientation defines you. It's a part of him and you have to find it in your heart to accept him, warts and all. A true friend would help him get help and remain friends even if he didn't.

The freak.

Hey, Woody!
I was out of town and picked up this really cute and inno-
cent guy. Innocent-looking, anyway. That's the last time I
pick up anybody wearing Polo. We're undressed, fooling
around, when the Polo Perv pulls out what looks like an
electric torture device. It was a butt plug wired to an elec-
tric generator! I practically ran out of the bedroom scream-
ing.
   Why would people use electricity for sex? Christ, isn't
dick enough? Now we have to play with electrodes to get it
up?
                                              —Grounded and disgusted

Dear Grounded:
I'm with you on this one. Of all the things I want to hear a guy say
in bed, "Let me run an electric current up your ass," isn't one of
them.

   I can just see the ER doctor patting my mom's hand, reassur-
ing her that lots of grown men get electrocuted when they hook
their sphincters up to a high-voltage generator. My mom's been
great about the gay thing, but she's got limits.

   Electrical toys originated from a device called a TENS unit
(Transcutaneous Electrical Nerve Stimulation). Doctors prescribe
it to relieve back, knee, shoulder, and neck pain. It works by
sending small electrical impulses into the muscles, replacing
pain impressions with a massage-like sensation. Apparently some
queen, bored with her career as a medical technician, thought "I
wonder what would happen if I stuck this live wire up my ass?"

   There seems to be two camps within the kink crowd about
"electric play." One swears by it, the other swears at it. Trust me
when I tell you swearing will be the least of your problems if you
hook yourself up to one of these contraptions the wrong way.

   The generators, which produce a high-voltage/low amp current, are fed to a butt plug, which is buried, you know, *down*
there. When the current passes through your body, they contract
the muscles surrounding the butt plug. The generators don't pro-

duce enough juice to be dangerous unless, unless.... Wait a minute. All you Potential Pervs out there lean in and read closely. UNLESS the current is passed directly across the chest. Don't ever put either the generator or the attachment (butt plugs, cock rings, etc.) above your waist or you're going to fry like the Colonel's chicken.

So why would you skewer your ass with an electrode? Because you have entirely too much time on your hands. That, and the lovely sensations. Some people say it feels like they're being fucked by a ghost.

If bottoming for a poltergeist is your thing, have at it. Just go slow and for God's sakes don't do it with your boyfriend. Do it with someone you trust. You don't want the guy who nags you about taking the garbage out at the controls. Nothing good can come of it.

For those of you who long for a photovoltaic sphincter check out the Folsom Electric Company website at www.folsomelectric.com. They're a main manufacturer of the devices. Or check out the book *The Guide to Electric Sex*.

Hey, Woody!
I've been going out with this guy for about six months and everything's going great. But lately he's been badgering me to get a little kinkier with him. I'm not totally against it but I feel awkward. And so does he, actually. He kinda wants me to tie him up and hit him. Not like, you know, breaking his jaw, but enough to hurt him. I'm sorta shocked that he wants that but kinda turned on, too. The thing is, neither one of us knows how to start. Any suggestions as to how two beginners can get over their awkwardness?
—Working out the kinks

Dear Working:
Don't do it. Don't go over to the dark side. It's immoral and you will suffer the consequences of such sick and stomach turning desires.

Oh, wait. I have your letter confused with the one about monogamy.

Let me be the first to welcome you to BDSM, or Bondage, Discipline, Dominance, Submission, Sadism and Masochism. I know—too many words and not enough letters representing them. Don't look for logic in Kinkworld, it'll just confuse you.

First thing is, don't beat yourself up about feeling nervous or awkward. Beat your boyfriend. It'll help get you into the swing of things a lot quicker.

BDSM houses the full spectrum of actions and intentions. Some people are only interested in physical techniques, from the lightweight (spanking) to the truly torturous (forcing people to read this book). Some people get off just on the power differentials of dominance and submission and some on the pleasure of giving or receiving pain.

Not all of these things are linked. Just because you want to be hog-tied to the bedposts doesn't necessarily mean you want to be dominated, or just because you want to play Master doesn't necessarily mean you want to hurt your slave.

One of the more interesting things about BDSM partners is that many just want to get off on the pain and not be explicitly sexual with each other.

Before you get started, explore with your boyfriend what it is that he wants. Is it purely the physical sensation of being hit, or is it to feel like he's being punished for some made-up transgression like going AWOL from a dangerous mission? Does he want a couple of thwacks on the arm or does he want to be pummeled all over his body? Negotiating beforehand may feel a little awkward, but it'll save you some enormously unpleasant consequences.

If you get confused, always look to Aretha Franklin for BDSM advice. She spelled it out years ago: R-E-S-P-E-C-T. If your boyfriend is giving you the "gift" of his submission, respect his boundaries.

Agree on a "safe word" beforehand, a mutually understood word that, when uttered, means STOP WHAT YOU'RE DOING RIGHT NOW. Don't pick the word "No" because part of the thrill may be pretending you don't want the abuse. Sort of like when guys are handed this book and they shriek "No! No! No!" It just means they want more.

Pick a safe word that's totally out of context, for example, "apple" or "book," or, if you really want to be stopped in your tracks—"Al Gore."

If you want to try some bondage action, proceed with caution. Novices tend to restrain wrists and ankles with handcuffs, silk scarves, and clotheslines. Don't. Wrists and ankles are delicate and it's easy to accidentally hurt your partner badly if you don't know what you're doing.

Get some thick, wide, padded restraints that distribute the pressure over a wide area. Don't tie him up so that he's suspended, or in a way that parts of his body will go numb, like tying his hands over his head. All you'll be doing is buying him a spot in the ER.

Finally, get a beginner's book. The best in the bunch is probably *Screw the Roses: Send Me the Thorns*, by Philip Miller and Molly Devon. The title alone makes me wanna hurt somebody.

Hey, Woody!
My partner and I have been monogamous for quite a few years. We are both HIV negative and healthy. Within the past two years, we have both been experiencing with water sports. About a month ago, while we were having anal intercourse, he asked if I could pee inside of him. At first I was apprehensive, but later decided to try it. It took much concentration, but when I was finally able to pee, the sensation was incredible for both of us. Are there any dangers involved?

—Top that one

Dear Top:
You are the very link to kink. I have heard of all kinds of things but a fresh urine enema is one for the medical archives. My first

reaction was a total gross-out. And then I asked my boyfriend if I could do it to him.

First, congratulations are in order. I have a medical advisory panel I consult with when I get complicated (and did I mention ridiculous) questions. Because they have a large gay practice, they have seen and heard it all. This is the first time they just stared blankly and didn't know what to say. So congratulations, you've stumped the band!

When they finally composed themselves here's what they agreed on: Using your boyfriend as a urine recycling plant carries very little risk. Urine itself doesn't contain much HIV to make it an effective transport for exposure. However, you'd be a fool to try it if your HIV status is unknown. If you immediately hose down your partner with urine after cumming, you'd flush semen all over his colon and bowels, increasing the area for HIV exposure. But since you said both of you are HIV negative you don't have to worry about it.

Urine does carry toxins (urea being one of the big ones). If your partner's colon and bowels protest the use of their property as a toxic waste dumping site by carrying NIMBY placards (Not in my Back Yard), tell them they needn't worry. Urine is a sterile fluid containing no bacteria (unless you have an infection), and even its toxins are harmless.

So harmless in fact, that my panel agrees your partner doesn't even need to rinse the urine out of his bowels after you've filled him to the rim. Imagine that! Doctors—educated, sophisticated, wealthy men—saying you don't have to flush after going to the bathroom.

It's true, money can't buy you class.

If the ick factor doesn't bother you (and hey, one man's ick is another man's schtick), there's no reason to stop doing it. But I say flush it out after you're done, man. That's gruesome.

Hey, Woody!
What kind of gay sex advice columnist has never tried or worse, even heard, of a piss enema? I've had lots of guys

piss inside me after they've fucked me. You need to get out more and try a different flavor besides vanilla. I can't believe you pass yourself off as a sex expert. You're so full of judgment, how do you expect to open people up to new possibilities when you publicly gross out at anything different? If you're going to write a sex advice column you better open yourself up to a wider range of experiences, or you're going to lose readers like me whose sexual tastes have matured past the missionary position.

—Kinky and proud of it

Dear Kinky:

You know what grosses me out more than hearing somebody say they want to be pissed in after they get fucked? Hearing your sanctimonious bullshit.

A lot of you kinks have this really annoying hornier-than-thou attitude. As if somehow you're more evolved than the rest of us because you like to play skanky toilets in kinky psycho-sexual dramas. Please.

Weighted down as you are with all your chains, leather straps and butt-chaps, it's astonishing how quickly you can get up on your high horse. Why is it okay for you to tell us what turns you on but we can't tell you what turns us off? What, everyone gets freedom of expression as long as they agree with you? Wake up and smell the feces, man. You are not, I repeat, not more sexually sophisticated just because you built a True Value Hardware franchise in your basement.

The difference between vanilla and tutti frutti are the ingredients. Like sex, both require a lot of enthusiastic licking and an intense desire for the cone. And of course, both contain the motivating force of sex: Cream.

One flavor isn't better than the other; it's a matter of taste. Spare me the sexual high-priest pose. I say revel in your kinkiness but don't act like it's somehow better than the traditional approach to sex.

And one more thing. Your contention that I can't advise it till I try it? It doesn't hold any water. Or in your case, urine. A great coach doesn't have to be a former player.

Hey, Woody!
I love my new boyfriend but his obsession with me kinda scares me. He loves my cum on his chest so much he won't shower before work and I swear you can smell it on him. Is this a sign that it's going to get worse? How can I get him to wash my cum off?
                                        —The smell that refreshes

Dear Smell:
Geez, I remember when liking a guy meant wearing his ring, not his cum.

Unless he's going to work shirtless I wouldn't worry about it. I say treat it like a good blow job: Sit back, relax and enjoy the show.

Or spray it on his face and hair instead. If he goes to the office without washing the crud off, *then* we have a big problem.

I'd only worry if his obsession escalated to something truly harmful, like cutting off your toe and hooking it to a key chain. If that's the case, God help you if you ever break up. There's nothing worse than a gay *Fatal Attraction*.

First, you'll be the victim of a drive-by doiling, and next, you'll find your pet bunny on the stove in an exquisite tarragon, rose petal and saffron demi-glace encrusted with pecans, hearts of palm and a delicate mint-fennel sauce. I hate mint-fennel sauce on my pets. It ruins the taste.

Hey, Woody!
I can suck my own penis and cum into my mouth. I even swallow it. Sometimes instead of going out to the bars or the circuit parties, I figure, hey, the party's in my mouth,

**why go out? I like doing it but sometimes I feel guilty, like
I'm doing something wrong. Do you think I am?**

— **Roastin' my own weenies**

Dear Roastin':

Ahh, the problems of the double-jointed. Listen, you should be
proud that you can do it. Kinsey found that only two or three out
of every thousand men can make their bumpers shine like
chrome. The only thing you're doing wrong is not advertising it.
Hell, I'd pay your bar tab, taxi and breakfast just to see it. The
real question is, can you fit two in your mouth at the same time?

Kinsey observed a close tie between manual masturbation
and "oral eroticism" and recommended that scientists see self-
fellatio as just another form of masturbation. He called it a "biologically normal aspect of sexuality." And if there's anything I
love, it's the biologically normal.

Most guys consider oral self-service hot—there's a thriving
business of "solo" acts in porno. Don't feel guilty about what the
rest of us wish we could do. That's like feeling guilty for beating
off.

The only thing you should feel is warm, wet and satisfied.
Sucking yourself and washing it down with some self-produced
milk carries no health risk, so I say party on, man. And invite me
over.

Hey, Woody!
**My new boyfriend wants me to talk trash to him in bed.
I'm pretty good in the sack but I'm too bashful to talk
dirty. If I ever made it to the World Heavyweight Sex
Championship I'd be promoted as the "Thrilla-in-Vanilla."
How can I loosen my tongue and let the trash flow freely?**

— **Tongue in chic**

Dear Tongue:

Tabasco Talk is a real art. Too little and it's tasteless, too much and it burns. Like adding the sauce to chili, adding wordplay to foreplay is a great way to spice things up.

First rule: Forget the flowery prose. Your boyfriend doesn't want to hear he's got a velvety vulva; he wants to hear he's got a great ass.

If you're really shy, start by simply narrating what you're doing. If you go to a baseball game you're going to talk about who's pitching, who's hitting, who's doing what to whom. Do that in bed. Describe what you're doing and feeling, and more importantly, what you're going to do: "I'm gonna take my X, put it in your Y, and make you Z stars."

Remember the royal rule of the restless: Treat a queen like a whore and a whore like a queen. Meaning, your boyfriend doesn't want Aunt Bea in bed, he wants Ahnuld to terminate him: "Hasta la Pinga, baby."

A great way to jump-start the process is to practice on the phone when you're out of town. Some people find it easier because there's no eye contact and there's only one way to communicate on the phone—verbally.

Lastly, don't forget the Three G's in bed: Groan, Grunt, and Grab. Not many syllables to them, but animal sounds can speak a thousand dirty words.

Hey, Woody!

I'm white and my new black boyfriend wants me to call him "nigger" in bed. Now, Woody, I'm a good liberal. I can't say shit like "Take this big white cock, farm nigger," like he wants me to. What can I do to talk him out of it? He's really angry with me, calling me sex-negative and too vanilla. I feel like I'm violating my own social values just so he can get off in bed. What should I do?

—Shocked right out of Compton

Dear Shocked:

I'd do it while blasting rap music in the background. Then you'll just be part of the chorus, and you won't hear yourself say it.

Look, lots of people want to be dominated in bed. Some people want to be punished with belts, your boyfriend wants to be punished with epithets.

I agree with you—it's pretty sick, but when you think about it, is it really any different than a guy who won't have sex unless you promise to say, "Who's Your Daddy?" Or the guy who makes you say, "Open wide, bitch, I'm coming in." You know, like Elton John did with Eminem.

Your boyfriend clearly wants to be dominated and he wants you to club him with racist talk. The only way this could work is if he agreed to, or more importantly, was capable of, separating the role-play from your relationship. Imagine if, in the heat of an argument, he throws up your racist language in bed as proof that you don't respect him?

Another thing you might talk about is whether being called a nigger is a role-playing fantasy or some manifestation of an inferiority complex, which you'd be aiding and abetting. If that's the case, forget it, don't do it. Let me. I'm a professional, you know.

Is it going against your value system to say things you don't believe in a role-play? No. I don't believe in stealing but I can do it in a play when a scene demands it and not feel like I compromised my values.

Hey, Woody!

I recently picked up a 65-year-old guy in a bar and had the best orgasm of my life. I am 25 and now can't stop thinking of geriatric sex. It grosses out all my friends but I can't stop fantasizing about having sex with very old men. Do you think I'm sick? If not, how do I meet older guys? They're not at the bars.

—Penchant for pensions

Dear Penchant:

Do I think you're sick? Of course. You're reading this column, aren't you?

And speaking of sick, I recommend watching every ill person's favorite movie: *Harold and Maude*. Harold is 20, very rich and very suicidal. Maude is 80, very poor and full of life. They fuck like rabbits and fall in love.

It's a brilliant movie about a love affair between a pup and an artifact. You will see yourself in it and you will have all your feelings validated. Rent it. Your wrinkly future awaits you.

I'd place a personal ad in the gay paper. Just warn them beforehand. A 25-year-old looking for a geriatric? They're going to have to back up a truck to haul out all the mail.

Just be prepared for some of the exasperating consequences of dating really old people. Both my grandparents are in their 70s and they're really forgetful. Once, I saw this incredible exchange between them: Dad was on his way to the kitchen and Mom asked him for ice cream with Cool Whip and strawberries. "Do you want to write it down so you don't forget?" she asked. Irritated, he waved her off. Twenty minutes later he hands her a plate of bacon and eggs. Mom stares at the plate for a minute, looks up and says, *"You forgot my toast."*

Hey, Woody!

Not only do my boyfriend and I have house-shaking sex, we also do three-ways, groups, baths, and sex clubs. He is the nastiest, biggest fuck pig I've ever run across.

God, I love him.

So here's the problem: Last month we were in a sex club where he was being gang-fucked in a sling. In the middle of everything he bursts into tears, holds my face in his hands and tells me how much he loves me. Talk about embarrassing. Try to be a dick pig in the middle of that.

I adore this man but I don't understand his timing. The raunchier the sex act the more emotional he gets about

me. What can I do to keep his legs spread and his mouth shut when we're being pigs?

—Stop it, you're embarrassing me

Dear Stop:

I kept holding your letter up to the light to make sure it wasn't a counterfeit. But then I remembered, truth is stranger than fiction.

The therapists on my advisory panel agreed on two things:

1. Raunch scenes trigger your boyfriend's emotional outpouring because he sees your approval of these scenes as the ultimate testament of your love for him.
2. Your boyfriend is one sick fuck.

Well, the therapists didn't actually say that. Slandering potential patients isn't a good career move. There are mortgages to pay, you know.

So allow me: Your boyfriend is one instrument short of a band. You don't have to listen very long to know something doesn't sound right. He declares his eternal love for you while complete strangers are fucking him into hamburger meat? Listen, I know sick. *That's* sick.

Most relationships would disintegrate with the kind of openness you guys have. There's only so much pounding a couple can take before their relationship collapses, spent from all the bodies they have to dig through to get to each other. Damn, I'm getting half a stock just typing that last sentence.

Now, where was I? Oh, yeah. Your boyfriend blubbers about love in all the wrong places because he's emotionally overwhelmed by the sexual freedom you've given him. He can be totally uninhibited with you and not be judged. He sees this sexual freedom as a loving gift from you. Sex with strangers in your presence puts him in touch with that love and he wants to express it. On the one hand, his gratitude for the sexual freedom you've given him is understandable. On the other hand, his timing is absolutely ghoulish.

The solution is pretty simple. Pull him aside before your next date with Caligula's friends and say, "Look, dear, I love to hear you say you love me. But that's really personal and I don't want strangers to hear our deepest intimacies. It's one thing to share our bodies with other people but it's another to share our love. Our love is special and I want to keep it just between us.

"You Sick Fuck."

Hey, Woody!
I've been a regular reader for a while but your riff on the leather and SM communities was the last straw. Since you're not into BD/SM or any of its dynamic, why do you feel that you should make people like that the brunt of your humor? I am not into vanilla sex, but I don't belittle those who are. I think the phrase "It takes all kinds" should apply here. We as a community suffer enough prejudices from the het population without internalized prejudice from within. I'm the chair of my city's leather alliance and we all agree: You suck and we're not going to read you anymore.

—Fuck you

Dear Fuck:
You poor, put-upon leather guys. Some mornings it just doesn't seem worth gnawing through your leather straps, does it?

I've said it before and I'll say it again: The leather community sucks. Not because you're engaged in absurd sexual practices but because you radiate with the kind of monumental arrogance that makes me wanna tie you up and keep beating you way after you've screamed the safe word.

Your letter is a perfect example of leather arrogance. You say you've been a faithful reader of this column, which attacks everyone and everything. You never wrote to complain when I jabbed and poked other groups, but I train my guns on you and suddenly I'm out of bounds.

In other words, it's okay for me to make fun of everyone but you guys, the exalted ones, the ones hog-tied to the bedposts. Know why you think that? Because you believe the leather and kink community isn't having sex, but some elevated spiritual practice manifested through the union of two men who blah, blah, blah, and yank, yank, yank, and (insert the sound of Charlie Brown's teacher here).

"It's okay to make fun of everyone else," you're wailing, "but not us leather guys because we're too tender and sensitive."

What a crock. Your letter proves the difference between leather and feather is a letter. You're not men, you're hens.

Hey, Woody!

I was reading somewhere that there's going to be a "slave-camp" put on by some organization to teach people how to be "slaves" and "masters." What a goof! I know these guys are serious, but how can anyone keep a straight face through a weekend like that? Could you?

—Laughing too hard to breathe

Dear Laughing:

No way. It'd be like watching Congress in action—grave and weighty men, flatulent with self-importance, engaged in ridiculous activities. And always resulting in the same thing: Someone getting fucked in the end. Who could keep a straight face through that?

Sorry, but this whole slave/master thing is lost on me. All that theater for a tablespoon of semen. Why not just be an extra in *Gladiator* and be done with it?

The weekend you're talking about is "slavecamp," an event hosted by the Master's Association. Don't confuse them with the benefactors to Golf's greatest tournament in Augusta. The main difference between the groups is their goal: Getting a hole-in-one versus getting one in the hole.

According to the Master's Association website, their mission is to "provide both Masters and slaves with a platform and an environment where they can seek each other out." Notice how Masters is capitalized and slave isn't. Nice touch, huh?

The great thing about membership in the organization is that if you're a slave owned by a Master and you register at the site, you can have your $59 membership revoked without refund if your Master does not approve. They'll delete you from the slaves registration and place your name in the "Wall of Shame" directory. It's the gay, grown-up version of being put in "time-out."

But wait, it gets better. Masters can drive directly to the weekend's campsite event, but slaves must meet at one of the pick-up points at the airport. The event will include slave training sessions, chain-gang hikes, daily slave exercise, bondage and discipline.

Weird. I mean, why go to a retreat for something you can get at home. You *really* want to experience bondage? Try marriage.

"Slavecamp," which promises to teach you the art of being a human ash tray, starts with a slave auction. Each Master acquires one for the weekend. Or, if you're a Master in the mood for sharing, you can bring your own slave and allow "it" to be auctioned to another Master. As a point of pride, the Master's Association never refers to slaves as men, but as property.

Are these guys white males or what?

Slaves set up the camp, cook meals, polish their Master's boots, clean their tents, and memorize slave regulations. Each night, they entertain their Masters around the campfire and massage their Master's feet. Throughout the weekend slaves will be drilled in obedience, discipline, correct behavior, and how to properly address Masters.

I know what you're thinking: What's in it for the Masters?

There's only three reasons to go to something like "slave-camp":

1. You just don't have enough going on in your life.
2. See point number one.
3. See point number two.

So with these three points in mind, my recommendation for the errand boy within you is to sign up for the retreat.

Hey, just because I think the weekend is ridiculous doesn't mean I don't think you should do it. I think you should do whatever turns you on sexually—as long as it involves a consenting two-legged adult mammal. The way I see it, you have the right to do anything you want, and I have the right to make fun of anything I want. It's what makes this column click.

So go to the Masters website (www.mastersassociation.com) and sign up if you want. Just beware, you have to be a member in order to participate in the retreat. The best part of signing up is at the end where you're asked to send all the info (including your credit card number).

The click button is adorned with a slave's face brutally bound by a blind-fold and mouth-lock with the words "SUBMIT NOW!"

Geesh. They don't sound like Masters. They sound like editors.

Hey, Woody!
I went home with Mr. Stuff because of his first name—Hot. But when we got to his place he made me sweat for all the wrong reasons. We were naked and fooling around in his living room when he asked me if I'd "plate" for him. I was like, "huh?" He takes everything off his long glass coffee table and gets underneath it. Then he asks me to get on top of the glass and take a dump, so he could jerk off to it looking at it from underneath the table. I thought I would yak. Then he offered me $100 to do it.

I can't believe someone so all-American looking could be so perverted. I haven't returned any of his calls, even though he's wonderful in every other way. Have you ever heard of "plating?" Do you think I'm wrong for not calling him back?

—Letting voicemail pick up

Dear Letting:

"Take a hike" is a perfectly natural response to being asked to take a shit on a coffee table. A lot of guys have problems peeing in front of other guys, let alone taking a shit in front of them. Or over them, as the case may be.

"Plating" is so over-the-top, so absurd, it almost qualifies as an urban legend. But of course it's not. Dildos don't come in a one-size-fits-all; why should sexual obsessions? Some men are obsessed with feet, some with feces. A few to the point that they'll actually eat feces right out of men's asses. Hmm, nothing like steaming, fresh-baked pastries pulled right out of the oven.

I looked up the word "disgusting" in the dictionary and it said "see 'plating.'" There's no way around it—eroticizing shit is another way of broadcasting the fact that you ain't right. Throughout time, feces have always been associated with human degradation. Nobody says "eat shit and die" or "I don't give a shit" as terms of endearment.

While I personally find "scat" disgusting, I also believe that people who love disgusting acts have the right to find other people who love disgusting acts so they can gross each other out in the privacy of their own homes.

Still, your date was a smellier asshole than the one he wanted you to bare. Not because he shared a disgusting fantasy, but because he tried to railroad you into it. Getting someone to participate in your fantasy requires enrollment, not coercion. I say forget about him. There's plenty of fresh water in the dating bowl, why go after what you already flushed?

Hey, Woody!
I like to have dirty, hot, sweaty, nasty, piggy sex, but my boyfriend is one of those people who blow-dries his hair before going to the gym. The idea of having pre-showered, pre-baby powdered, pre-anti-perspiranted, pre-cologned, pre—mouthwashed sex leaves him less than limp. I, on the other hand, pop zippers when I smell glandular malfunc-

**tion in the arm pit area. How do we bridge the grime gap
between us?**

—This little piggy went to bed without any

Dear Piggy:

You've got your work cut out for you. Getting Nancy Drew to lick
your stinky pits when you can't even get her to look at your dirty
shorts is going to be a real accomplishment. But it can be done.

First, sit down with him *when you're not horny* (this is critical) and tell him that making him sexually fulfilled is important
to you. Ask him what he needs you to do to him, or for him, to
keep him peaked. You'll score points for asking and more for de-
livering. And by all means deliver. Once you've brought home the
goods, it's time for him to deliver. But don't demand. Ask. And
one of the things you should ask is what would make it easier for
him to enjoy the pigginess you so crave.

In other words, don't dirtbag him all at once. He might be willing to let you sniff the smelly pits as long as your underwear is
clean. Soil him slowly, if you get my drift, and you'll desensitize
him to the joys of a pungent man-marinade. Remember, the difference between rape and seduction is salesmanship.

Hey, Woody!
**I was in New York City for Pride a few months ago, and a
dude approached a friend with the opening line, "Hey,
you've got cute feet" and handed him a card inviting him
to a private foot fetish party. I'm not feeling left out, just
curious: What makes for cute feet? Any guidance would be
much appreciated.**

—Not your sole admirer

Dear Not:

What makes a good-looking foot? I don't know. What makes a
good-looking man?

A friend pointed to a "gorgeous" guy, once. I thought he was
kidding. The guy had a face that would make a train take a dirt

road. There's no accounting for taste in men, so why should there be for feet?

As far as the foot fetish parties, use your imagination. They're not comparing hands. They're doing everything you can do to feet: Toe sucking, sole sucking, foot tickling, boot licking, shoe worship, and of course, foot massage.

Oh, and let us not forget the ultimate in a foot fetish party: sock sniffing. Now *there's* an activity I don't get nearly enough of. There's nothing I'd rather do than pull up a chair and inhale a soiled sock like a line of cocaine.

Sorry, but if I got stuck at a party like that I'd be eyeing the exits and thinking, "Feet, don't fail me now."

Private foot parties often have "theme" nights. In New York, for instance, they have annual events like "The Annual Foot Ball," proving that it's not the sweaty stinky feet that make you nauseous, it's the incessant puns.

"Sole Train: Feet of Flava," is another. Stand back, I'm getting hard.

Sometimes the foot freaks hold contests like "Biggest Feet, Stinkiest Socks" and "Best Foot Strip Tease." We can only hope the guys at these parties aren't marketing experts. Imagine their first product: A peanut butter and toe jam sandwich.

There are lots of websites that'll give you a whiff of things to come. Feetishes.com specializes in "soles of color." Feetonline. com has videos they describe as "Toe-tally Great." Groan. The site with the most comprehensive links is probably malefeet.net/links.html. They list the free non-commercial sites first; something you don't smell too often.

Hey, Woody!
My boyfriend is addicted to pornography. He'd rather masturbate to naked men on the videos than make love to me. I'm not some skanky guy, Woody. I'm 6 feet, 170 lbs and I work out every day. I've tried to get him to read articles or get help, but he won't do it. We're having less and less sex, and I'm getting more and more unhappy. I don't want to

break up with him, I just want it to go back to the way it was. How do I do it?

—**Fuck You, Falcon Video**

Dear Fuck You:
Your boyfriend is suffering from osteopornosis. It's a degenerate disease that can only be cured by stealing his video collection and sending it to me.

The problem is that your boyfriend doesn't just like porn, he *needs* it. No fetish is a problem until it becomes a problem. He has a problem. And the biggest one is that he won't admit he's doing something that's endangering your relationship. He's gotten himself so used to beating off to porn that he can't get aroused from proven pheromone-ish stimulants, like say, this book. Oh, yeah, and you.

There's nothing wrong with "married guys" looking at porn. I agree with Pornmaster General, Larry Flynt, the publisher of *Hustler*. He once said, "There are two kinds of people who oppose porn. Those who don't know what they're talking about and those who don't know what they're missing."

But if porn's the only way your boyfriend can be sexually satisfied, it means that the porn is starting to matter more than sex itself. Your boyfriend needs professional help. Talk to him. Let him know what you love about having sex with him. Then tell him how disappointed you are that sex with him is getting less and less frequent. Tell him you think the porn has made him lose his attraction to you.

He'll have one of three responses: Denial, Defensiveness, or . . . oh, wait. I forgot he's gay. That means his first response will be to walk to the mirror and make sure his hair's okay.

You'll probably have to give him an ultimatum. It's either you or the remote. There're lots of 12-step programs for sexual compulsives, as well as therapists who specialize in these situations. Find a licensed sex therapist and offer to go with him. Remember, you can lead a whore to semen, but you can't make him swallow. If he refuses to get help, you might have to refuse dating him.

Hey, Woody!
I love pissing on my boyfriend during sex, but he won't let
me anymore because my urine suddenly changed. It's
darker and tastes awful (well, I'm taking his word for it;
***I'm* certainly not going to taste it).**

I want to get back to watering his lawn on a regular
basis but first I need to fix the sprinkler. How do I get my
urine back in shape?

—Pissed off

Dear Pissed off:

Change your diet and quit drinking alcohol. Food and liquor are
the two most common reasons why urine changes color and
smell.

Even small changes in diet produce big changes in urine. Not
getting enough water, drinking too much caffeine, or having too
much salt can piss off your urinary tract and that can make your
boyfriend all pissy about getting pissed on.

Vegetables are also a prime culprit. Beets can darken urine
and asparagus can make it smell like, well, like somebody just
pissed on you.

The only way to find out why your pee went kerplunk is to
keep a diary of everything you eat and track the color and smell
of your urine. While this system works to determine the cause, it
also works to determine that you're a fucking loser with way too
much time on your hands.

If it's not your diet, it may be a urinary tract infection, in
which case you'd also be suffering from frequent urination or a
burning sensation. You know, like the kind you get when you
read this column.

If so, the cure's easy: Stop reading the column. Or go to your
doctor. He'll have you do a "clean-catch" urine sample (meaning
you don't pee into the sample container until you're in "mid-
stream." That way you get a sample free of contaminants normally present in the opening of the urethra, like white blood
cells, or in your case, your boyfriend's saliva).

If you test positive, he'll give you an antibiotic. If you don't, it's back to the diary.

Hey, Woody!
My tits are my favorite sex organ. They've been growing from all the action, and at first I liked it as they approached the pencil eraser stage. But now they're the size of quarters and I can't stop playing with them! I fear I'll have nipples the size of cauliflowers if I keep this up, but I don't want to curb the action (I've graduated from squeezing and pinching to clamps to calf castration devices, even electrodes). How do I keep up the tit work but keep down their size?

—**Titty Shame**

Dear Titty Shame:
You're out of luck, tit-for-brains. The damage has been done. You can't undo it without plastic surgery.

Our bodies aren't made of Play-Doh. Extreme sex has a very high likelihood of mutilating you.

It's kind of pitiful when you BDSM people finally discover that actions have consequences. "Another Day Another Collar" may be your philosophy, but I wouldn't be so blasé about sex acts that end up making you embarrassed to take your shirt off. And calf castration devices on your nipples? As my mom used to say to me all the time: *"What are you, some kind of freak?"*

Hey, Woody!
I love getting plugged with sex toys, and this guy I went home with last month picked up on it right away, reading me like a large-type *Readers Digest*. He pulls out a box of sex toys and, of course, there were hearts in my eyes. Until I saw some crud on them. I wasn't stupid enough to use them but it got me thinking about my own toys. Namely,

am I cleaning them the right way? I just use soap and water. Should I use anything else?

—Toyman

Dear Toyman:

Soap and water is enough to clean most dildos and vibrators if you're only using them on yourself or the same partner. But if you're diddling so many guys your bed has an odometer, it isn't enough. You need to sterilize them. Your toys, I mean, not your tricks. Though that could be fun too.

Silicone or acrylic toys can be run through the dishwasher or boiled in water (at least three minutes) to destroy microorganisms. Or use diaper wipes, but make sure they're made with nonoxynol-9, alcohol, and benzylkonium chloride. Or just use diluted household bleach (one part bleach, ten parts water).

Chapter 5

Relationships: How to Fit Large Feelings into Small Openings

Most of the letters I get about relationships boil down to three main issues:

1. How do you get your boyfriend to do what you want in bed?
2. How do you get into and stay in a relationship?
3. Is monogamy the highest expression of love or the dyslexic spelling of monotony?

The first one's easy—pistol-whip him. The only problem is that the use of weaponry is inconsistent with the spirit of love. I'm still working on how to resolve that.

The real answer to getting your boyfriend to do what you want is simple, yet it's the kind of simplicity that's beyond the reach of us emotionally constipated guys.

The answer is talking. But "talking" has a universally hated little brother called "listening," and nobody wants him hanging around, ruining the hanky-panky.

What I find in my letters is not just the inability to talk, but also the fear that doing it will cause more problems. It's a well-justified fear, given the way most guys go about it. Let's face it, we don't talk; we tell. We don't have conversations, we have demands.

What you say to your partner is secondary to how you say it. You know how, when you're single, the difference between rape and seduction is salesmanship? Well, when you're married, salesmanship has to give way to diplomacy, which as everyone knows, is the art of stealing more on Tuesday than what you gave on Monday.

The second most common question—"How do I get me a relationship?"—reveals how hard it is for many gay men to start meaningful relationships. You only have to be male for about a minute to understand the duality of our natures that make lasting emotional connections so hard. Namely, that we think like women and act like men.

How do we resolve our conflicting desires? How do we work out our need for tenderness, security, and love with our desire to stick our dicks in anything with a pulse?

If you figure it out, write. It's as good as published.

I've written this column as a "married" man and a single man. I looked at all my columns to see if my answers on relationships reflected my marital status in any way. Here's what I noticed: When I was "married" I tended to rail against monogamy; when I was single I tended to glorify it.

If that doesn't tell you something about the male psyche, I don't know what will.

* * *

Hey, Woody!
I've had several "fuck buddies." You know, guys who I get together with on a regular basis just to have sex, not to date. My buddies never seem to last more than a few months, though. One of us starts falling for the other, or one of us loses interest. Either way, it ends. I'd love to keep a stable of FBs but I just don't know how to do it. Is there such a thing as long-term "fuck buddies?" What's the secret of keeping them?
—Dying to know

Dear Dying:

It's the same secret to a good marriage. Be a whore in bed and a mute outside of it.

It's almost impossible to keep long-term fuck buddies (FBs) because it goes against our natures. Men love casual sex. But once you have it, casual goes out the window and guess what comes in the door? Love or tedium.

Like you said, somebody either falls in love or loses interest. FBs are the no-man's land between groom and trick. You don't want to marry them, you don't want to date them, but you don't want them just once either.

It's the difference between being "involved" and being "committed." Think of it as a bacon and eggs breakfast. The chicken was involved; the pig was committed.

You want to be involved.

This poses a special problem. You can't "work" on an FB relationship the way you "work" on a romantic relationship because the first rule of a good FB relationship is NO WORKING. It gets in the way of fucking.

Of all my promiscuous friends, I am . . . wait. That's redundant. I hate it when I waste words. Of all my friends, I am the only one who's had a fuck-buddy for over four years. And from my experience, I can tell you the only way to keep an FB relationship going is to understand the role of silence and distance in the context of a mutual sexual attraction that neither party wants to manifest through dating or marriage.

English translation? Shut up and don't get together very often. A FB is a treat, not a staple. Understand that sexual familiarity breeds scheduling contempt. Put another way, absence makes the hard grow yonder.

Here's what the successful FB relationship requires:

1. A mutual physical obsession. It won't work if only one of you is into the other's body. That's called marriage.
2. A mutual disinterest in seeing each other outside the bedroom. It won't work if you want to have dinner. That's called dating.

3. A mutual disinterest in doing platonic things, like running around with your buddies. That's called friendship.
4. A mutual agreement to play hide the salami in secret. If it's not a secret, it won't last. That's called gossip.
5. A mutual agreement to leave as soon as you've both ejaculated. No lingering, no cuddling, no post-coital heart-to-hearts. That's called lesbianism.
6. A mutual agreement to having sex no more than once a month or so. Although that's also called marriage.

It's hard for two men to agree on the last six points. That's why long-term FBs are so rare.

About three and a half years into it, I had the first real conversation with my FB about our relationship. I even poured a glass of wine before we broke some bedroom furniture. We both agreed the reason it lasted so long is that we have a profound understanding that sex is the only thing that binds us together.

We raised a glass to toast this wonderful relationship, a relationship that wasn't central to our lives, a relationship that would never take the place of true love, but a relationship that for an hour or so every month or so, gave us the kind of sex people dream about.

And then I fucked him senseless.

Hey, Woody!
My boyfriend and I have rock-'em, sock-'em sex, man. I'm like a walking light bulb around him—just waiting to be screwed so I can light up the room. Here's the problem: As soon as the sex is over, so's his attention. I like to cuddle and he doesn't. How can I get him to cuddle more?
—Wanting more

Dear Wanting:
Personally, I love cuddling; it's one of the best parts of sex. It feels so primal I'm sure it's biological. In fact, it is, for women.

Scientists have discovered a female hormone, oxytocin, that makes women want to cuddle.

But there's no such hormone for men. I believe the only hormone that gets released in men after sex is . . . damn, I forgot the name of it. But you can find it on the web at heartlessbastard. com.

How do you get the stud puppet to pay more attention to you after sex? The same way you get a gay man to pay attention to anything—make sure lots of mirrors are involved. That, and talk to him. Ask, don't demand. Don't make him feel bad or defensive. That's my job. Your job is to talk to him when you're not in bed, when you're sharing a glass of wine and you're both mellowed out.

Take his hand and put it on your chest so he feels the heat of your heart, and get into a conversation about sex and how wonderful it is with him. Tell him you love to be held in the warm afterglow of his embrace and that it's really important to you that it be a big part of your sex life. If you say it with warmth and sincerity, it'd be really hard for him to say no.

Unless he's my ex-boyfriend. Then, he'd probably point to his empty ring finger and say, "You want some more milk? Then buy the fucking cow."

Hey, Woody!
I've been seeing someone off and on for about two years. Four months into the relationship things kinda went downhill when we were unable to come to an understanding about commitment. Namely, I understood the meaning of the word; he didn't.

We continued to see each other more as lovers than just friends. I really love him and I feel confident he feels the same for me. The problem is every time I start seeing someone else, he gets obsessively jealous and starts showing me a lot more attention. When he feels the risk of losing me to someone else, he does everything in his power to

get me back, to the point of suggesting we move in together. But when I stop seeing the person to be with him,
he goes back to his uncommitted mode.

I really don't know what to do about this, Woody. I really love the guy. I'm afraid I will never be able to have a
relationship with someone else until this crazy cycle
stops. On the other hand, I cannot imagine putting him out
of my life. I'm 22 and he's in his mid-30s. Do you think the
age difference has anything to do with it?

—Little boy left out in the blue

Dear Little boy:
Face it, you're his bitch. Every time he howls you spread like
you're in heat.

Believe me, I know his type. I'm one of them. I've done exactly what he's doing to you. Only at some point I had the decency to see how much I was hurting the other guy and stopped
it. *Even though I wanted to keep seeing him.*

I hope the surgeons performed his decency bypass without
anesthesia.

You've got three options:

1. An open relationship. Sounds like you've ruled it out, but if
    you're determined to keep him as a boyfriend then revisit
    the question.
2. Learn to live with ambiguity. This means you go about life
    partaking of its joys, releasing its miseries, blessing both
    the arrival and departure of love. Or in your case, the ar-
    rival and departure and arrival and departure and arrival
    and departure and arrival and departure of love.
3. Take control of the relationship. Declare the end of your
    current relationship and the start of a new one. Sit him
    down and ask him to be fair to you. Ask him to respect the
    boundaries that you want in place to support the friendship
    and prevent you from getting on that schizophrenic eleva-
    tor you hate so much.

Figure out what those boundaries should be. Here are a couple: No late night booty calls. No coming over for dinner or watching TV—classic plots to get in your pants. He wants dinner? Go to a diner. Watch TV? Invite three other friends.

The key is to gain his commitment to fairness, to respect your choice because it's coming from a genuine desire to heal and move on.

I learned this from a six year-old, believe it or not. I was tickling my nephew, annoying him like he was one of my readers. Like them, he commanded me to stop, and when that didn't work, he begged me to leave him alone.

And you know how I love to be begged.

Of course, I didn't stop. Even as an uncle, Woody wants what he wants when he wants it. But then my little nephew said something my sister had taught him: *"Uncle Woody, you have to respect my words."*

God, I hate my sister. How the hell was I supposed to keep tickling him after a line like that? I'd be a complete shit if I did. Try it on Yo-Yo Man. If it stopped an annoying prick like me, it'll stop an annoying prick like him.

If you really want to get on with your life you have to change. And here's what you've gotta change: Stop being his bitch.

Hey, Woody!
How come you never talk about Viagra's emotional side effects? Believe me, there are plenty.

After years of impotence my boyfriend started taking it. He loves it, I hate it. I find it insulting that he can't get it up for me without taking a pill. I thought I wanted to have sex with my boyfriend, but now I realize what I really wanted was to feel like I could turn him on.

With Viagra everything about sex has to be planned. We can't have it when I want it, only when the pill kicks in. Sometimes I just fall asleep waiting for it to raise my boyfriend's dick from the dead. Then I get to be woken up

by someone driven by the medication, not by his feelings for me.

Of course, now my boyfriend wants to take it regularly, and I don't want him to. What do we do? Before, the lack of sex was ruining our marriage. Now, it's the sex that's ruining it. Help!

—Sick of the pill

Dear Sick:
You don't need a pill, you need a couch. If there's a relationship that could serve as the model for couples therapy, yours is it.

As you've found out, the little blue pill doesn't just make dicks salute, it also makes unresolved problems stand at attention.

Urologists report that many couples in sexless relationships come unglued when they resume having sex. In some cases, men refuse to try Mr. Blue because the idea of getting "pill-fucked" is so upsetting to their partners. Also, Mr. Blue can sometimes have an annoying social side effect: Mid-life crises. When formerly impotent men get their dicks back they want to wave it at every Tom, Dick, and Harriet.

Obviously, Viagra's not a magic cure-all. Throw it at a problematic couple and all you do is throw an erection at a problematic couple.

So go to a therapist and the three of you make a plan about using Viagra (when, where, under what conditions, if at all). You need to solve something more important than sex right now.

Wait. Did I just say there's something more important than sex? Somebody shoot me.

While you're waiting in the therapist's lobby counting up all the ways your boyfriend's wronged you, let me clear up something. You've assumed that Viagra works by increasing the level of desire men have for their partners. You're wrong. Mr. Blue does nothing for desire. That is a well-documented scientific fact.

If you're not with somebody that turns you on, Mr. Blue will not help you fuck. Viagra does not give you erections; it improves the blood flow to the penis when you get aroused. No arousal, no erection.

The fact that you're boyfriend wants to fuck you when he's on Viagra is a high compliment, but you've managed to make it the ultimate insult. You are projecting your insecurities onto your boyfriend's motivations. You need a jolt of self-esteem. Too bad you can't borrow some of mine. People are always telling me I have too much of it.

For anyone who's thinking of taking Viagra here are a couple of caveats: Don't take it if you're going to use poppers. That's like riding a jet-propelled bicycle through downtown traffic—you're going to die a very ugly, messy death.

Also, don't eat before you take it or you'll reduce the effects. And beware of the side effects: flushing, lightheadedness, headaches, sweating, and a belief that guys are more interested in your accomplishments than your dick.

Take my word for it, that last symptom will go away in a hurry.

Hey, Woody!
My boyfriend won't go down on me. It's driving me crazy. I go down on him all the time and he loves it, but he won't reciprocate. He says he doesn't feel right about it and that he plain doesn't like it. How can I get him to change his mind?

—Dying for head

Dear Dying:
You'd never hear me say "my boyfriend doesn't suck dick." However, you might hear me say *"my ex-boyfriend doesn't suck dick."*

(But enough about how I'd handle the problem.)

It sounds like you're into missionary work, so your best bet is to sit him down for a heart-to-hard talk. Find out what he doesn't like about giving head and then ask him what you can do to make it more pleasurable for him.

Is it the taste he doesn't like? Would it help if he tried it right after you showered? Does he feel too submissive doing it? Find a position where he feels more in control. Is he choking on it too much? Show him how to use his hand to control when, how far, and how fast to take you in.

Experiment with him and ask him how he feels every step of the way. You may not get him to suck the chrome off a Buick, but you may get him to do it without resorting to the unholy triangle of threats, bribes and begging that have served me so well with uncooperative boyfriends.

Often, a revulsion toward oral sex is a reaction to sex abuse or just plain bad experiences as an adult. Was he forced to perform oral sex in the past against his will? In other words, did he date me?

His hesitancy may be a manifestation of childhood sexual abuse. If that's the case, be prepared to have another man in your life: His therapist.

Hey, Woody!
When we first started dating my boyfriend admitted he cheated on all three of his ex-lovers. He said he changed his ways, and that he wanted a committed life partner. He's cheated on me a few times throughout our three-year relationship. Each time, we talked about it and he swore it would never happen again.

The only time he seems to straighten up is when I threaten to leave. I'm filled with doubts, but then I think, aren't people allowed to make mistakes? Shouldn't I be more forgiving? I don't know whether I'm being played for the fool or whether he really does care about me. Either way, he's just got this problem keeping it zipped. What do you think I should do? Leave? Stay? Do you think it's possible for him to be monogamous in the future? Help!
—Wringing my hands

Dear Wringing:

What are you, a straight woman? Didn't anybody tell you there are only two kinds of men? Men who cheat, and men who get caught cheating. Lucky you, you got stuck with both kinds.

Your story reminds me of an ancient Indian riddle: *"Of all things on earth, what is most strange?"* The answer is, *"That a man should see death all around him and not believe that he will die."*

Of all things in your letter, you know what is most strange? That you could date a man who cheated on all his lovers and still believe he wouldn't cheat on you.

You've made it clear that monogamy is a core criterion for a relationship and he can't give you that. Unless you're willing to open the relationship I see nothing but heartache in your future. I say dump his cheating ass.

Hey, Woody!

My boyfriend and I vacationed at a friend's gay guest-house, where Chi-chi LaRue, the famous porn director was shooting the next "Falcon" video.

One day, my boyfriend goes to the gym, and wouldn't you know it, one of the porn stars starts cruising me on the set. He whispers something to Chi-chi and that big old mascara'd mess lumbers over to me and announces, *"The star of our show wants you to fluff him for his next scene."*

Well, Woody, what was I supposed to do, say "No?" So I went into the kitchen, got down on my knees and fluffed until I could fluff no more. My question is, do I tell my boyfriend? We've never talked about "cheating." Which brings me to my next question: Did I cheat? My clothes never came off. The porn star never got off. I didn't have sex with him; I merely prepared him for the sex he was going to have with someone else.

—Fluffy

Dear Fluffy:
It always amazes me what convoluted excuses we make to let ourselves off the hook. Was it sex? Give me a break! Of course it was sex. There's a reason the word "sex" appears in the phrase "oral sex."

Is a test any less of a test because it's an "oral exam"?

I, as judge and jury, pronounce you neither innocent nor guilty of infidelity. I'm throwing the case out on a technicality. How could you have broken a rule if there was no rule to break?

I don't think you should tell him about the fluffing unless you have a worthy reason for telling him. Unburdening yourself isn't a worthy reason. Honesty is not the highest value here; love is. Love and honesty are often at odds with each other. If you don't believe me, answer honestly when your boyfriend asks "Honey, does this shirt make me look fat?" and see where it gets you.

If you're going to tell him about the fluffing, tell him because you want to open the relationship, because you love him too much to lie and hide, and because you want to establish mutually agreeable terms.

Every couple makes rules, whether they're aware of it or not. Even you guys. Your rules are to not talk about the rules. Trust me, that's no way to have a relationship. If your relationship has a chance of surviving, it'll be because you talked about, set, and respected the rules. I know; I lost a great boyfriend because I didn't pay attention to my own advice.

Hey, Woody!
I have a long-time fuck buddy that has the two things I like most in a man, that is, very pretty feet and a plump and contoured butt on a small slender frame. Each time he comes over to get fucked, he never fails to shave his beautiful little ass at my request.

The problem is I'm from the old school where it's only appropriate to "lick it before you stick it." The few times he has let me eat his ass, he always expresses his dislike about the practice.

I've always felt that our encounters were one-sided—always to his favor. He loves to get fucked and I love to fuck him. I like licking his smooth butt hole, although he's always reluctant to having me lick it. He loves to suck my cock and lick my balls, but won't let me reciprocate. Finally, he knows about my foot fetish; he knows how much I enjoy sucking his pretty little toes, but he insists on getting into bed with his socks on. This makes me boil.

Our fuck-buddy relationship has lasted for several years now and we have had numerous heated arguments each time I express my concerns of the relationship being one-sided.

Overall, I like what we have (considering the fact that he doesn't want to date) and I don't want to lose it. He's several years younger than I am and doesn't respond well to interpersonal discussion. What should I do at this point? Are there formal rules of play and etiquette for fuck-buddies?

—This Bud's for me

Dear Bud:

First off, you don't have a fuck-buddy, you have an unrequited love. Your letter aches with passion thwarted and love denied. You're pretending this is about sex, when it's really about you being in love with someone who doesn't love you back.

You asked if there were formal rules of play and etiquette for fuck-buddies? Yeah. Rule #1: No talking! Rule #2: No letters simmering with anger or jealousy. Rule #3: No references to the "relationship being one-sided." Rule #4: No communication that goes past the words "fuck me," with the possible exception of "now" or "harder."

Dude? Are you there? Look at me when I'm writing to you. Better yet, look at the writing on the wall: You're a penis to him. And an annoying one at that. Nobody likes a penis that talks. He's playing his role perfectly. You're the one who screwed up. He wants to fuck and you want to take him to couples' counseling.

As I see it, you have two options: 1) Tell him that you'd like to start something more serious and hope he responds positively (at which point your calls will probably go mysteriously un-returned, but at least you'll be putting something woefully miss-ing back into your interactions—honesty). Or, 2) Shut-up and keep fucking him. I vote for #1. You're too emotionally involved for #2.

Hey, Woody!
Why is it that after I cum, I just want to roll over and fall sleep? Almost every guy I know is the same way, except my boyfriend, who, I swear, is like a chick. He wants to talk and cuddle and have all kinds of heart-to-hearts after I cum. I've tried changing him but nothing works. Is there something I can do to change?
—Snoring but satisfied

Dear Snoring:
Yes. Become a woman. Or just be honest. Say "Honey, after I come I need something only you can provide: Your absence."

If you're still alive after your honest communication, then ex-plain the science behind your sleeping: When you ejaculate your adrenal glands release epinephrine, a chemical that accelerates pulse, elevates blood pressure, and increases blood flow to mus-cles.

This "rush" depletes your muscles of glycogen, a carbohy-drate your body depends on for energy. Glycogen converts to lactic acid during strenuous effort like working out at the gym or going out on dates with me.

That, sleepyhead, is why we go from the bump-and-grind to the slump-and-slide in a bathhouse second. Generally speaking, the effect is less pronounced in men who have less muscle mass. So I guess your only hope of changing is to eat like Kate Moss.

Hey, Woody!
I'm in a committed relationship with a wonderful guy. I
want to stay in the relationship but the sexual spark is
gone. I love this guy and we're the best of friends, but I've
taken on a boyfriend on the side who I also feel strongly
about. My husband does not know about this, ahem, "ar-
rangement."

I don't want a divorce because I want to live up to my
commitment and I don't want to give up what does work in
our marriage. My husband and I have sex infrequently but
we do have it. And that's the problem. I know this is going
to sound fucked, but it's the truth: Whenever I have sex
with my husband I feel like I'm cheating on my boyfriend.
How can I get rid of this guilt? It's really starting to
bother me.

—Committed but confused

Dear Committed:
Let me get this straight. You feel like you're being disloyal to
your boyfriend when you're making love to your husband?

Christ, I gotta get a better gig.

Look, you sperm-burping fuck, not once in your letter did you
mention the impact your cheating has had on your husband. Or
the fact that he might deserve better.

It isn't guilt about "cheating" on your boyfriend you should be
feeling. It's a deep shame you should feel about being such a
prick to your husband. What amazes me isn't so much the
breathtaking inversion of guilt you've managed to construct, but
the utter disregard you have for your husband.

You need to read my favorite Philip Roth book. He must have
been sipping a latte in a coffee shop, trying to think up a good
title when he saw you walk in. He ended up calling it *The
Human Stain*.

In the book he talks about the "ecstasy of sanctimony," a condition in which arrogant hypocrites like you get to do morally
reprehensible things and still manage to look pious.

You say you're great friends with your husband. Bullshit. Friends don't do friends like that. You say you want to live up to your commitment. Bullshit. You call that a commitment? I can imagine the promise you must have made him when you exchanged vows at the ceremony: *"I'll stay in this relationship forever, even if it means I have to treat you like shit and sleep with other men behind your back to do it."*

Here's my advice: Cleanse yourself. Stop seeing your boyfriend. Live up to the commitment you say you're so proud of. Get couples' counseling and try to make it work.

Making it work might even include an arrangement with your boyfriend. But it cannot include deceit and dishonesty.

Hey, Woody!

Last week I went home with a guy I had a crush on ten years ago. I hadn't seen him in a few years and we ran into each other at a bar. He seemed to have really aged and put on some weight, while I've gotten all buff at the gym.

He was really into me that night and I found myself going home with him more out of once having a crush on him than actually liking him now. He kissed me in the bar and it sort of but not really turned me on. He practically begged me to go home with him. I did, but not without saying we probably wouldn't have sex, that I'd have to leave his place real soon, and on and on with more rules and demands.

When we got to his place I basically took a "blow me" approach and I left before he came. I really feel shitty about what I did. Looking back, I realize I was angry that he never paid me attention ten years ago, but now that he's getting older and pudgier, suddenly I'm acceptable. Anyway, I'm feeling like I should call him and apologize but then I think, he's just a trick, you don't call tricks to apologize. What do you think?

—Ashamed

Dear Ashamed:
There are lots of reasons to go home with somebody. Personally, I prefer going home with guys because they turn me on, not because I want to teach them a lesson.

All your "rules and demands" smack of vindication, a power payback for his not having wanted you back then. Basically, you went home to lord it over him.

Should you call him? Absolutely not. What would it accomplish? You've done enough damage. What you did was completely understandable but it was mean and shallow. I won't have you encroaching on my territory. You stick to being principled and leave the cruelty and superficiality to me.

I joke a lot about men being pigs (well, actually, that's no joke) but just because someone's been a pig to you, does not mean you should be a pig back. You cannot grow as a person until you can be kind to the people who were cruel to you.

Instead of going home with him you should have said, "You know, I used to have a crush on you ten years ago and you never paid me attention. Now, you have a crush on me and I'm only interested in being friends. Isn't life funny?"

Hey, Woody!
I've been seeing this guy for three years but he's not out. He hangs out with straight friends and every two or three weeks he pops in with a bag of cocaine and we fuck. The guy thinks we're boyfriends; I think we're fuck buddies. He even said if he ever caught me with another guy we're through. I lost it at that point and yelled, "WE'VE NEVER DATED AND WE NEVER WILL BECAUSE ALL I WANT IS YOUR COCK!"

He said "fuck you, pass the cocaine," and we fucked again.

So here's my question: How do you tell someone he's a fuck buddy when he insists he's a boyfriend?

—Confused

Dear Confused:
You're confused? Try reading the letter you wrote.

Actually, I was fucking a guy like that once. He kept insisting he was *"The One"* for me. Yes, I told him, *"Of Many."* He still didn't get it. But then how could he? He once spent twenty minutes staring at a carton of juice because it said, "concentrate."

In addition to stupidity, the problem with these guys is that they don't listen very well. You say, "You're nice, but..." and they hear, "Your nice butt..."

My advice is to keep fucking him till he goes away. Don't have any conversations about your "relationship." If he brings it up, just do what I do: push your cock farther into his mouth. Works every time.

If he really wanted to date you, he'd ask you out. When he does you'll know your fucking days are numbered. Even idiots end up asking themselves why the guys they're fucking should buy the pig when the milk is free.

Hey, Woody!
I love getting fucked by my boyfriend. After he comes inside me I lift my legs so high I practically do a headstand because I want his semen to flood my insides. It's almost like taking sacrament. But I'm wondering what happens to the semen inside me? I know it seeps out but not all of it. What happens to the part that doesn't? And is there any harm to having his semen inside my body? We're both negative and monogamous.
—Awash in a sea of white

Dear Awash:
Dude, can you say "obsessed"? Man, I can just see the bunnies boiling on his stove if he ever leaves you.

Semen is the fluid that carries sperm. It will either travel farther into your rectum or trickle out and dry up. You know, like bar flies spilling out the door after last call.

I hate to feed your obsession even more, but the semen that doesn't seep out will carry sperm that'll survive for three to five days. Yeah, you read it right. You can walk around knowing your boyfriend's sperm is flopping around your insides for up to five days looking for an egg. I can hear the squish in your walk from here.

As far as the semen that seeps out, it evaporates in the open air, killing the sperm with it. How long does sperm last outside the body? No one knows because it depends on the humidity, body temperature, consistency of the semen, and what body part it lands on. But it isn't very long. The macho gazpacho turns out to be girlie-milk, crying out, "I'm melting" as soon as it sees daylight.

It goes without saying that you're playing with fire when you let someone cum inside you during receptive anal sex. Someone needs to introduce you to a condom.

Hey, Woody!
Last week you wrote about the guy who let his lover come inside him (he practically did a handstand so the semen would trickle far into his body. Yuck, but that's another letter). Here's my beef: You told him he should wear a rubber even though they were in a committed, monogamous relationship.

What are you, some kind of AIDS Nazi?

I read your column because you're a funny, insightful bastard, but there's nothing funny about believing gay men can't trust each other. Telling your readers to forget trust, forget monogamy, forget LOVE, is just way too cynical for the world I want to live in.

Basically, you told him "Don't trust each other—wear a condom." There is no AIDS expert that would say that to a straight, married couple, but you're perfectly willing to say it to a committed, monogamous gay couple. What a double standard. You surprise me, Woody.

I love my husband, I believe he's faithful, and sharing

our juicy fruits is just one reward for trusting each other. Your advice may be exactly right for single men, but it SUCKED for those of us who really do practice monogamy and don't lie to our partners.

—**Loads of love**

Dear Loads:

You're right that by telling committed, monogamous couples to use condoms I implied that trust between men is impossible. You're also right that by advocating condoms I implied the impossibility of monogamy for gay couples. And you're right that most AIDS experts would not have given the same advice to straight, monogamous couples.

So an apology is in order. I believe in my heart that gay men can be monogamous. I believe it because I've been in monogamous relationships and I know lots of couples who can say they're exclusive without their friends bursting out laughing. My advice contributed to the rampant cynicism about gay relationships, a cynicism I don't share.

HOWEVER. (And you know, there's always a *however* in my apologies.)

Nobody goes into a marriage thinking it's going to end in divorce. Yet over half of marriages end up panhandling on the corner of Trust and Betrayal.

If that's the track record between men and women, what is it between men and men?

We can't predict the future. Relationships change over time. The love and commitment that exists today may be gone tomorrow (notice I said "may," not "will"). And in that sense, wearing a rubber buys you health insurance in the same way a prenuptial agreement buys you financial insurance.

Speaking of insurance, does getting car insurance mean you're breaking a promise to drive safely? Does getting life insurance mean your promise of growing older with your lover is a lie? Preparing for the worst is not an indictment of the present nor a callused view of the future.

Still, I was wrong because my advice smacked of absolutes

and in the complicated world of safe sex, absolutes don't work. Whether it's dieting, drugs, alcohol, or unsafe sex, absolutes are a recipe for failure.

On the risk scale, getting fucked by a married, monogamous, partner is not equivalent to getting fucked by a single, promiscuous guy. Should the advice for sex acts with wildly different risk levels always be the same? Not if you're a realist willing to exercise reasonable precautions to live a passionate life.

My advice shouldn't have been "Wear a Condom." It should have been "Weigh the Pros and Cons of Wearing a Condom." Condoms may not always be the answer, but they are always the question.

Hey, Woody!
My physician turns me on. And I think he's interested too, but he's not making a move. I want to tell him it's his turn to drop his drawers but I don't know how to do it. Any advice?

—Hangin' on the examination table

Dear Hangin':
No self-respecting doctor would lose his license to win your pants. If it's really unbearable, tell him you will no longer see him in his office because you'd rather see him in bed.

If he's interested—and ethical—he'll tell you "Great! See you at my place in six months!" That's the time frame the American Medical Association recommends for doctors to take their ex-patients into their arms and still keep their license. Not to mention their integrity.

Hey, Woody!
I had a date with a dreamboat last week. After an enchanting dinner we repaired over to his home, where I tried to kiss him on the lips. He put his hand in the way and said *"I don't do that."* At first I thought he was kid-

ding, but he wasn't. Woody, this guy didn't want to kiss, didn't want to hold hands, didn't even want to have oral sex. He said the only thing he'd do is fuck me. This, from a guy who swears he's interested in me. I refuse to get fucked without a kiss—I'm no Log Cabin Republican. Still, I really like this guy and he wants to keep dating. Should we? Or am I just kidding myself?

—Fuckable but not kissable

Dear Fuckable:

He wants you to get fucked without getting kissed? What does he take your for, a Log Cabin Republican?

Ten bucks says if you fuck he'll insist on no lube. Sounds like the only part of him that came out of the closet was his crotch. If you want real dating material, you'll have to wait till the rest of his body and mind come out.

Falling for a hot guy with a neon "DANGER" sign blinking over his head sets up an interesting dilemma: Walk away now and cut your losses, or go for it knowing you might get hurt in a big way.

The answer depends on your tolerance for pain. Nobody wants to throw a good-looking fish back in the water—unless it's a piranha. Even if you're a dick pig, you might want to take a pass. How good could this guy be if there's no kissing, no foreplay and no oral sex? That's not a date, that's a boyfriend.

On the other hand, you could go for it and see if you can change him. Pay no attention to the laughter in the background—it's just nature's laugh-track. It kicks in whenever I say something ridiculous.

Hey, Woody!
You've gotten a lot of flak from people about your position on monogamy. Reading you week to week, it's actually kinda hard to pin you down. Sometimes you defend it, sometimes you attack it. Are you waffling on us?

—Unsure myself

Dear Unsure:

Monogamy is either a necessary ingredient for couples to stay together or a new Milton Bradley bored game. Like the rest of you, I can never make up my mind.

I've defended and attacked monogamy because it needs defending and attacking.

On the one hand, monogamy is a wonderful way for couples to experience the high of exclusivity. And it can be quite a high. Emphasis on "can."

The other thing arguing for monogamy is the nature of all worthwhile things. Namely, that they require sacrifice. To have a great body you have to sacrifice fries and chocolate shakes; to have a great income you have to sacrifice hanging out at the beach on weekdays; to own a great porno collection you have to sacrifice the cheaper rentals.

To have a great marriage, do you have to sacrifice sex with others? I pose it as a question because the answer is different for different people.

Personally, I don't believe that sexual fidelity is the primary measure of a man's love for another man. Mostly because sex isn't the highest expression of love. Celibate priests know that. So do the handicapped and people with medical conditions that prevent them from having sex.

It's not that I think there's something wrong with monogamy, it's that I don't think it's the only route to experiencing true, genuine love and commitment for another man. I believe the highest form of commitment isn't sexual, it's emotional. I'd much rather be in an open relationship with a partner who would stand in front of a bullet to protect me, than in a monogamous relationship with a partner who'd sit in front of the TV and ignore me.

Hey, Woody!

I live in a one-bedroom/one-bath apartment with my boyfriend, and his bathroom habits are driving me nuts. He won't close the bathroom door when he shits because he wants to feel "intimate" with me.

He thinks I'm being a hypocrite ("Why is it okay to see things go in my ass but not out of it?"). Geez, all I'm asking for is a little privacy. Do you think I'm over-reacting? I love this guy, but does love mean never having to close the door?

—Load-phobic

Dear Load:

Sitting on the toilet farting, grunting and wiping in front of your boyfriend isn't intimacy. It's terrorism.

I don't want to see my boyfriend brush his teeth, let alone wipe his ass. Nobody shits out a bouquet of flowers. Shit stinks. It makes you gag, it's unhealthy, and it makes you lose your erection. You know, like marriage.

Your boyfriend's assertion that you're a hypocrite because you like to put things up his butt but don't want to see anything slump out of it is nonsense. Our butts have dual natures. They're "manginas" at night and shit factories in the morning. Confuse them at your peril.

It's wonderful that your boyfriend has no shame about his bodily functions. In some ways, he's more enlightened than the rest of us. As children we were often humiliated in our toilet training and learned to associate the natural process of elimination as something shameful. And Lord, if you were a bed wetter, you were subject to enormous shame and guilt.

Your boyfriend would've fit in perfectly in ancient Rome. It wasn't unusual for slaves to haul silver urine pots into the middle of a royal dinner for the guests to relieve themselves *while they talked to each other.* You didn't dare tell people to piss off back then. They would've done it right in front of you.

And get a load of the French. King Louis XIII had a "rumble throne" where he would literally defecate while conferring with his advisors. The man didn't take crap from anyone.

Hell, maybe your boyfriend was born a few centuries too late. But it doesn't matter. That was then, this is now. There is such a thing as privacy. Everyone's got boundaries. He should respect yours and not give you any shit about it.

Hey, Woody!
I've known this guy for seven years and I have always
wanted to sleep with him. Problem is he is close friends
with my best friend and I think that would make things very
weird. He also used to date my ex-boyfriend who is still
weirded out whenever I even look at another man. Oh, he
also has a boyfriend who is very nice and I have never been
able to figure out what the deal is with their relationship.
Any advice on how to lure this guy into my bed?
                                    —Wondering how I could

Dear Wondering:
You remind me of the guy who steps in dog shit, tracks it all over
the house, and then wonders where the odor's coming from.
Dude, both your sole and your soul need a little cleaning up. I'm
all for grab-it-and-growl sex, but Christ, not if it's going to leave
dead bodies piled up on the floor.

Anybody who's willing to lose his best friend, bust up a romantic relationship, and anger an ex-boyfriend just to free Willie
for an hour is a smellier asshole than the one he's trying to fill.

Your dick hurts and that makes it okay to ruin relationships?
Here's my advice: Go to Radio Shack, where they sell those
satellite-based navigational sensors—the kind that guide cars to
their destination—and ask them if they have a gizmo like it for
the morally blind. Cuz you run over honor and dignity like my
grandmother runs over parking meters. At least she'd be morti-
fied if she knew the damage she was causing. You ARE aware
and you still don't care.

Until you do, I say get back in the closet and give me the key.
I'll let you know when you're ready to come out.

Hey, Woody!
I was having a fight with a friend of mine because he was
bragging that he's never cheated on his boyfriend. I re-
minded him of a certain night a few weeks ago when he

went home with a friend of mine and got blown, as he said, "to Kingdom Come."

I said to him "You don't think getting blown constitutes cheating?" He disagreed completely. We both read your column. Settle it for us. Who's right?

—Oral quarrel

Dear Oral:

You're both right. There isn't a sex therapist in the world that wouldn't classify blow jobs as sex. Whether it constitutes cheating, however, is a different story. It depends on what agreement your friend has with his lover. If they both believe that oral sex isn't "real" sex then, no, your friend didn't cheat on his spouse.

Signed,

Hillary Clinton

Hey, Woody!

Here's my problem in a nutshell—I'm in love with a man I can't have. He's in a committed relationship with another guy. All three of us are friends, and I don't want to hurt anyone, but every time we're together, all I can think about is how happy I could make him. To make matters worse, I have been spending a lot more time with the guy I love and the attraction is getting stronger and stronger. I'm afraid if I'm not careful, the attraction will become obvious, and I'll wind up losing two good friends. What should I do?

—Guilty on the Gulf Coast

Dear Guilty:

What should you do? Run like hell. Go to Blockbuster Video if you want that much drama. Your job is to build a happy home, not wreck one.

You have an obligation to yourself to have a satisfying sex life, but you also have an obligation to respect the boundaries of friendship and committed relationships. My advice is to act like you were just about to step on a rattlesnake and back away slowly. You can do this in one of two ways:

1. Tell him why you're backing away (you're falling for him, it hurts too much, and you have too much respect for your friendship and his relationship to mess them up).
2. Just back away without saying anything. Say you're too busy to meet. And then get busy.

Hey, Woody!
I'm stuck on a crossword puzzle about sex. What's an eight-letter word for "Monotony?"
—**Just curious**

Dear Just:
Monogamy.

Hey, Woody!
I've placed some ads in the personal classifieds that turned into actual dates. The majority have been duds. However, there are some dates where both parties had a good time. My question is, what is the proper etiquette as to who calls whom first? The guy placing the ad or the answeree?
—**Unclassifiable**

Dear Unclassifiable:
The one with the smallest dick has to call first. What the hell kind of question is that? You're sitting there scratching your ass, going "Duh, I really like this guy, but I'm not going to call because I placed the ad and everybody knows the placer doesn't call first." For all you know he's already called but the ringing in your ears drowned out the phone.

Here's the rule: There ain't no rule. You do what feels natural in the context of the signals you pick up from the other guy. Translation: Call the next day if he snorted and pawed at the ground to get at you. Call a day or two later if he snorted and pawed through the personals as he talked to you. Call immediately if he snorted K and tried to pawn you off on somebody else. Yes, call *immediately*. The paper, I mean. You'll need to extend the ad another week.

Hey, Woody!
I figure with the amount of attitude you pack in each response you'll be able to give me the kick in the ass I know I need. Besides, I think you're really a woman who's hiding behind the pen name Woody Miller (either that or you're a passive bottom). My boyfriend has beat the shit out of me twice. I only came back after promises that he'd stop and gut wrenching pleas for me to come home. He said he had been crying for days and couldn't live without me.

Now I'm home and afraid. I tried leaving again and he said he'd hurt me or himself badly if I did that. I want out—but don't want him to hurt me or himself. Should I just pack up and leave and hope for the best, should I call the police, what should I do?

—Dazed and confused

Dear Confused:
Only a gay man can find the time to launch a few bon mots before enduring a violent attack. I admire your pluckiness in the face of adversity.

First off, I'm not a woman. There's a stylistic difference between cranky and bitchy. Maybe if your boyfriend wasn't boxing your brains so much you'd understand the subtlety. And I'm a passive bottom the way Hillary Clinton is a befuddled wife.

There's a lot of bravery in your humor. I hope you can use it to get yourself out of this horrible situation. I turned to The Partnership Against Domestic Violence for help. They say your situation is a textbook case of domestic violence.

It starts with intimidation and threats, progresses to the actual battery, and then settles into a "honeymoon phase" (where the batterer apologizes profusely, begs you to take him back, and swears it'll never happen again). Then the cycle begins all over again. Sound familiar?

If you're in imminent danger (and it sounds like you are), the best thing to do is call the National Domestic Violence Hotline at 1-800-779-3512. They'll link you up with a local center, where they'll suggest safe havens, provide support groups and counseling, as well as help with legal and law enforcement options.

You HAVE to leave, but ironically, leaving puts you in the greatest danger because that's when Mr. Control Freak redlines the asshole meter. If you're not in imminent danger, don't just up and leave. "Plan your escape," instead.

First, do not move in with family or friends. It's the first place he'll look, and you'll be putting them in danger. Find an apartment with security. You may have to switch jobs. Make the arrangements BEFORE you leave. While you're making the arrangements, slowly pack your stuff in unnoticeable ways. Like, every time you do your laundry, take two or three items and salt them away in a bag. When all the arrangements are solid, do not announce that you're leaving. Just leave with what you've stored away—when he's gone.

May God watch over you, but not before he sees me kicking your ass out the front door for coming back to your boyfriend in the first place. The average person attempts to leave their batterer seven times before they make a permanent break. They come back, like you did, because their shit-for-a-boyfriend turns human for a couple of months during the "honeymoon phase."

There is no such thing as a one-time batterer. You were a fool for coming back after the first time. So get some courage, get a plan, and get out.

Note: For additional information, visit the National Coalition against Domestic Violence's website at www.ncadv.org or call the local chapter of Men Stopping Violence.

Hey, Woody!
I slept with my best friend's boyfriend. It was a drunken
mistake and I have no desire to repeat it. I want to tell
him but I'm afraid of losing his friendship. What should I
do?

—Honest Indian

Dear Indian:
Most professionals would recommend that you acknowledge
your dirty deed and pay the price, even if it means losing your
best friend.
    Lucky for you, I'm not a professional. I say silence is golden.
Act like you're in Fort Knox. Honesty is an incredibly overrated
gesture in situations like this. If any good could come out of your
best friend knowing, I'd say do it. But unloading your guilt doesn't
qualify as a selfless, beneficial act. It's like taking a dump in his
living room. Sure, you'll feel unburdened but what's he supposed
to do with a hot, steaming load of shit on his rug?
    I say keep your mouth shut, your fly zipped, and resolve never
to repeat the same mistake.

Hey, Woody!
I'm a very prominent drag queen here so please don't print
the town. I'm in love with a good friend of mine I met
when I first started dragging. He's a gorgeous pretty boy,
and I'm just a drag queen. I look like a drag queen in and
out.
    I'm not interested in him for his body, I love him for his
heart and his soul. I don't know what to do. He's a good
friend of mine. I don't know how to approach him. I need
an outside party to help me out. I'm really, truly in love
with him. Everyone wants him. He's with everyone else ex-
cept with me. I think about him all the time. Everything
he's ever given to me, I put on a high pedestal and never
take it down. Do I tell him? Or do I suffer in silence?
                              —Smilin' on-stage, cryin' off-stage

Dear Cryin':
Sweetheart, there is nothing I can say that's going to take the hurt away. The only thing I can give you are three very painful options. The first is to tell him. Ordinarily, I'm very big on being direct, but in your case I'm not. Why? 'cause he already knows, sweetie. And he hasn't responded.

Contrary to popular belief, men aren't morons. We may be cruel selfish pigs, but stupid we're not. Well, most of us, anyway.

We know when somebody carries a torch for us. By confronting him you cross a boundary and risk his friendship (most people when confronted by a friend confessing a crush start distancing themselves).

Your second option comes from the "outta sight, outta mind" school of healing. Cut him off so you can heal, move on, and point your lipstick case to reciprocal love opportunities. But the disruption this will cause among your other friends and in yourself has some pretty painful consequences.

My vote is to minimize your contact with him without making any pronouncements or making your friends crazy by forcing them to "warn" you when he's going to be somewhere so you can avoid him. I know it hurts but you don't have the right to drag your friends—and him—into a pain you created.

There isn't a man alive who hasn't been in your, er, uhm, pumps. We got over it by being kind to ourselves, confiding in trusted friends who can take the sting away, and mostly by receiving the wisdom and perspective only time can bestow.

Or you can do what I did—buy a therapist his first pool.

Hey, Woody!
I'm concerned about my "past" which has been, uhm, colorful. But I'm on the straight and narrow now, looking for real love, unpaid love, if you know what I mean. But I'm depressed about it cuz I figure I'm going to scare off men when they find out about my past. How will I explain it?
—Turned my last trick

Dear Turned:
There is nothing to explain. First of all, it's nobody's business. Second of all, a true gentleman won't inquire. Besides, potential suitors are not interested in your resume, they're interested in your eyes, your mouth, your dick, your ass, the way you touch them, the way you talk to them.

Congratulations on your new life, by the way. I wouldn't worry about future dating prospects. Just remember when they ask you to whisper the three magic words, they're not "Master-Card or Visa?"

Hey, Woody!
So I meet Mr. Creamy with sugar on top, and we have balls-to-the-wall sex (literally!) for a couple of months. We're dating, we're screwing and I start to fall. Then he stops calling. Won't return my calls. I just can't believe it. We were sparking the wire and suddenly the line goes dead. We never had a fight, a disagreement, nothing. I'm pissed and I'm hurt. I just want to know why. I deserve some closure but he won't give me any. Should I keep trying to reach him, if only just to acknowledge that it's over?

—Over but not out

Dear Over:
You were probably too distracted by the gorgeous sites in Manland to notice the sign at the entrance of town—"Welcome to Hell." As a long-time resident, let me be the first to welcome you.

Scientists have recently found the "pig" gene in men. It lies dormant waiting to be expressed at the right moment. His moment came. All over you. It's shocking when it happens because you don't understand how you could have felt so magical about your time together and he didn't. You almost feel like you can't trust your own feelings.

But don't lose faith in your own "radar." What you felt was

genuine, what you read was not. You didn't read the signs, guy, and believe me, men with pig genes drop signs like horny deaf guys prowling the bars.

The truth is, he's allowed to change his mind about who he's fucking. He should have given you what the Army gives when they want to get rid of a guy without taking away his dignity—an honorable discharge.

While I feel your pain, you need to give up on the idea of "closure." There ain't gonna be any. Pigs don't know how to close, they only know how to root around. So stop calling him, don't write letters (well, you can write to let off a little steam, but don't send them), don't communicate with him.

You were a piece of meat to him. Own it, grieve it, get support for it, then get over it. The best thing you can do is remember how awful it feels, and swear never to visit the same crap on somebody else.

Hey, Woody!
I love kissing. As far as I'm concerned if you're not a good kisser, you're not a good lay. Even when I watch porno, I notice I get extra hard when I see the on-screen studs kissing deeply. I've been dating this creamy guy for a few months, and to my shock and horror, he doesn't really like to kiss much. He's told me I'm the best kisser he's ever had but that he just doesn't get into it that much. What can I do to turn this around? He's perfect in every other way.
—Tonguing for more

Dear Tonguing:
I'm right there with you, babe. Sex without kissing is like eating dinner alone in a steak restaurant—even when you're served a sirloin, the meat's still missing.

Many men, myself included, consider kissing more intimate than sexual intercourse. Breathing somebody else's breath, caressing their cheeks, tasting their tongue—these are all incredibly intimate acts.

In fact, that may be the reason why Mr. Creamy won't spread his lips as far as he spreads his legs. If he's been deeply hurt, one way of protecting himself is not to get too intimate too fast, and that may mean putting his lips on ice. If that's the case you're going to need time, patience and understanding to overcome it.

If you haven't already, tell him how important kissing is to you. Don't blame; request. Don't say what I'd say ("Look you self-ish prick, you're in this relationship to service me and I want some tongue NOW"). Instead say, "Kissing is the best part of sex for me. What can I do to make you want to kiss me more?"

Give him some time and enjoy him without putting a lot of demands on him. If he doesn't come around, you have some tough choices ahead of you.

Chapter 6

Anal Sex: Cracking the Case Wide Open

Even in the fudge-packing world of butt pirates I'm a contrarian. I've often been asked what position I prefer, top or bottom. I always answer truthfully and consistently: None of your fucking business.

I won't even answer the question when friends ask it. Why? Because unlike my readers, I'm allergic to labels.

The only thing gay men seem to like more than assuming the position is assuming an identity. Oddly, we've created whole identities out of sexual positions.

Sex has a glorious, unlimited horizon. It's uncharted territory no matter how many times we've been there before. It's a journey toward discovery, an extreme sport, an escapist plot. It's a tactical game, a tactile trade, a longing proscribed, a desire for bribe. It's a criminal act, a loving act, sometimes purely an act. It's all these things, none of these things, some of the time, none of the time, and sometimes *at* the same time.

And the best description we can come up with is "top" and "bottom"?

We suck.

Labels take you from liberty to limitation in sixty self-adhesive seconds. If you perform a sexually aggressive act, labels demand you take on a sexually aggressive persona. If you perform a sexually receptive act, labels mandate the conception of a submissive identity. Label-love turns the principles of pleasure into the politics of penetration.

So why do we do it? Read the fucking chapter. This is just the intro.

Other than label-love, the letters in this section tend to focus on guys who can't seem to put anything up their butts, guys who can't keep anything out of it, and guys who have a love/hate relationship with the whole mess.

The most interesting questions, as always, are not the medical ones, but the ones that reveal something much greater than the sex acts they're inquiring about. For instance, the letter from a butch guy who didn't want his nelly boyfriend to top him. Interesting question. Would you let a nelly queen fuck you?

* * *

Hey, Woody!

I'm lucky enough to have a boyfriend with a lovely piece of equipment. It's not mammoth, but far longer than average. I love it when he plows into me, but sometimes it really hurts. I mean the pain can be frighteningly, sickeningly bad. It's not just stretching and friction at the orifice; it's as if his head is pounding on some internal organ.

Last weekend was the worst yet. All his long strokes just about killed me, each one a real sharp pain at a specific spot deep in my gut, a little right of center. The pain lasted about three days.

Is it possible that I bruised my bladder or my colon? What can I do to avoid this awful pain? I tried it doggy style but that hurts too. I know guys take on guys with bigger equipment than my boyfriend all the time and I've never heard of this problem. What's wrong with me?

—Gotta have it

Dear Gotta:

What's wrong with you? Do you want it numerically, alphabetically, or categorically?

You have what's commonly known as an "Ignoranus," an anal opening surrounded by an ignorant queen who endangers her life by fucking through excruciating pain.

Look, how many times do I have to say this to you crack whores? If you're having sex and your crack hurts, STOP. Pain is a signal that something's wrong. If pain were a traffic light it would not be a yellow "oh, what the hell, floor it" caution light. It would be a blinking red "Game Over" stop light.

When I went to my advisory board (usually at midnight in a cemetery. They don't want to be associated with a gay sex advice column and I don't want to be associated with respectable people. We're all terribly conflicted. Reminds me of my family)... Anyway, my docs took one look at your letter and said (a) I have truly stupid readers, (b) you could easily be describing colon or prostate cancer, (c) you need a urinalysis to see if there is blood in your urine, (d) you need a screening colonoscopy, (e) you need to have your ass kicked.

I can't help you with A through D but hold on for E, I'm looking for the right boot. While I'm lacing up, here are a couple of other things. It's possible you could simply have a bruised colon. Remedy: Stop fucking for a few weeks and take sitz baths (sit in a tub of warm water for twenty minutes a day).

If you're lucky and you're not suffering from any of the conditions listed above, you'll probably have to resign yourself to getting half-fucked and not letting your boyfriend go in all the way.

And what's with the "lovely" package? What are you, some kind of British poofter?

You're never going to know what you have unless you see a doctor. If you don't have one, get one. If you have one but he's not gay, dump him. I don't know many straight doctors who can hear about buttfucking without blanching.

Until you see your doctor you must stop getting fucked. If your boyfriend gives you grief about it, tell him why Jewish women like Chinese food so much. Turns out Won Ton spelled backwards is Not Now.

Hey, Woody!
I've been bottoming with gleeful abandon lately and I've
noticed something kinda gross—I'm not near as tight as I
used to be. I'm leaking into my underwear. What can I do?
And don't tell me to stop fucking—it ain't gonna happen.
—Fucked coming and going

Dear Fucked:
I would never tell anyone to stop fucking—unless it was a delaying tactic till I could get there for the three-way.

Your sphincter is a muscle designed to keep your butt closed. The more it stretches, the more elasticity it loses and the more likely it won't contract to full closure.

Put the bounce back in your ass with "Kegel" exercises. Tighten your anus like you were stopping the flow of urine, hold for a few seconds and let go. Typically you want to do them for a few minutes, but in your case, Trampolina, I'd be spending at least 15 minutes a day feeling the burn.

I pitched Jane Fonda on an exercise video to repair over-stretched sphincters, figuring the experience of marrying one made her an expert. Security escorted me out of the building before she had a chance to answer.

Anyway, if you don't recuperate your sphincter's elasticity, you're going to find even uglier surprises in your underwear. Ultimately, you might need surgery to close it up. If that doesn't get you yelling " . . . 5, 6, 7, 8!" I don't know what will. Having a surgeon up your ass is fun only when it's a date, not when it's a procedure.

Hey, Woody!
My boyfriend of approximately 14 months is a hardcore
bottom. I've always been the top and that's the way we
both like it. He's never topped another guy and wouldn't
even consider it. The problem in our relationship is that
he's a wimpy bottom. Sometimes I have to beg and plead
for me to fuck him.

Anyway, he claims he's sore a lot and I have to admit he's in so much pain it sometimes sounds like I'm raping him. I'm frustrated because most hardcore bottoms in my past have been "eager beavers" and were always ready and willing to get plowed. I love this guy, but I'm frustrated. What can we do? How do those other hardcore bottoms take it all the time, everyday and for several hours? How can I make my sweet wholesome boyfriend trashy in the sheets, but not in the streets?

—Hard and hoping

Dear Hard:

There are two issues here—his libido and your stupidity. Solve your problem and you'll probably solve his.

Listen to yourself, blockhead—*"he's in so much pain it feels like I'm raping him."* God Almighty, you fell out of the stupid tree and hit every branch on the way down. Never, ever, proceed with a sex act when someone is in pain (unless pain is the goal, but that's another column). I'd claim a low sex drive too if I knew my ass was in for a turkey-stuffing reaming by the Fistmaster General.

Without meaning to you've taught him to associate fucking with pain. You need to undo what shrinks call "negative reinforcement." Here's how: Stop fucking him. Back off and let your fingers do the walking. With lots of lube. Explore his love hole with only one thing in mind—finding out the difference between his pleasure and pain points. Go from one finger to two to sex toys. Back off when he feels pain. Figure out what he likes. There's a real easy way to do that: Ask him. "Do you like it when I do this? How about when I do that?" These are the questions every good top asks.

Eventually he'll be ready for the real thing, but don't give it to him. Make him go from begging off to begging for it. After a couple of weeks of stuffing everything but yourself into him, he'll be climbing the walls for it. Learn to generate desire in him. Remember, the fastest way to get what you want in bed is to slow down and give your partner what he needs.

He needs a kinder, gentler lover. You need a shot of common sense—straight up with no chaser.

Hey, Woody!
I'm a surgeon working in the operating room (OR) of a major hospital. One night, a man walks into the ER complaining of an "unfortunate soft drink accident." Meaning, he got a Coke bottle stuck up his ass.
Well, Woody, this was no ordinary man. He was the CEO of a Fortune 500 company. He walked in with his wife and a number of our staff recognized him. They made a small attempt to remove the bottle in the ER, but they quickly gave up and made a call to the OR requesting we put him to sleep and do the excavation under anesthetics.
We put him to sleep, turned him over belly side down in a jack-knife position, hoping everything would relax and I could pull it right out using the same instruments we use to deliver a baby in a difficult lie. But it just wouldn't come out!
We couldn't be too forceful or rough in our attempts, because if the bottle shattered inside him ... well, we would probably cause him to die a slow, awful death.
The anesthesiologist gave him more relaxants than is normally recommended to "loosen him up," so to speak. Everyone on the surgical team had their favorite position to conduct the reverse penetration—on his back, in stirups, on his side, and so on. We spent many, many hours with every instrument in the book with this guy, snickering over how it might have happened.
Since his wife accompanied him to the hospital, we sort of concluded she was in on a playful sex act. I assume, being a public figure, he didn't dare go out and buy a dildo, so they resorted to common household items.
Around 5 a.m., after several hours of attempted removal, the only option left to us was to turn him over on his back and cut him open to remove it through his ab-

domen. The procedure was called "laparotomy for removal of a foreign body from sigmoid colon." But I called it a "Cokectomy."

We had to take a picture of the "foreign body" (standard procedure) and then send it to pathology so they could examine it for an official path report.

The most amazing part is that the crisis did NOT make it to the rumor mill and he survived professionally. Clearly, he had inside help because the picture of the Coke bottle disappeared and the final path report did not specify what the foreign body was.

As a medical doctor I don't have any questions for you. Obviously, this is a cautionary tale to all your readers. When you put something in your rectum, make sure the distal end (the last part to go in), is so big and broad there isn't a snowball's chance in hell that it will slip all the way in.

—Dr. Excavation

Dear Doc:
I don't think having consumers admitted to the ER with a bottle up their ass was the company's intent when it came up with the slogan "Have a Coke and a smile." But, hey, to each his own.

Obviously I can't publish the name of the CEO, but I've seen him in business magazines invariably described as a "hard-ass." Thanks for letting me know why.

Hey, Woody!
I'm just coming out and I love to make out and go down on guys. But the intercourse thing has my "wanna/don't wanna" meter bobbing up and down like a buoy in the Pacific. I know nothing about "the forbidden zone" down there and I'm too embarrassed to ask any of my friends. Can you give me an "Anus 101" intro class?

—Future Ass-Master

Dear Ass-Master:
Kinsey, the thinking man's pervert, said half his survey respondents considered the anal area an erotic zone. And he wasn't just talking about gay men, either.

In a recent survey of 100,000 *Playboy* readers, 47 percent of the men admitted having tried anal intercourse (calm down, they were talking about penetrating their girlfriends. Most of them, anyway).

Intercourse is the least practiced form of anal sex, according to sex researchers. The most common? Touching the anal opening with a finger while masturbating, or stimulating a partner's anus during oral sex. "Rimming" is another way to play without going all the way. There are two dots in this scenario—a tongue and an opening. Let your imagination make the connection.

Anal intercourse is fraught with pain and complications if you're not careful. With its high concentrations of nerve endings the anus can produce thrills or agonies, depending on your approach to it. Finger, penis or dildo, the anal muscles go into a spasm when you first insert a foreign object into it. Or even a familiar one. If you don't wait for these muscles to relax, it's going to hurt like hell and you run the risk of tearing the anal lining.

Chronic anal tension is the most common cause of anal discomfort during sex. Like any sales call, the best way to relieve the tension is to make some introductions: "Mr. Rectum, I'd like you to meet Mr. Finger. He's with Hands, Inc. and he's going to make sure all your needs are taken care of."

The best place to make your introductions is in the shower. Start by inserting your finger about a half-inch into your anus and press the fingertip against the side. You'll feel two sphincter muscles, about a quarter-inch apart. The external sphincter is controlled by the central nervous system, which means you can voluntarily tense and relax the muscle. The internal sphincter twitches to a different master, though. It's controlled by the autonomic nervous system, which governs involuntary functions like your heartbeat.

The internal sphincter is what keeps most men from enjoying

anal intercourse. As it tenses around the finger-penis-dildo, it can create enormous pain. It's possible to gain voluntary control of the internal sphincter, but you can't do it directly like you can with the external sphincter. You do it by inserting a finger (do it every day for a couple of weeks) and desensitizing it. Basically, you're training it (rather than ordering it) to relax.

Like your love life, there's nothing straight about the rectum. After the short anal canal that connects the anal opening to the rectum, the rectum tilts toward the front of the body. A few inches in, it curves back—sometimes as much as 90 degrees. Then, after a few more inches, it swoops toward the front of the body once again. Hence, the high demand for Rotor-rooting tops.

Before you get laid, get the lay of your own land by using a dildo. Try different angles and body positions and concentrate on how it feels. For heaven's sake, make sure it has a flared base in case you lose your grip and slip it into the abyss. There's nothing worse than finding yourself in the ER announcing an unfortunate gardening incident.

Being thoroughly at ease and familiar with your own cracks and crevices will make you a better lover. You need to do a lot of homework before earning a degree in the ass arts. Fortunately, you can begin with a self-study course.

Hey, Woody!
Are some people's butts just built differently than others? I mean on the inside. My boyfriend and I both enjoy playing bottom, but he could swallow dining room furniture with so much as a hit of poppers, and I struggle with the basic big dick. It makes me jealous that he can take so much more than me, and I think he must have some physical advantage up there. Is there anything I can do to take on more cargo?

—Tightass

Dear Tightass:

Yes, people have different butts. I myself have three different butts scheduled this week.

Your boyfriend isn't that unusual. Lots of guys have black holes so dense even light can't escape their gravitational pull. I have a friend whose motto is "If it didn't fit, it wasn't my hole."

The rectum is not a straight tube. The pubo-rectal sling pulls the rectum in an "S" curve. The more pronounced the "S" curve, the more pain you'll experience with larger objects. Your boyfriend probably has little "S" in his ass and that's why he can take everything from A to Z in it.

So how do you match your boyfriend's cavernous welcomes? Practice.

Here's how: Stick a joy toy past the anus into the rectum. Always aim for your belly button. After a few inches it'll most likely start to hurt. You've hit the curve. Pull it back a smidge, then move your aim up towards the head and slide it back in slowly.

Did I mention SLOWLY? Remember, a fraction of an inch feels like a foot in your ass.

Because of the rectum's "S" curve, it's important to use a flexible dildo. As you relax more, the pubo-rectal sling elongates, lessening the curve. Eventually, the rectum takes a left turn into the sigmoid colon. If you go that far pack a lunch, because you ain't coming back.

Hey, Woody!
I've always been the raging top and my boyfriend the insatiable bottom. But lately he's been bugging me to reverse our banging sessions. He wants to bury the bone for a change and I don't blame him. But here's the thing. I like my guys a little on the nelly side (I have this dominance thing, what can I say?). It's not like a purse drops out of my boyfriend's mouth when he talks but he's not exactly butch.

The thing is I don't want to be fucked by someone who isn't completely masculine. The idea of getting topped by a bottom shuts me down completely. How do I get over this? I know I'm not being fair to my boyfriend.

—Topped out

Dear Topped:

Be honest. Sit him down, hold his hand, look him in the eye and say, *"You're not butch enough to fuck me, dear."*

Next Question.

You're buying into all the ugly stereotypes of receptive anal sex. You're not alone; most people do, and the reason stretches back thousands of years.

As much as man-on-man sex was accepted in ancient Greece and Rome there were strict rules about anal sex. Namely, that boys, not men, received it. And when they did, it was something to be endured, not enjoyed. Getting fucked was a rite of passage. Once you became an adult, you were supposed to switch roles and become the penetrator. The Romans even had a word for it: *vir*, a man who would shtuup, but not be shtuupped.

It's hard to play the nail for years and suddenly become a hammer. Exclusively, anyway. Many boys, upon becoming men, wanted to keep getting nailed. And they were—to the cross, if society found out.

In ancient societies, nothing could be worse than acting like a woman. And nothing made you more like a woman than doing what women do in bed—receiving an erect penis between your legs. So while Greeks and Romans celebrated man-on-man sex (or more accurately, man-on-boy sex), they only celebrated it if you were a "top." There was only scorn and social ostracism for "bottoms."

We still live out these ancient and patently false ideas of sex. You can hear it in our snide asides *("Oh, there's nothing in this town but bottoms," "He's nothing but a big bottom").*

But hear me now, girlie-man, when was the last time you heard something derogatory about people who like to penetrate. Ever heard anybody say "He's nothing but a big top?"

So call me a freak, I don't believe that "bottoms" are sissies and that getting fucked by someone less masculine makes you less masculine.

I never advise people to perform sexual acts against their will (unless it's me they're dating), but at the same time, it strikes me as unfair that you're not willing to do for your boyfriend what he's doing for you. You've got two competing values here: Your right not to do anything you feel uncomfortable doing, and your obligation to keep your partner sexually satisfied.

You can do both. Here's how: Your current interpretation is that you're going to be topped by a bottom. A better one might be, "I have the opportunity to know the man I love in an entirely new way."

Ask yourself what needs to happen to make it acceptable. Like, tell your boyfriend you have a fantasy about a leather-clad cowboy dominating you. In other words, butch him up without hurting his feelings. Now, go, get fucked.

You big nelly bottom.

Hey, Woody!
I'm 100 percent gay but I've been having cyber sex with four straight guys. I use a female screen name, complete with nudie pictures I downloaded from a website.

I'm on it every other night and I've developed strong relationships with these guys. We've had great talks and even better sex. Whenever they want to meet I always remind them I have a boyfriend (I don't, but it's the only way to put them off).

I like to get cyber-fucked by these guys, but the thing is, Woody, I'm a total top. Never been fucked by a guy and don't really want to. But for some reason, acting like a girl and typing out stuff like "fuck my pussy" to straight guys sends me to the moon.

Do you think it's wrong to pretend I'm a girl to get straight guys to cyber-fuck me? It's not that I have trouble picking up guys. Hell, I'm 23, in great shape and scored an

8 in that awful website, amihotornot.com. Why do I have fantasies of being fucked by a straight guy but not by a gay guy? Am I hopeless?

—A fucked top

Dear Top:

Let me get this straight. You're a gay "top" who fantasizes about straight guys fucking his pussy? Christ, I gotta find another job.

Okay, here are two scenarios. Put them in your hole and see which one fits.

Scenario One: Your fantasy is to have sex with straight guys. Welcome to life. But the only way to have sex with straight guys is to ride the pussy express, baby. You can't have fantasies of topping a straight guy, not just because Falcon already made that movie, but because that scene is gay and your weenie wags for straight action.

Scenario Two: You want to get fucked by a gay guy and this is the only safe way of expressing it. You have what the shrinks in my panel like to call "Issues." Note the capital "I" in the word. I put it there especially for you.

You've got to figure out what those "Issues" are and work through them. Since I doubt you can afford my rates, you'll have to take it up with someone else.

You don't say what your hesitation is about getting fucked by a guy so I'm not going to go there. I have no recommendation but I do have a prediction: Once you start getting fucked by a guy, your straight cyber sex fantasies will slowly go away. Because once you get a taste of the real thing, you're going to take an ax to the computer.

Hey, Woody!
I met this guy at a circuit party where we were both whacked on meth. He told me he's a top, and instead of discussing the shallowness of labels I went home with him. His comment to me as we were heading back to his room

was "So, let's get you spread out." Hmmm ... well, things happened but not the main event. Need I say the goddess (Tina) was involved in all major decision-making at that time, bless her crinkly, plastic-encased white self.

Now this guy has called and he wants to finish the job Tina interrupted. I'm leery of getting into a situation SOBER that I was into when imbibing (i.e., getting plowed into the box springs). My recent inclinations are to run the show in bed, to get back in the saddle. The problem is this guy is a handsome, humpy 6'3" Latino who is fluent in English, except for the word "No." It must mean something very different in Spanish.

I really do want to hook up cuz I'm attracted to him, but I don't want to bottom. I'm afraid it might get ugly cuz he's expecting something I'm not sure I wanna provide. Do you think I should hook up with him and take my chances or just write him off?

—Sleepless in Atlanta

Dear Sleepless:
Here's the thing, snort-boy. You've got two problems. Well, three, if you count me.

First, you have this mistaken notion that a promise to put out one night is a guarantee for the next. Fuck that shit. *You* are the bouncer guarding the entry to your VIP room. You get to decide who gets in and when, not the Latin patron behind the velvet rope.

Tina has a wonderful disposition but she gives terrible advice. She's actually got you believing in the need to submit to something you don't want to do. You need to put Tina in her place (which, by the way, is in my dresser, two drawers down on the left). You don't have to do shit if you don't want to, I don't care what was done or said to Enrique Iglesias in the past.

It's true that Latinos hear "know" when you say "no," but remember you're in charge, not him. If you feel physically threatened by him and think there's a possibility of rape then don't go home with him. If that's not the case, I'd call him, tell him you want to hook up, and be, be . . . okay I know this is a foreign word in Gayland . . . HONEST with him.

Say something like "I really want to hook up with you but here's the thing: I'm big on respecting people's boundaries and I feel like you really haven't respected mine. If you're open to hooking up without pressuring me into doing something I don't want to do, then name the time and place and I'll be there."

As for Julio, Enrique, or whatever the hell his name is, I have a feeling he's going to be one lousy lay. Any guy who believes penetration is the only acceptable sexual act is a guy bound up in regimentation. And nothing kills a good roll in the hay than regimentation.

As for you, you need to replace your ON/OFF button with a dimmer switch. You shouldn't be saying, "I won't go home with this really hot guy because I don't want to get plowed." You should be saying, "This guy's really hot. I'll go home with him and I'll do whatever feels right to me. If it doesn't feel right to get plowed, we'll just do something else."

Hey, Woody!
I'm too ashamed to ask my doctor so you're it. I'm a famous bottom from way back and lately I've developed hemorrhoids that are getting pretty bad—there's blood in my stool when I go to the bathroom. My doctor is giving me some medication and "toilet tips" but I just couldn't get myself to ask him if (a) I should stop having protected anal sex, and (b) if the anal sex is what caused it. Should I, and did it?
—Wondering if I should ever throw my legs in the air again

Dear Wondering:
No and no. I'll forgive you the ignorance of thinking anal sex causes hemorrhoids because it's a common myth. What I can't forgive you for is that you've actually been having anal sex when you know the lining in your rectum has torn and you're actively bleeding.

Don't give me that "protected" shit either. You have to be as thick as concrete not to understand that condoms aren't 100 percent effective. Somebody needs to bitch-slap you across the bed and hog-tie your knees together.

As for the hemorrhoids, any rectal surgeon will tell you they're caused by straining too hard in the toilet and passing hard bowels that tear at the lining of the rectum and sphincter. Everyone has hemorrhoids, three to be exact. They only flare up when you strain to get cylindrical objects out of your rectum, not when you strain to put them in. You can tear the lining of the rectum with anal sex but you can't inflame hemorrhoids.

My advice:

1. Stop having anal sex until the blood clears up. You idiot.
2. Drink lots of water and take lots of fiber (in combination it softens the stool, so when they "pass" they're less likely to rip or inflame anything.
3. Lose the magazine rack in the bathroom. You should be on the toilet no more than five minutes. If it doesn't come out, get out. Reading on the bowl practically guarantees hemorrhoids in men.
4. Lose your doctor. It's especially important for common-sense impaired people like you to have a doctor they can say anything to without shame. Otherwise, the risk of self-inflicted stupidity is too high.

Hey, Woody!
Most times when my lover and I have sex, I end up getting shit on my dick. We usually have sex at bedtime and his body cycle is timed so he doesn't have to use the toilet until morning. We have tried using an enema a few times and that works, but then we lose all spontaneity having to kinda plan when we're going to have sex. So I ask you, what can we do?
—Getting the shitty end of the stick

Dear Getting:

When you drill in an oil field, you're gonna get oil in the damnd-est places. Short of an enema, there's not much you can do. Your boyfriend needs to have good bowel movements so he doesn't retain sludge in the rectum. The best way of doing that is to increase his fiber intake (it flushes the system).

Have him eat fruits, vegetables, cardboard, wood chips, maybe even take Metamucil at night. He'll have fabulous bowel movements the next morning—the kind you write home about.

Hey, Woody!

Most of my out life I've tried to pass myself off as "versa-tile" but I've "hit bottom" and accepted the fact that I love to be bottomed and *only* bottomed. Now I'm obsessed with it, and l literally can't get enough. My last overnight partner pulled out the biggest toy I've ever seen and wanted me to, um, swallow it without using my mouth. As I did it, my face turned white, numb, then ecstatic! I feel like I'm getting hooked on bigger and bigger things to the point that I'm afraid sex with regular-sized guys just isn't going to do it for me.

Am I ruining myself for real sex by playing "Hoover" to bed-post sized toys? And am I in danger, physically, by stuffing myself like a Thanksgiving turkey?

—Lookin' for one more inch

Dear Lookin':

I'm worried about the psychological and physical harm you may be doing to yourself. Physically there is a load-limit to your cargo-carrying capacity. Although your rectal muscles can be stretched, with each larger stretch you risk a tear.

When you convert a one-way street into a two-lane boulevard, small tears in the lining of the rectum can occur. And it sounds like you've turned your quiet neighborhood street into a six-lane super-highway.

If you get rectal tears ("fissures") they can become fistulas and then you've got a problem bigger than your toys. Without treatment, fistulas produce pus that literally burrows a hole from the inside of the rectum to the outside of the butt cheek, usually within an inch or two from the anus. Yeah, sounds like a party to me.

To avoid this you need to hear the three words every crack whore should repeat to his tricks: "Proceed with caution." Go slow, use lots of lube and avoid alcohol and drugs (they dull the senses—you'll go faster and rougher and increase the likelihood of a tear).

Psychologically, you seem to be focusing exclusively on how far and wide you can go with a toy, rather than how near and dear you can get to a man. You say in your letter you haven't had a long-term relationship though you've been out for over ten years. Do I need to connect the dots for you?

I think your obsession with stuffing your hole helps you stuff something else—your feelings. I say, be the hottest bottom you can be but not at the cost of connecting with guys in a meaningful way. Therapy might help you bridge the chasm between your heightened sexuality and lowered ability to enjoy men.

Remember, hot and healthy aren't mutually exclusive terms. You got the first part down, now work on the other.

Hey, Woody!
Every time I try to get fucked by a guy I have to stop because it hurts so much. I don't get it. How is a port that small supposed to fit cargo that big? What can I do to "limber up" so my middle name doesn't become "Bottomus Interruptus?"

—Trying to take it

Dear Trying:
Go fuck yourself.

I mean it. When it comes to learning how to receive, you are your best teacher. By "fucking yourself" I mean with your own fingers and store-bought toys. By controlling the movement, speed and size, you can find out the best way to minimize pain and maximize pleasure—without having your partner put you through a stress test.

The first lesson in "Woody's Way" is to get yourself comfortable and remember three things: Start small, start sober, start lubricated.

Start small by letting your fingers do the walking. And start sober because alcohol numbs sensations. The lining in and around your sphincter can be safely stretched, but it's easy to tear something if your buzz makes you do things you're not ready for.

Put a towel under you and forget about your normal masturbation sessions because you're going spelunking in the love cave. By all means, put some porno on—anything that will get you in the mood.

Insert one finger gently. Don't rush it. Remember, this is about sensuality and sexual satisfaction, not about how much you can stuff in there. Go deeper only when you're completely comfortable. It's not a race, so relax. Too much too quick is a good way of tearing the delicate linings. Use the same rules you use when you're in line at the grocery store: Don't shove.

When you're ready, try two fingers, all the while masturbating so you associate it with pleasure. This is no time to be cheap with the lube—slather it on in gobs and keep replenishing when you need it.

Next, graduate to a small dildo. For heaven's sakes, do not use anything but a dildo with a wide base so you can pull it out. Don't find yourself in a hospital emergency room trying to explain why you're walking so funny.

As you get more comfortable, go to a medium-sized dildo. Soon, you'll be ready for the real thing. By fucking yourself before you let others do it, you can control the pain and learn the pleasure. Everybody assumes that getting fucked is an art that comes naturally. It isn't. You get to sexual nirvana the same way you get to Carnegie Hall: Practice.

Hey, Woody!
I recently had my prostate removed (by a doctor, thank you, not by rough trade) and now I can't get it up. My doctor basically told me I have to live with it; that it's better to be soft and alive than hard and dead. Is there no hope for me?
—Hardly hoping

Dear Hardly:
The number one side effect of prostate cancer surgery is Willie's Attention Deficit Disorder. Close to 60 percent of men who have their prostates removed end up becoming impotent. About 10 percent also lose bladder control. Great. Now you can't get it up or keep it in.

There is some good news, but unfortunately, not for you. The University of Washington developed a new surgical technique that could keep as many as 50 percent of post-prostate surgery patients from becoming impotent. Unfortunately, the surgery must be performed at the time of prostate removal.

Why is impotence a high likelihood after removing the cancer? Because removing cancerous prostates rips out nerves near the bladder and the penis. The new nerve transplant surgery basically reconnects everything. The fascinating thing is how they do it: They remove a small nerve in the ankle and use tiny microscopes and an electric probe to sew the nerve between the bladder and penis areas. What a kick in the ass, huh? Or near the ass.

As for you my friend, there's not much that can be done. Your days of charming the cobra out of the basket are gone. There's nothing to do about it but grieve, heal and come to the realization that while sex makes life worth living, it's not the only thing that makes it worth living. You still have all the other ones.

Hey, Woody!
Speaking as a recent prostate cancer survivor, your advice to the guy suffering from impotence after having his prostate removed ("sorry, there's nothing you can do to

get hard") was dead wrong. I couldn't get it up after the surgery either, but thanks to the wonders of medical science I can plow any willing ass. There are at least four options to choose from: Viagra, vacuum pumps, a urethra suppository, and injections. Since your answer seemed to suggest a real need for knowledge in this area, you should know that it's even possible to cum! I hope you'll be man enough to admit your mistake publicly and offer more hope to people who need it.

—Half-assed but fully-bonered

Dear Half-assed:
You are quite correct that there are options for guys to grab their goobers and growl after prostate removal. But your Pollyanna, "isn't-life-grand-you-can-fuck-with-the-best-of-them" advice is as fat as my "there's-nothing-you-can-do" advice was skinny.

There are stiff penalties (pun intended) to the options you've described. First, some facts. According to the *Journal of the American Medical Association*, almost 60% of men who've had their prostates removed end up impotent. And about 10% end up incontinent. The cause? Surgery rips out nerves connected to the base of the penis and bladder.

The treatment options for post-surgery impotence are as likely to get you nauseous as they are to get you hard. Case in point: Alprostadil is the current drug darling of the I-can't-get-lift-off crowd. It opens blood vessels to the penis. Sounds great, right? Except you have to inject it into your penis. Now *that's* what I call foreplay. Imagine the sexy pillow talk: "Honey, can you hold onto my penis while I stick this hypodermic needle into it?" It doesn't quite have the ring of "yeah, baby, suck that cock," does it?

Or maybe it's just me.

The other option for Alprostadil is to inject it through an amusing little device called the Muse System. Basically, you insert a plastic tube into your penis through the urethra, press a button releasing a pellet containing the drug. Studies show

Alprostadil can work for up to 67 percent of people taking it (though the latest study showed only 27 percent benefited).

When it works, you've got Willie saluting for about 45 minutes. Then he turns into Wilma. Twelve percent of users reported a burning sensation in the urethra for up to 15 minutes and 29 percent reported pain in the penis. Gee, I wonder why. Shoving a plastic tube up my dick doesn't sound like it would hurt.

The good news is that Alprostadil is being developed as a topical cream, but it's too early to tell how effective it will be.

The vacuum pump may be the best option. You place the prize inside a plastic cylinder and create a vacuum, which causes blood flow to the penis. Then you put a band around the penis to trap the blood and you're ready for action.

For God's sakes, if you're going to try the pump don't order it from those horrible mail-order people that sell rainbow stickers, porn, and tight shorts (the holy trinity in gay life). You're liable to free willie in the most unexpected way. Look for medical brand names like Erecaid, Catalyst, or VED.

The least invasive option—Viagra—is also the least effective. Only 20 percent of men who had post-surgical nerve damage reported increased erections after taking it.

The effectiveness of all these options is determined by how much nerve damage resulted from the surgery. The more damage, the less effective these options are.

My original advice was accurate, but only in the technical sense. If you're impotent from a prostate removal, you're never going to experience erections like you once did. Still, I was wrong for not mentioning the options, despite the seemingly insurmountable psychological obstacles.

Hey, Woody!
You scared the bejeesus out of me when you said the most common after-effect of getting your prostate removed is impotence. It got me to thinking—is there anything I can do to avoid prostate cancer?

One of my friends said, "Get fucked as much as possible. The more you use it, the less cancer you get." For some reason, it doesn't sound factual, although it may be. Please help. I'm 28 and I have sex maybe once every two months, which isn't a lot, so maybe he's right. I don't want to end up impotent. Is there anything I can do?

—Worried about Willie

Dear Worried:

Yes there is something you can do: Get rid of your ignorant friend. Everybody knows fucking doesn't prevent cancer. It prevents heart attacks.

I wish. Actually, the only thing fucking prevents is boredom. Too bad it doesn't prevent your friend from saying asinine things. My trusted medical advisors tell me there is nothing you can do to prevent prostate cancer. The consensus is that it seems to be genetic. Some men are predisposed to it, just like some women are predisposed to breast cancer.

Prostate cancer is second only to lung cancer as the leading cause of death among American men. Forty thousand men die every year from it. The good news is that screening tests can detect it early, before it becomes life threatening. So keep getting physicals every couple of years and get yer arse checked out.

At 28, you don't have much to worry about. Almost 80 percent of men diagnosed with prostate cancer are over 65. Oddly, the risk of prostate cancer is higher for African-American men. Is it because blacks get fucked all the time? Ask your friend. He's the expert.

Actually, there really is a medical condition fucking might help prevent—prostatitis (inflammation of the prostate). The treatment for prostatitis is antibiotics and . . . are you ready for this? . . . Regular massage of the prostate!

Shhh! Listen—do you hear it? It's the unmistakable sound of a coast-to-coast "SCHWING!"

It's true. If you're diagnosed with prostatitis, doctors recommend you come in at least once a week to get your prostate massaged by Doctor Digit who'll lube his finger up and dig for gold.

"You should see the look on straight men when I tell them what we have to do," said one of my medical advisors. "They act like their house burned to the ground."

On the other hand, some men are a little too happy to jump up on the examination table, according to Herr Doctor. Once, a patient came in, handed him a dildo and announced, "If you're going to massage my prostate, do it right."

Doc politely refused, not wanting to violate the sanctity of the doctor/patient relationship. Well, not in his office, anyway. I don't know what the big deal is. Doctors always ask their patients to "Open wide and say 'aahhhh'" before they stick wood in. If it's okay to put wood in your mouth, why not your ass?

Hey, Woody!
I have this love-hate thing with anal sex. It turns me on but at the same time it grosses me out. I'm not sure what to call myself. I've never been bottomed so I'm not a bottom, but I rarely top guys, even though I want to, because I get squeamish. The *idea* of being inside a guy turns me on, but when I start putting my large, prized possession into that rabbit hole of fecal sludge, it makes me droop like a week-old party balloon. I've completed the act before (and liked it) but I don't try very often. One whiff of what I'm pumping and my gonads start shrieking "I'm melttiiinng." And I don't even want to go into what the rubber looks like after I'm done. How can I get over this and give my sex partners what they want, and me what I need.

—Topless in America

Dear Topless:
You bring up a taboo subject in the gay world—the fact that there are some ugly realities to beautiful sex. Nobody ever talks about the messiness inherent with anal sex. And that's a shame because *"Where in the world am I putting my Thing?"* is a more common reaction than you think.

In some ways porn contributes to the jolt many of us receive when we play "hide the salami." There's a reason why Jeff Stryker's movies don't come with Scratch-N-Sniff cards. You'll never see Jeff pull out of a pounding with a gooberish wad of brown mucus sludged all over his tool like a glaze in a walnut apple cake. So if you watch a lot of porn—and who doesn't?— you get an artificial insemination of just what anal sex is all about. Namely that it's clean, wholesome fun the whole family can play.

The first thing you need to do is quit putting pressure on yourself. What you're feeling is completely normal. Nobody ever pinched a loaf in the toilet and waxed romantically about the full-bodied bouquet. It's natural that you'd have some misgivings.

Second, it's important you have several good penetration experiences in a row to give you the momentum to crack the inner top trapped inside you. Here's how: The next time you're in bed with a guy who wants you to ride him like a lawn mower, tell him you will—the next time you meet. Be honest. Tell him that you're a clean freak and need to make sure he's clean all the way to his ears. If he's an experienced lawn mower he'll understand it's douche time and he'll do some spring cleaning (like Stryker's buddies).

When you get together again it'll be time to cut some grass. When the moment of truth arrives, the important thing is to get him to guide you. Place his hand on your cock to signal that you want him to pilot even though it's your plane. Right now, you're too squeamish to be doing anything down there with fingers and homing devices—it'll just make you concentrate on the wrong things. Instead, let him be in total control and just submerge yourself in the feeling. By doing this several times (well, maybe not on the same night!) you'll begin to desensitize yourself to that part of penetration that turns you off so that you can concentrate on the part that turns you on.

Hey, Woody!
I know this is a stupid question, but what do two bottoms do when they hook up?

—**Just curious**

Dear Curious:

Hair and make-up.

What kind of bullshit question is that? What, you think sex is so one-dimensional, so inflexible, so unimaginative it can only be performed when one partner is exclusively the penetrator? Christ, what a bore you must be in bed.

Hey, Woody!

I'm the top in our relationship, but my partner's constantly complaining that I don't take charge of our sex life like I should. Huh? Who's pluggin' who? I'm doing all the work in bed—he's just layin' there taking it. He's getting more distant and we're having less and less sex. Do you think if I let him top me that we could jump-start our sex life again?

—Topsy turvy

Dear Topsy:

You're asking the wrong question. You're asking who should be the top or bottom when you should be asking who's the giver and who's the taker. Besides, spreading your legs to make somebody happy isn't a good way to solve sexual dissatisfaction. Well, unless I'm involved.

Sexual roles aren't just about who gets to doodle the noodle. They're also about who makes the decisions. Who's responsible for the sex you're having? Who initiates? Who comes up with new positions? Who is constantly accommodating? Who gets to lay there in a post-ejaculatory catatonic state while the other hauls out the mop and the pine-sol?

Just because you're a top doesn't make you a giver. In fact, you sound like a "taker" to me, forcing your boyfriend into the role of "giver" he doesn't like. Takers tend to think they don't have to be creative, assertive, or expressive in bed—that this is their partner's job. They reap the benefits of all the attention without contributing anything but their presence. How noble.

Givers start resenting that they have to do all the work in

bed—initiating, creating the ambience, caressing without being caressed back, coming up with new positions, and so on. It just may be that your boyfriend feels resentful and burdened by all your taking. Don't think that penetrating him is your only responsibility. Sexual balance means being a giver one day, a taker the next. Talk to him about it, and play "giver" for the next couple of weeks to see if things don't straighten out.

Hey, Woody!
It's been almost two years I've been shtuuping my partner. I play the role as the top, but I do like being a bottom every now and then. But my lover doesn't like topping me. He's such a bottom, he can't even think about it. We're fighting about this. How do we straighten it out?
—Tryin' to be versatile

Dear Tryin':
Your partner owes you a good fuck—it's a central tenet of good relationships. The trick is to get him to realize it without exploding some clearly sensitive issues he has about entering you. And without making him feel defensive or guilty.

Many men see themselves as receptacles, not deliverables (and vice versa). Their identification has powerful psychological roots—it's not just a matter of physically changing positions. You might make him more comfortable if you tell him how much you like to fuck him and that you want to get better at it. Sometimes being a better "giver" means understanding what it's like to be a "receiver."

Don't pressure him to be inside you right away. Get a toy (and uh, don't go to Toys-R-Us—they don't stock the recommended brand). Get him on top of you and have him insert his faux self in you. Play-act the whole thing. That way you can get a reasonable facsimile of what you want, and he can experience being a giver without performance anxiety. From there, hopefully you can move into the real thing.

Hey, Woody!
Somebody was talking about the "taint"—that licking and
massaging it is a real turn-on. I want to try it, the problem
is, I don't know what or where "taint" is and I'm too em-
barrassed to ask.

                                            —Tainted by ignorance

Dear Tainted:
It's the small strip of tissue called the perineum. Its "street" name
is "taint" because 'tain't your balls and 'tain't your ass. There is a
high concentration of nerve endings there just begging to be
touched, kissed, or licked.

Hey, Woody!
What is it with gay men when it comes to being a top or
bottom? I mean, why do we still look down on bottoms?
Without bottoms there wouldn't be any tops. Am I right or
am I right? So many bottoms out there are still saying
"Oh, I'm a top," when in reality, they're not. Like they're
ashamed of admitting their bottom tendencies. I say to
them, "enjoy being a bottom, it's like having two penises
to play with." And what could be better than that? And to
all those tops I say, "good for you." Because I'm sure it is.
But, guess what? The bottoms are having more fun.

                                        —Ceiling-pattern expert

Dear Ceily:
I'm with you except for the part that bottoms have more fun.
People who love what they do are the ones having more fun.
Top, middle, bottom, sideways, it doesn't matter.

    First of all, I think the whole idea of reducing your sexuality
to a binary classification system reeks like a clean-up towel you
forgot to put in the hamper. It perpetuates the notion of a sexual
hierarchy, when there is no such thing. Here's why most bottoms
are closet bottoms: Society says (and we as gay men completely

accept) that "masculine" is better than "feminine." To the masculine goes the power, the riches, the influence, the admiration. To be masculine is to dominate, to be superior, to be "on top."

To be on the bottom is to "admit" (that's society's belief, not mine) that you're not masculine, therefore not due all that comes to the masculine. Who wants to be known as the recessive gene in a pool where the dominant ones get all the goodies?

You'd think a subculture that gets hammered with strict and narrow definitions of what's allowably masculine would rebel against it. But we don't. We've got the keys to the gender jail, but we happily stay behind the bars, playing wardens to ourselves.

To say that a top is more masculine than a bottom is bullshit. First, the preference for a sexual position says NOTHING about you as a person. Just like your sexual orientation says nothing about your character, your preference for being a bottom says nothing about your masculinity. I once plowed a boxer who could kick my ass into the middle of next week. Trust me, there wasn't a nelly bone in his body.

The other reason I don't like the "top," "bottom," or even "versatile" descriptions is that they're labels. And while labels can sometimes be a relief (and act as linguistic short-hand), they almost always morph into psychic prisons preventing you from experiencing all that there is to experience. There is no shame in being gay; there is no shame in liking to receive. The only thing shameful is how willing we are to buy into such bogus identities.

Hey, Woody!
Don't laugh, but my boyfriend fucks me when he's asleep. I know he's not pretending because he snores while he's fucking me! It doesn't do a whole lot for my self-esteem. In fact, it's really getting annoying, and creepy to boot. What can I do?

—Nocturnal omission

Dear Nocturnal:

I'm not laughing. "Sleepsex," or sex activity that occurs during sleep, is a recognized phenomenon in sleep research.

Most sleep researchers don't believe it's classifiable as a distinct sleep disorder like sleep apnea (a temporary stoppage of breathing), and think it's a variant of sleepwalking. Also, they're leery about classifying the disorder separately because of the potential for abuse ("But, judge, I was asleep when I shoved my throbbing penis into my 14 year-old daughter . . .")

Like you, most partners of sleepsexers find the episodes disturbing. People have broken up about it. But that's only because they haven't written to Woody. I say throw caution—and your legs—to the wind. Use the disorder to improve your sex life.

There's a great example of that possibility in a report published in the *Archives of Sexual Behavior.* A sleepsex sufferer was a lot more aggressive and dominant with his girlfriend during sleep, biting her and talkin' trash. Though she was disturbed about the whole thing she found that she liked his late-night persona better, so they incorporated it into their daytime sex. You go, girl.

What causes "sleepsex"? Many scientists believe it's caused by reading this column late at night. But I pay them a commission for saying it, so I'm not sure how well the theory will stand up to scientific scrutiny.

Sleepsex occurs mostly in men. One theory flashing its girdle around scientific circles is the classic Freudian repression vibe about doing in dreams what you're too afraid to do in life. But some researchers think that theory should be a little more modest on account of there's so much flab around it. They point out that sleepsex doesn't always occur when a person's dreaming. There's just not enough research to make any theory hard enough to penetrate the scientific community.

Chapter 7

The Utter Cream: How to Milk Your Man

Ever been told you suck in bed? By straight men, yes. But I'm talking about your partners. I have. By someone I really cared about, too. Boy, did it hurt. Took months to recover. In fact, he's still walking funny.

The truth is, most of us aren't very good in the sack because:

    a. We're male, a species that does not particularly concern itself with the needs of others.
    b. We're gay, so every session is a three way—you, your partner and your ego.
    c. Nobody taught us how to do it right. Society says we're not supposed to be doing it at all, let alone doing it well.

The best way to get better at sex is to do whatever the guy was doing to you that made you moan like a whore.

Copycat sex is the shortcut to greatness. That's why there isn't much about technique in this book. Besides, learning how to ride a man from a book is like learning how to ride a bike from a manual. You'll never really get it till you mount it.

The expression of desire needs no introduction to tactics. Expressing yourself freely, losing yourself in his smell, finding yourself in his touch, these are the things that make memorable sex. Sex isn't about technique; it's about how you express your desire.

And speaking of expressing, that's exactly what most of the

letters in this section are about: Expressing the very milk of human kindness.

"Why do I drip when I want to shoot?" "What's this stuff made of?" "Is it nutritious?" "Should I swallow?" "Should I spit?" "Should I pasteurize?" The questions about man-milk are endless. As they should be. No point to the cone if you can't get to the cream.

It does make you wonder, though. All that drama for three lousy tablespoons of joy juice.

* * *

Hey, Woody!
I have great orgasms but nothing comes out. My partners think I'm "faking" my orgasms, but I swear I'm feeling as much if not more than what they're feeling. I know there's something wrong but I can't figure it out.
                    —Tired, with not much to show for it

Dear Tired:
If all the sensations are normal but there's no fluid, you probably have something called retrograde ejaculation. It's a damaged bladder neck that causes semen to be expelled backward into the bladder. Basically, you're shooting a pistol with the barrel curved towards you, robbing you of the pleasure of seeing your fine work splat all over a humpy chest.

Anejaculation is another possibility. It's caused by blocked ejaculatory ducts. Or maybe you were born without seminal vesicles, which make most of the ejaculatory fluid. Whatever it is, you need to see a doctor.

Unfortunately there's no cure but the good news is that in most cases you can continue to have sex. Look at it this way: Your partners will never have to choose between spitting or swallowing.

Hey, Woody!
Is the color or consistency of cum a sign of health? I notice sometimes my cum is whiter than at other times, and

sometimes it's thick and sometimes thin. What do the changes mean?

—**Cumin' 'n goin'**

Dear Cumin':
Semen is composed of secretions from a lot of different sources. Only two percent of semen is actually made up of sperm. The rest is alcohol. Well, at least in my friends. Incidentally, that two percent factor is why our straight brethren don't notice any difference in semen volume after they get their wings clipped (vasectomies).

Research shows that consistency or viscosity of semen varies significantly but has little clinical significance. The majority of semen comes from two glands, the prostate and seminal vesicles. The seminal vesicle fluid contains sugar fructose and proteins that cause your cum to coagulate. The prostate vesicles put out (and oh, do they put out—like my boyfriend after a couple of martinis) enzymes that break down the coagulation. So basically, your cum gets it coming and going—it coagulates as soon you launch it, then immediately goes into "liquefaction." God, if only my tricks would do the same.

Hey, Woody!
To my eternal regret, my roommate discovered the gym. Now that he's down to a 34 inch waist his eyes narrow every time I go near the fridge or crack open a beer. Is there anything worse than somebody who's gotten religion at the gym? Now he's on me about working out, promising my sex life would be better. He swears he gets harder and stays up longer now that he's "in fucking shape." Is he making this shit up to get me to the gym, or can you really improve your sex life by getting in shape? I have this sneaky suspicion the flat-bellies say this just to justify all the vanity checks they cash at the gym.

—**Say it isn't so**

Dear Say:

Well, I'd love to be able to tell you to go ahead and eat that second helping of pie, but I'd be lying. Most studies show being overweight drastically increases your chances of developing some form of Erectile Dysfunction.

The Harvard School of Public Health presented a study to the American Urological Society showing men with a waistline measuring 42 inches or more were almost twice as likely to be impotent than men with a 32 inch waist.

Inactive men (bedsores like you) who didn't exercise at least 30 minutes a day were also much more likely to suffer sexual problems. The study brings up two important questions: 1) Does whacking off for half an hour count as exercise? and 2) Did they use penis-shaped pointers in the presentation? My medical advisors assured me the answer was no on both counts.

So, sorry guy. If you've retrofitted your front door with a garage opener, it's probably time to hit the gym, the street, your friend, *something*. Losing weight really will improve your sex life. Why? Because being overweight or inactive isn't good for blood circulation and that ain't good for erections.

Look at it this way: Because of your weight, your sex life is probably limited to men who got trapped in your gravitational pull, right? By slimming down you can expand the number of people willing to throw out their welcome mats.

Hey, Woody!
I notice that some guys I go home with have no "pre-cum" and others run like a drippy faucet. What's the deal with that?

—Running with the runny

Dear Running:

Sex researchers say 30% of men do not produce pre-ejaculatory fluid. 25% have one drop, 10% two drops, and 35% need to give their partners scuba-diving gear.

In about a quarter of men, pre-cum has enough sperm to impregnate a woman. Which of course, is useless information to us.

Hey, Woody!
I was accused by a trick of being lousy in bed. Now, every time I see him in the clubs I'm embarrassed as hell cuz he's been telling people behind my back. The thing is, I AM lousy in bed. I guess my only excuse is I just came out. Is there some G-spot in men I don't know about? Where is it and how do I work it so I don't get the reputation I'm getting?

—A newbie

Dear Newbie:
Whenever I end up in bed with lousy lays like you I think, "Either he's dead or my watch stopped."

Unfortunately it's easier to put life into a dead watch than into some of the corpses I've taken home. But there is good news: The first step in improving your sex life is admitting you suck at it.

The G-spot was named after Berlin gynecologist Ernst Grafenberg, who "discovered" in 1950 that women had a spot on the inside of the front wall of the vagina, which when firmly stimulated produced an intense desire for Beluga caviar.

No, wait, that's not right. Actually, when stimulated it produced . . . oh, who gives a shit? If you want to know more about vaginas go someplace else.

Do men have G-spots? Some experts believe the prostate gland is analogous to a woman's G-spot. Do I? I don't know, but I love the first four letters in the word analogous.

There are three hot spots in most men. First is the frenulum, the sensitive area just on the underside of the penis, where the folds of your glans (the head) come together. The second spot is the perineum, or if you live in the South, the "Tain't." Cuz it tain't your dick and it tain't your ass. It's the area of skin between the testicles and the anus. Last and certainly not least is the prostate, an internal gland behind and under the bladder. The gland produces fluid for the semen. Stick a well-lubricated finger up there, move it around and eventually you'll feel this spongy object. It can be manipulated to produce intense feelings. You know, like a man's ego.

As for getting better at sex, there really isn't any mystery to it: Pay more attention to your partner than you do to yourself.

If you're gay you probably didn't understand a word I just said. In a lot of gay circles every encounter with a guy is a three-way: You, your partner, and your ego. The best way to practice my advice is to PRETEND there's another human being in your bed that might have needs that aren't yours, and try to meet them.

I'm losing you, aren't I?

Seriously, it's not technique that distinguishes great sex; it's desire and energy. That means paying attention to what's going on in you and around you, and getting involved mentally and physically in the expression of that energy. Techniques without that fundamental sense of desire, exploration, and expression don't mean shit.

Hey, Woody!
My boyfriend won't swallow my cum because he thinks it tastes terrible. Would changing my diet improve the taste? Also, I've heard there's something you can do to make cum taste like chocolate. If that's true, what do I need to eat?
—Trying to feed his sweet tooth

Dear Trying:
There really is a way of making your semen taste like chocolate—spray Hershey's chocolate syrup in your lover's mouth right before you cum in it.

What kind of crap are you reading, man? Chocolate-tasting cum? Fuck Mars, NASA oughta send the Polar Lander to whatever planet you're living on. There's no telling what it would beam back.

You can't change the taste of your semen by what you eat. Not on this planet, anyway. At least that's the consensus from people with medical degrees. People without medical degrees, however, believe otherwise. Truth is, the only way you'll know is to try it out. I seriously doubt it would work. Semen is produced in the reproductive tract, not in the digestive tract.

The prevailing thought—by the cum-obsessed, not doctors— is that dairy products, which contain a high bacterial putrefaction level, create the foulest taste. Though to my mind, there's no such thing as foul tasting cum. Asparagus is the whipping boy of the Cum Purification Committee. Eat it, they say, at the risk of driving your partner away.

So what to eat? Fruit and alcohol are supposed to give bodily fluids a pleasant, sweet flavor. But processed liquors are supposed to be a no-no. So if you're going to drink (and who isn't, if you're hoping to get some), drink naturally fermented beers like Rolling Rock or Kirin. Talk about branding. "Tastes Great, Less Filling" could take on a whole new meaning.

But all this is supposition. A friend once told me he could tell if his boyfriend had eaten a Whopper with onions at Burger King by the taste of his semen. Personally, I think along with his boyfriend's cum, he swallowed a load of bull. Still, there's no harm in adding or eliminating different food groups to see if there's an effect.

Hey, Woody!
I can get it up no problem, but I can't orgasm. No matter what I do or whom I'm with, there's just no climax to my story. I've talked to my doctor about it, and he thinks there's nothing physically wrong with me because I get wet dreams all the time. I don't want to go to therapy for something so embarrassing. Is there anything I can do or take to prime the pump?

—Backed up

Dear Backed up:

Yes, me. But I don't come in pill form.

Sounds like you have "anejaculation," the inability to climax and ejaculate during sex. Some men with this condition can ejaculate with masturbation, but most can't under any circumstances while they're awake.

Nocturnal emissions (wet dreams) are common, though. Your best bet is to see an urologist for a detailed history and physical examination. Anejaculation can be a symptom of endocrine and neurological disorders, so your doc will probably give you a nerve stimulation test.

If Dr. Dick says it's psychological—and there's a good chance he will—don't worry. The odds of getting more bang out of your pistol are very good with behavior modification therapy.

Assuming there's nothing physically wrong with you, your inability to off-load may be an issue of letting go. Some guys have control issues, distrust sex, their partners, or men in general.

And who could blame them on the last point?

Hey, Woody!

I've been told I'm a great kisser but I couldn't tell you why—I just do whatever comes naturally. I mean, I don't say to myself things like "okay, dart your tongue in three times, back off and finish with a lick over his teeth."

Still, I'm wondering, if I wanted to get even better, what would I do? Since I don't know what I'm doing right in the first place, how do I know what I should do to improve?

—The kissing bandit

Dear Bandit:

You're a good kisser because you love to kiss and you're into the guy you're kissing and you live for the effect it has on him.

I doubt you need much technical advice but here are a few tips if you want to add a little hooch to the smooch:

1. Be rhythmical. Move smoothly from passive to active, from slow to fast to back and forth, from dry to wet, to gentle and wild.
2. Breathe through your nose. It prolongs the kiss.
3. Close your eyes. They'll look like two giant beach balls to the guy you're kissing if you don't. And who wants to kiss big balls? Wait. Bad example. Just keep your eyes closed and quit confusing me, dammit.
4. Make sounds. Small, almost imperceptible sounds. A tiny rumble here, a soft moan there. Communicate what you like and what you're feeling through noises, not words.
5. Kiss your partner's eyes. The heat of your lips on his eyelids will drive him crazy. Just make sure his eyes are closed. There's nothing worse than getting your corneas licked.
6. Let your desire show. Look at your partner with a deep, rapacious, insatiable hunger. The way Republicans do when they see the Alaskan wilderness.

If you want more tips, send your online pictures. I do house calls, you know. Or read William Cane's excellent book, *The Art of Kissing*.

Hey, Woody!
I'm a great fan of porn, but mostly the written form. I've noticed in these stories that buttfucking ALWAYS ends with the bottom having a MASSIVE handless orgasm! Well, I've never seen that happen in any movies I've seen! My question then, is: is this really possible or are these writers blowing smoke? If it IS possible to "hit that perfect beat" JUST from riding the spike, is it something that can be learned? Where do I sign up for lessons? This would be SUCH a handy skill to have!
—Willing to learn, no matter how much practice is needed!

Dear Willing:

Wow! You write with so many exclamation marks! If you put half the energy of this letter into your bed you must be one good lay! Either that or one big headache, which is what I got from reading through your letter. Calm down, Trampolina. Try ending your sentences like women end their months—with a period.

Yes, it's possible to cum without touching yourself. Guys who can do this are intensely focused on their peri-rectal area, particularly on the prostate as it gets massaged by that vicious, insensitive boyfriend who just barges in without foreplay and expects you to spread like peanut butter at a moment's notice, and if you had any sense you'd send him packing but hell, while he's there, why waste a perfectly good erection?

You can learn how to cum without touching yourself but why would you want to? It would feel dreadful. At the moment of ejaculation we men don't want a light and airy finale. We want a show-stopping, door-busting, barn-burning finish. Haven't you ever noticed when you masturbate that the closer you get to cumming the harder you jack off?

If you really want to cum without touching yourself, train by concentrating really hard on your peri-rectal area. And get plowed like a snowy Minnesota freeway. Believe me, it'll help.

Hey, Woody!
I was on vacation with my boyfriend, staying with some friends with exquisite taste. When they were gone, we did the unthinkable and had sex on their prized Mies van der Rohe sofa. Well, we got carried away and next thing you know there was blood on the couch. I don't know which was worse—the blood on a work of art, or the fact that it was MY blood and it came out of my dick when I came. We lost our friends. Am I going to lose my dick?
—Bloody fool

Dear Bloody:

You had sex on their van der Rohe? If they murdered you, there wouldn't be a jury in the world that would convict them. Talk about justifiable homicide.

I'd say you should worry more about the thoughts getting into your head than the blood coming out of your dick. Bloody ejaculate (hematospermia) is not that uncommon and if it just happened once, it's probably the result of a burst blood vessel. If it does happen more than once you could be looking at an infection, maybe even a tumor, so get yourself to a urologist.

And, uhm, when you're waiting in the lobby? Don't use the chairs for anything but sitting.

Hey, Woody!
What do you think of "non-goal-oriented" sex? Is this a legitimate way of having sex, or is it just sour grapes from people who have a problem ejaculating and want to hide it by proclaiming that "full-body orgasms" are superior to ordinary cumming? Sounds like nonsense to me.
—I'll take mine with cream

Dear Creamy:

Sex without coming can sometimes feel like you've thrown a party and the guest of honor didn't show. You can take the negative view that the party's a bust, or you can take the positive view that there's less liquor you have to share.

The truth is, when all you can think about is the destination, the journey can suffer. The best thing about not cumming during sex is that it forces you to pay attention to other pleasurable feelings ignored in the rush to detonate.

Choosing not to cum can make you a better lover. Not only will you pay more attention to the subtler sides of your sensuality, it makes you more attentive to what's-his-name laying beside you. I don't think it's an either/or, is-one-better-than-the-other question. It's like asking which is tastier—strawberries or blueberries? Like gay men, it's all fruit—it just depends on your mood.

Your point is well-taken, though. Sometimes the "non-goal oriented" advocates are just covering up their problems with ejaculation. Urologists say nearly a third of their visits are from men having ejaculatory problems. Problems range from premature ejaculation to "retarded" ejaculation (making an exceedingly stupid face when you cum). No, that's not right. Oh, just read on.

About 30 percent of all men are premature ejaculators. About 8 percent have "retarded" ejaculation problems ("it takes me an hour to cum"). It's often an undiagnosed medical or psychological condition. Or it could simply be the side effects of certain medications (some drugs affect the orgasm reflex). If that's the case, your doctor could prescribe an antihistamine like Sudafed to counteract it. Whatever the reason, I say sex is good whether you cum or not.

Hey, Woody!
I agreed to donate my sperm to a lesbian friend, but no matter how many times the sperm lapped the egg, nothing took. Finally, her gynecologist ran some tests and pronounced my sperm "impaired." My friend couldn't get pregnant and I couldn't get an explanation. Not that I'm going to be using my sperm for anything but irrigating manly chests, but what the hell is "impaired" sperm?

—Shooting blanks

Dear Shooting:
"Impaired" is the medical euphemism for deformed. About 40 percent of all male sperm comes out deformed. As long as the other 60 percent aren't, the egg has a good chance of getting parboiled.

"Normal" sperm have oval heads and long tails. Heads that are round, pinpointed or crooked are signs of impaired sperm.

It's important that sperm move quickly and straight forward otherwise they can't get past the cervical mucous and penetrate the hard outer shell of the egg. Moving slowly and side-to-side is a sure sign of damage. Especially in a bar. You'll never get laid walking that way.

The most likely cause of impaired sperm are varicocele veins. They're similar to the varicose veins that many women get in back of their legs. When one of the testicular veins becomes inflamed, the valves get worn out, forcing the blood to run in the wrong direction—toward the testicles instead of away. Blood overheats the testicles, damaging the production of sperm. Overly warm temperatures destroy sperm. That's why the "manufacturing plant," the testes, are located outside of the body where it's two degrees cooler.

"Tying off" the varicocele veins is an easy outpatient procedure. If you want to get another girlfriend pregnant, I'd consider it (but first, get a diagnosis from an infertility specialist). About 70 percent of post-surgery patients show improved sperm count and quality, and 40 percent go on to become fathers.

Hey, Woody!
Are there any secrets to giving great head? I'm 21 and most of the guys I date are the same age, so none of us have that much experience. Got any tips?
—Sitting at the foot of the master

Dear Sitting:
It's not my feet I want you to sit on, but it's a start. If you want call-backs from your sexual prey, the first thing you need to know about giving good head is never stay with one technique or rhythm for more than about a minute (unless you want him to cum).

Here's one example of how to do it: Put him on his back, with you on all fours perpendicular to him, like this: →I. If you're the arrow in this configuration, it gives you access to his crotch and his torso, which you'll need. Wet your lips and produce as much saliva as you can. You want a lot of steak sauce on the sirloin. Remember, too much is never enough. Fill your mouth with the head of his cock and slowly, but ever so s-l-o-w-l-y, start moving up and down. At first a few millimeters then a couple more, then all the way. Get a good rhythm going then slowly disengage your mouth from his cock (be sure it's plenty wet) and give him a long French kiss.

Suck his tongue like you sucked his cock. Linger a minute in his mouth, then go back to his cock. Linger on his cock a few moments then go back to his mouth. Back and forth your mouth goes, between his mouth and his cock. Mouth-cock-mouth-cock-mouth-cock.

When you establish the rhythm, make a pit stop at his left nipple. Now take your wet mouth from his cock to his nipple to his mouth to his nipple to his cock. And just when you establish that rhythm, add his right nipple to the mix. I call it "full-bodied head." He'll call it heaven.

Hey, Woody!
Most times guys just dive for my crotch like they were bobbing for apples. I mean, it's like 30 seconds of kissing and, wham, next thing I know my underwear's around my ankles. I don't want to sound like I'm complaining cuz I want the prize as much as the next guy, but a slow hand (and mouth) goes a long way with me. How do I tell other guys not to exceed the speed limit in my neighborhood?
—Rarin' to go, but need some cranking up first

Dear Rarin':
The first rule in "Woody's Way" is never say what you can show. Especially if your sexual prey is new. The bedroom is no place for conversation between strangers. You can get your point across much more powerfully by demonstrating what you need than by languaging it.

Instead of saying "Whoa, how about a warm-up lap before the race?" tell him you want to enjoy his body by giving him a massage. It's a great way to form an intimate connection and more importantly, to lay hands upon ALL his wonderment, not just what you're wondering about.

The trick to a good massage is where you start and how you end. Never start at the genitals. Start at the head or feet. DO NOT give the kind of relaxing deep-muscle massage you'd get at a spa. You don't want him relaxed, you want him stimulated. Focus on his skin, not his muscles. You want your hands to feel like feathers. Forget massage oils or lotions. You can stimulate the skin's nerves better with dry skin. Mix it up with dry and wet kisses, blowing on his skin, and so on.

You're an explorer, mapping out the contours of his body, but only for about 15 minutes, because, like, he's there for a reason and it ain't for a rub-down. Like every explorer, there comes a time to plant the flag. The main thing is to enjoy his body. In real estate terms, if he's ocean-front property why not enjoy the view? If you go straight to his dick it's hard to do, because hey, once you go there it's hard to go anywhere else.

I'm all for grab-it-and-growl quickies but they're snacks, man, they're no kind of meal. If you want real sexual satisfaction, you'll start working it long before your underwear hits the floor. Basically, it comes down to this: If you wanna light a fire, you gotta start with kindling.

Hey, Woody!
I have a strange problem. Sometimes when I cum, I cry. I'm not sad, but the tears come anyway. It doesn't happen all the time but I've run off a few promising dates because they thought I had "issues." It's not like I blubber or anything, but it's noticeable. The thing is, it'll happen even with a trick I don't ever want to see again. What can I do to stop this?

—Reaching for the cum towel AND the Kleenex

Dear Reaching:

You're breaking my mom's first rule: Don't cry over spilled milk. Though I don't think she had you in mind when she said it.

There's nothing wrong with you. In fact, I think it's rather sweet. In addition to a physical release during climax, there's also an emotional release. There are men, for instance who convulse with laughter after they cum. Nothing strikes them funny, it's just the way their mind-body connection reacts to the release.

Like my boyfriend's moods, sexual response is multiphasic. Energy builds from excitement (the first stirrings) to resolution (the last dribble). By the time you're ready to "pop," all that built-up energy gets released in different ways. For you, it's crying. For others, laughing. For my boyfriend, a compulsive need to brush his hair.

Crying may be your body's way of saying "Thanks, I needed that." Be grateful. That kind of emotional juice doesn't come often.

As for scaring off partners, just treat it lightly. If they think you're crying because you're falling for them, just say "Don't flatter yourself, I cry when I beat off."

Hey, Woody!
I have this girlfriend who says she's allergic to semen. Poor thing—I'd kill myself. But it brings up an interesting question. Can men be allergic to other men's semen?
—Hoping against hope it's not the case

Dear Hoping:

It's true that some women are allergic to semen but not in the way you're thinking. They don't break out in a rash when the nectar hits their skin. Some women develop antibodies and immunity to sperm cells. Believing the sperm is a foreign threat (their systems are as paranoid as republicans), they mobilize against it and sic the jack-booted anti-bodies on the poor backstroking critters.

This search-and-destroy tendency makes it impossible for such women to conceive. There are no cases in the literature about actual skin allergies to someone's semen. Thank God.

Hey, Woody!
I keep hearing rumors every few years, of stars like Rod Stewart being rushed to the hospital to have their stomachs pumped because they swallowed too much semen. I'm assuming these are urban legends, but now I'm curious—is it possible to swallow too much semen? And if you did, would you have to have your stomach pumped?
                                                    —Curious and salivating

Dear Curious:
Every few years there's a rumor that pints or gallons of semen had to be pumped out of some famous stomach. I've heard it about David Bowie, Mick Jagger, even Alanis Morrissette. If you swallowed a pint of semen, two things would happen:

1. You'd have a bad case of heartburn.
2. We'd never get the smile off your face.

Semen, as my boyfriend knows all too well, is not toxic. If it was, he'd have Poison Control on automatic dial. Your body would process the semen like food—there would be absolutely no medical reason to have your stomach pumped.

Hey, Woody!
I've got a pet peeve I thought you might want to tackle. It's deep-throating! It seems the majority of gay men have somewhat learned this technique, but not as a continuing part of a stroke. Instead, they take the penis down their throat, and then STOP! They hold it down as long as they can hold their breath, and only then continue the motion

that brings pleasure to the recipient. I wish men would consider what is good sexual technique and what is a parlor trick. When men masturbate, do they simply grab their penis with both hands motionless? NO! They move their hands up and down continuously. It's the motion that brings pleasure, not just the contact. Tell them to stop slowing the momentum down, Woody!

—Got something caught in their throat

Dear Got:

You're complaining about guys who deep-throat? You probably came out of the womb complaining about the back-lighting.

Here's advice #1: Never complain when somebody can deep-throat you. Complain when they can't.

Advice #2: When somebody's doing something you don't like, don't bitch. Request. As in: "Wow, that feels great, but it feels better when you don't stop the motion." Grab his ears and gently show him how to swallow the sword without nicking his throat or stopping the mo'.

Your partners aren't the problem, guy. You are. You seem to think that your partners should know what you like before you tell them. Here's a hint: You can't move a man's mouth down your shaft through telekinesis. Why are you so unwilling to tell your partners what you like?

Hey, Woody!

I wanna spray like I'm hosing down my deck, man. But when I cum I notice that not a lot comes out. Is there anything I can do to increase the amount of semen I ejaculate? I'm not talking about sperm, but the actual load that ends up on my stomach (or hopefully, his chest).

—It's never enough

Dear Itsy:

As any long-term masturbator in Long Island would tell you, "Fuhgedaboudit." Outside of masturbating or having sex less frequently—the less you yank the more you'll blow—there's not much you can do.

The single biggest factor between a drip and an avalanche is how long you've gone since your last ejaculation. If you ejaculated several times in a row, you'd poop out a drop or two. If you waited several weeks, you'd better stand back, cuz she's gonna blow. But not too far back, because most men ejaculate less than three tablespoonfuls. Hell, that's barely a dosage of cough syrup. Nobody's going to drown in that.

And "fuhgedaboud" drinking lots of fluids or eating certain foods—they won't increase the volume either. Semen is not like urine—it doesn't come from the digestive tract or urinary system. The majority of semen comes from two glands, the prostate and seminal vesicles.

There is one thing that can influence the volume of your semen, and for once, it doesn't require months of exercise or licking expensive medicine. It's a hot guy with an even hotter technique. The more stimulation you get before the orgasm, the more likely you'll see your pearls turn to diamonds. And no, you aren't imagining that you cum more when you're getting fucked—massaging the prostate will do that.

For the most part your genes determine your load-bearing capacity. So if you want to complain about how much cum you ejaculate, take it up with your mom. I'd love to hear her response.

Hey, Woody!
Ever since we opened up our relationship to include sex with other guys my boyfriend's developed this weird thing where he can only come during group sex. He can't come when it's just me and him in bed.

I really don't know what to do because having sex with other guys has added a great dimension to our relationship. I don't want to stop the group sex thing; I just want him to come when we're flying solo. Should I put my foot

down and close the relationship for the sake of our private sex life?

—**Pissed off at the orgy**

Dear Pissed:

His inability to ejaculate when you're alone is most likely a sign of major problems in your relationship. Problems that probably need a therapist to be worked out. But since you're gay you probably don't believe sex has any emotional components, so let's pretend the problem is purely physical.

In that case, your boyfriend may be suffering from a physical arousal issue. The constant group sex could cause an unintentional "stimulus hunger" in your boyfriend. He needs higher and higher levels of stimulation to trigger his ejaculatory reflex. Like drug addicts who need more and more drugs to get the same high, your boyfriend needs more and more dick to get the same ejaculation.

You know when you constantly yell at your boyfriend to take the garbage out and he doesn't do it, and you have to resort to yelling louder and louder to get the same sense of superiority you used to get at a lower decibel? It's the same concept.

Let's face it, men like new meat. New arouses. It's why the "first time" is often the most memorable, because all your physical senses are on high alert.

That's why guys with beautiful boyfriends (or girlfriends) often cheat with people that aren't nearly as good-looking as their spouses. Case in point: Hugh Grant getting caught with that rat-faced hooker when he had Elizabeth ("Helen of Troy") Hurley waiting for him at home.

What to do? Talk to him. Not Hugh Grant; your boyfriend. You're gay and horny so you probably missed that last suggestion. Let me repeat it: Talk to him. Tell him you want to continue sticking your dick in anything with a pulse but sex with him comes first.

The only way an open relationship can work is to preserve the primacy of your bond. Sex with others is an amenity, a side dish, and side dishes should always complement the main meal, not take it over. If it interferes with the main course, you may have to switch restaurants.

Lastly, read the first line of my response again. And again, and again, until you get it.

Hey, Woody!
You've given some great advice on what to do when a slab of meat is laying next to you, but what if he isn't? Any advice for us loners? Are there techniques to make jerking off by yourself a more memorable experience?
                                   —Flying solo in a groupie world

Dear Solo:
You can masturbate just to get off (a worthy goal in anybody's book), or you can do it with the goal of being a better lover and flinging a future co-pilot to new heights. Why not do both?

More than a few readers tell me they jerk off in the shower because it's more efficient (they can just wash that cum right out of their hair). Next time a friend tells you he can't go out because he needs to do laundry, you'll know the kind of load he's washing. My point, and I do have one, is that efficiency is at odds with great sex. Making a mad dash for the cum line never makes you a better lover. Here's what the right kind of self-flogging can improve:

Staying Power: If your tricks are timing eggs from the time you enter them, you need to practice lasting longer. When you're masturbating, bring yourself to the point of no return then back off. Learn to recognize when you're about to blow so you can head it off. Fine-tune your early-warning signals. There's nothing better than watching your partner smell the eggs burning because minute man turned into marathon man.

Lunging Power: Practice letting yourself go soft and then bringing it back up. By doing this, you'll teach yourself that losing your erection isn't a reason to blow chunks into your Kleenex. This is important for guys anxious about "situational impotence." The way to let go of your anxiety is to let go of your hardness, knowing it will come back up again.

Positioning Power: Masturbate in different positions, especially the positions you fantasize about with that hunk at the gym, the one who'd lose half his body weight if he ever got circumcised.

Get off your feet, your back, however it is that you normally do it. For instance, if you fantasize about fucking, then masturbate belly-down and mimic the action, training for the real thing. Ease off from your Kung-Fu grip, too. You want to simulate how it's going to feel when you're dipping into the real stuff. Thrusting against a lightly held hand will more closely simulate intercourse.

Hey, Woody!

Have you heard about this new supplement that's supposed to make your cum taste sweet? Is this real, or one of those red flags being waved in front of ground-pawing bulls like me looking for the next big thing in sex?

—Sweet Tooth

Dear Tooth:

I love your bullfighting analogy because that's exactly what you have to do when you're faced with the claims of most supplements—fight bull.

The latest thing making nostrils flare in horny anticipation is a supplement called "Semenex," manufactured by MMOR Research. Semenex isn't the only thing the company is manufacturing. There's enough manure in their claims to make Ireland's pastures green with envy.

Semenex is a dietary supplement made up of fruits, vegetables, spices, vitamins and minerals. You mix the powder in a glass of water, and voila, 12 to 24 hours later your semen tastes like a new Ben & Jerry's flavor.

Hey, wait a second, what's that smell? Check the soles of your shoes, everybody. I think we just stepped on another pile of dietary supplement claims.

There is no proof whatsoever that anything can change the taste of your semen. Yes, there are all kind of "experts" claiming you can make your cum taste better if you do the Hokey Pokey and drink this unpasteurized pineapple juice with that hormonal strawberry. Only doctors with Caribbean medical degrees believe that.

If Semenex were practicing "truth-in-advertising," it would change its name to Excremenex.

Hey, Woody!
A lesbian friend I adore wants me to be a sperm donor, but she, ahm, wants it donated in the old fashioned way. Now, I love her and everything, but I'm still going to have a blindfold over my eyes and a clothespin over my nose. Needless to say, I want it to work the first time—is there a time of the day when my sperm count will be higher, and thus increase the chance for it to "take"?
—I'm what you call a REAL friend

Dear Real:
Sperm work the second shift. While everyone is winding down and driving home, they're just getting ready to go to work. Researchers in Italy compared semen samples collected from men at seven in the morning with those collected from the same group of men in the afternoon (don't worry, they didn't give same-day samples—my God, they'd be exhausted. They waited for the pumps to refresh after a few days). The semen collected in the afternoon contained 40 million more spermatozoa than the samples collected in the morning. That's almost a 30 percent increase. So wait till late afternoon/early evening, clamp the clothespin on and knock yourself out.

Hey Woody!
I have been with about four guys, sexually, and have no-
ticed that they all had considerable amounts of pre-cum.
The thing is, I don't. I don't have any at all. I have no prob-
lem reaching a point of climax, but there are no juices
flowing prior to that. When I do finally cum, I have varying
amounts from average to Oh My God. Is this normal?
                                                    —Cum-see, cum-saw

Dear Cum:
You need to fiddle with your worry radar because it's picking up
things that aren't there. Pre-cum is the penile version of salivat-
ing when somebody puts a big piece of meat in front of you.

Just because you don't drool doesn't mean there's something
wrong with you. The muscle contractions of sexual excitement
squeeze the prostate and seminal vesicles and force the fluid up
(usually just a couple of drops). There is no relation between
cum and pre-cum. If you don't have pre-cum, it doesn't mean
you'll have more cum at the moment of truth.

Pre-cum serves as a built-in reservoir of lubrication. Interestingly, some experts think it has an evolutionary purpose—to
neutralize the acidity of the urethra from any residual urine, thus
preventing sperm from being waxed before it can reach the egg.

Hey, Woody!
I know this is stupid, but why do we call it a "blow job" if
it's a sucking action? Why don't we call it a "suck job"?
                                        —Looking for any type of job

Dear Looking:
In China, fellatio is called "playing the flute;" in India it's called
"mouth congress," or "sucking a mango fruit." In Egypt it's called
"the great swallowing." In Woody's office it's called "come here."

I've searched high and I've searched low, but I haven't found
out how or why sucking turned into blowing. Any *sementacists*
out there who can help?

Hey, Woody!
I love making love to my partner and I'm trying to get better at it. Sometimes I cum too quickly, though. It's not a major issue but it's there. Any suggestions?
                                                    —Speedy Gonzalez

Dear Speedy:
Slow down. Especially when you're alone. Some sex therapists feel that we've conditioned our sexual climaxes to be overly fast because as boys we learned to masturbate quickly (hey, you had to get it done before Mom barged in on you).

If you cum right away when you're masturbating alone, you're liable to do it when there's somebody else in the bed. Lightning orgasms are fine, but try to work in some 15 minute sessions with yourself. Train yourself not to come too soon when you're alone so you won't come too soon when you're not.

Hey, Woody!
It's hard for me to cum inside my partner. I could go for hours and nothing. Are there any techniques I can use to deliver the payload in him rather than on him?
                                                    —Overnight delivery man

Dear Overnight:
I love it. On the same day I get a letter from a guy complaining of coming too soon, I get a letter from somebody complaining he can't come at all. Priceless. You two should have coffee sometime.

My advice is to: a) stop masturbating so much (you'll be more eager to spurt); and b) when you do masturbate, change the way you do it.

If you're like most men, you come best with fast, jack-hammer-like manual strokes. That's hard to reproduce when you're fucking, making it harder to climax inside your partner. You can get so used to hard, fast manual strokes that you can't come any other way.

So when you're alone, lighten up on the choke hold, and slow it down. Thrust yourself against a loosely-cuffed hand rather than pumping with your fist, mimicking the act of love-making. Try switching hands—it'll make you more conscious of what's happening.

Another thing that'll help is trying new positions and varying the thrust of your penis. Monotonous pumping can have a numbing effect after a while (never mind you, think about him). Change the depth, speed, rhythm, and timing of your pelvic thrusts. Start with shallow, slow thrusts and throw in longer, deeper, and faster pile-drivers. Mix it up. It'll help you come and him leave—with a smile.

Hey, Woody!
I've been thinking of getting my tongue pierced, really just cuz I think it looks hot. But lately I've been hearing that getting a blow job from somebody with a pierced tongue is awesome. 'Course, that just makes me want a pierced tongue even more. The question: Is it true?

—Wantin' to poke and prod

Dear Wantin':
Please. What makes a good blow job is a good blow job, not the metal you're packing. If you don't give good head now, you're not going to give good head just because you can pick up FM stations when you open your mouth.

Depending on the piercing, you can hang some "toys" on the barbell making your partner feel some interesting things, but come on. The way you slather mustard on the hot dog is far more important than the utensils you use to spread it with. Experts tell me if you are going to get it, place the piercing towards the back of the tongue—it's easier to blow someone that way.

Hey, Woody!
I'm a slurper from way back. I gave Folger's the slogan
"Good to the last drop." But just how good for you is it?
What exactly is in a man's nectar?
                                   —Just wondering

Dear Just:
Of the things you'd recognize, semen contains ascorbic acid, calcium, chlorine, cholesterol, citric acid, creatine, fructose, lactic acid, magnesium, nitrogen, phosporous, potassium, sodium, sorbitol, vitamin B12, and zinc.

Of the things you can't pronounce, semen contains aboutonia, deoxyribonucleic acid, glutathione, hyaluronidase, inositol, blood-group antigens, choline, purine, pyrimidine, pyruvic acid, spermidine, spermine, urea, and uric acid.

Hey, Woody!
Is swallowing semen healthy? Somebody told me that it
actually has good nutrients. I only do it with my boyfriend
and we're both negative, so I'm not asking about HIV or
other STDs, just like, the nutritional value of the stuff.
                  —Always looking for a better snack

Dear Always:
Cum as a nutritional snack? Hmmm. Somehow I think the boys at Nabisco will take a pass on that product idea. Semen isn't high in calories. It's made up of sugar, water, enzymes, protein, zinc, and citric and ascorbic acid (vitamin C). There's not enough of anything in it to cause harm or good.

Hey, Woody!
Last month I let a guy cum all over my face. It was great,
until he got it in my eyes. It stung like hell and I spent the
rest of the night flushing my eyes out with water. What

caused the stinging? Was it the sperm crawling all over my eyeballs looking for a wayward egg?

—Don't let this happen to you

Dear Don't:

Sperm in the eyes can cause terrible conjunctivitis (inflammation of the outside of the eyes). And no, it's not the sperm burrowing into your eyeballs looking for a good egg that causes the irritation. It's the enzymes in the semen (they help sperm get into the egg).

If you do get the joy juice in your eyes, flush it out with warm water immediately. There's plenty of good resting places for your partner's semen. Your eyes aren't one of them.

Hey, Woody!
My problem, and I'm not being frivolous, is that I have a big cock and enjoy being blown immensely. But I get tooth scratches all the time, which are painful, because my partners want to take it "all the way." How can I make my cock more tooth-resistant? After sex, I wash with soap and water and pour peroxide over the area and follow up with first aid cream such as Neosporin, but it takes several days for it to heal. Any suggestions?

—Fun way to prevent cavities

Dear Fun:

"How do I make my cock more tooth-resistant?" What, are you an idiot? You've actually let someone suck your penis when the skin was broken? Christ, I've got to get smarter readers. That's it—either my editor starts paying me more, or he starts being more selective about who reads this rag.

My advice is to apply for Poster Boy in the "How to Get HIV" ad campaign of your local health department. Then, after they boot you out on account of too many candidates applying for the position, you can follow this advice: NEVER have sex with broken penis skin, NEVER let it get to the point that your skin breaks. Stop your partners the second you start feeling their teeth.

You can't "teeth-proof" your penis anymore than a woman can "teeth-proof" her breasts. Skin is thin down there for a reason—it makes the area more sensitive. If you could "teeth-proof" your dick it would feel like your arm, and whoever heard of an "arm job"? What you *can* do to keep penis skin healthy is moisturize it. With a cream, dummy, not a mouth. That'll help avoid breaks and cracks through the skin's surface.

Hey, Woody!
It seems to take me forever to cum. I'm hard and all, but it takes me about an hour to cum when I'm having sex. At first, my partners love it (especially bottoms) but after a while it gets old. Even some of my more patient partners start drumming their fingers on my back and asking for the remote control. How can I speed myself up?
—Slow-poke in the fast lane

Dear Pokey:
About 10 percent of men seem to have delayed or retarded ejaculation ("inhibited orgasm" for those of us who love pretending we're schooled properly).

In a case like this, the first thing I'd do is let your fingers do the walking—straight to the phone for a doctor's appointment, preferably a urologist. Have him check you out to make sure you're not dealing with a physical condition. Oh, and see if he'll show you his before you show him yours. I'm just curious.

If he rules out a physical condition, you might need to do some emotional surgery on yourself. Often, delayed orgasms are a manifestation of emotional blocks: fear of being abandoned, fear of rejection, lack of trust, religious values, intimacy avoidance, or fear of not having enough towels to clean up the mess.

The inability to let go in the presence of your lover (or a hot stud) robs you of one of life's great joys. Get yourself to a therapist if you can't solve it alone.

Hey, Woody!
I love giving head, but I hate getting spooge in my mouth.
What kind of early warning system can I develop for guys
who deliver their payload without telling me?

—Lickety splat

Dear Lickety:
Most men who are still conscious tend to say something before their shots get fired. "Oh, God I'm gonna cum!" is usually a clue to let your hand take over what your mouth loves so much.

Sometimes, what they say is more subtle. Like "mommy." Or more often, a simple "yes" in three or more consecutive sets. If you're attracted to bed mutes who won't even mime a groan or moan, you can still tell by their shallow breathing. It goes without saying that getting cum in your mouth significantly increases the chances of HIV infection (if you have cuts, scrapes or gum disease). You might want to consider telling your partners before you go down on them that you want them to "call their own shots." Loudly.

Hey, Woody!
Sometimes after a really hot, intense bout of sex my
boyfriend doesn't want to cum. It bothers me more than it
does him. He says he doesn't need to cum to make hot sex
complete. Do you think I'm just not that good in bed and
he's just sparing my feelings?

—Lots of sugar, but no cream

Dear Sugar:
Great sex isn't just about an orgasm. In fact, defining an intense sexual experience by the orgasm is like defining a great ice cream sundae by the cherry on top.

If we'd all be as evolved as your boyfriend and focus less on a "goal" (like a torrential semen downpour), we'd all be a lot more satiated. Stop making sex so goal-oriented—it'll open up a world of possibilities.

Hey, Woody!
I cum way too soon, not just when I'm entering somebody,
but even when they're just jacking me off. I'm tired of
being a minute-man. What can I do to keep my piece from
going to pieces too soon? I've tried all the herbal crap and
my doctor said I check out fine. Any suggestions?
                                                    —Count down

Dear Count:
No herb or prescription medication is going to help with premature ejaculations. The good news is that ejaculatory control can
be learned.

Assuming your urologist shook your thang and pronounced it
in good working order, it sounds like you need to develop an
ability to stop and not collect "Go" after a point called No
Return.

All men have their own point of "ejaculatory inevitability"
(usually preceded by the words "Oh, God, I'm gonna cum!"). You
gotta know BEFORE you get there, and practice mental and
muscle control.

Experts cite the book, *The New Male Sexuality* by Dr. Bernie
Zilbergeld as one of the best self-help programs out there. Get
the book. Try out the exercises, and if you're still not satisfied,
forget about getting your money back. Nobody's gonna accept a
book return with skank smeared all over it. At that point, I'd seek
a board-certified sex therapist or clinical sexologist.

Hey, Woody!
Is it possible to cum without touching yourself? I have a
friend who claims he can do it. Do you believe him?
                                              —Hands across the water

Dear Hands:
Yes, I believe your friend if your friend is a woman. It's possible
for some women to have an orgasm without any physical stimulation. But this is a gay sex advice column so who cares? There is

no documented case of a man being able to "think off." If your friend really can, you'll have to start offering him more than a penny for his thoughts.

Hey, Woody!
I'm dating Mr. Right, except he turns into Mr. Fright when he kisses. It's like he's sweeping for land mines with his tongue. I give him tongue too but it's more of a flanking maneuver to stop the onslaught. How can I call a truce to our tongue wars, and teach him how to kiss better, without hurting his feelings?

—Awash in spit

Dear Awash:
You want advice on how to say something inoffensive and you came to me? Try *Ladies Home Journal.*

I always go by the theory that men are dense but pliable. Meaning, they're stupid but not stupid enough to leave you over something stupid.

Most guys are receptive to changing their techniques as long as you frame it as a request, not an insult. For example, you could say something like "Look, you moron, you kiss like a pack mule and I'm choking on all the spit you're hosing down my throat." But I don't recommend it. I mean, it worked on my boyfriend, but you need a certain finesse to get away with it.

Now, where was I? Oh, yeah. Try this approach instead: "You know what really turns me on? When you do *this.*" Then show him how you want to be kissed and say, "Now you try it." Then moan like a whore when he does it.

Chapter 8

Drugs and Alcohol: Substance Abuse or Seduction Technique?

Alcohol and drugs are the great thigh-openers. I gleefully recommend mood enhancers as indispensable seduction techniques. Which of course, sends gay schoolmarms to the moon. It's always the same guys complaining, too. The guys so frigid even Moses couldn't part their thighs.

Let's face it, sex is better with a buzz. Critics can't stand it when I say that. Perhaps it's my favorite cheer that bothers them so much ("One tequila, two tequila, three tequila, floor!"). Or perhaps it's the increased risk of unsafe sex ("I hate cheap wine—I always wake up with a sore asshole"). Or perhaps it's because you can die from excessive drinking or drugging ("I'll just do another ounce of GHB").

Whatever the case, my stand on alcohol and drugs has nearly gotten me kicked out of some newspapers. But I remain steadfast. Drugs and alcohol, when used responsibly, can not only enhance the sexual experience, they can get you up the crack of his ass faster than a thong.

I first learned the magical properties of mood enhancers with a recalcitrant date, who later turned into a boyfriend. This guy was wound so tightly light couldn't get through the spaces in his teeth. A little liquor and poof! Out came his guilt and shame, along with his penis.

Another satisfied customer.

If it weren't for alcohol I probably wouldn't have slept with half the people that I wanted to sleep with. No, not because I got them so drunk they didn't realize whom they were going home with. Quite the opposite. Because I was too scared to approach them. A couple of drinks later, the fear diminished enough for me to take a risk. There's a reason why the Irish say they drink beer "for the courage that might be in it." Read on and find out.

* * *

Hey, Woody!
After thirty hours with no sleep, which included two nights of dancing, drinking, using Ecstasy and "G," someone slipped me an overdose of this new thing called Liquid X.

In about an hour I was so messed up I couldn't complete a sentence. Before long I was vomiting. But not just vomiting, I mean VOMITTING. As the medic said, I almost drowned in it.

Within another hour I was in a coma, unable to breathe for myself. The medics took me to the local hospital and put me in the ICU (Intensive Care Unit). The doctors told my friends there was a good chance a vessel busted in my brain and I may have incurred brain damage and/or possible brain death. They said the next six to twelve hours would be critical. Of course, I have no memories of all this.

About six hours into the coma, I found my way back into consciousness and I was horrified at what I saw: A tube was down my throat, breathing for me. I was connected to all kinds of wires and other not-so-pleasant things like a catheter jammed up my dick to siphon the urine out.

It's a miracle that within forty-eight hours of being taken into the hospital in a coma, being kept alive by a machine, I walked out on my own two feet. But unfortunately, right into PTSD (Post Traumatic Stress Disorder). I can't sleep and when I do, I have nightmares that I'm choking. My doc has given me Ambien to sleep and Klonipin to calm me down, which has helped a lot.

For a few weeks, I cried all the time, though that's getting better too. I've been a circuit boy for a while now and needless to say, this near-death experience has changed that part of my life completely. I don't touch the stuff anymore and I'm telling everyone to stay away from it.

Woody, would you print this letter and tell everyone to flush all their drugs down the toilet? Everyone I know in the circuit reads your column. Do the responsible thing and tell them to stay off drugs.

—Over it

Dear Over it:

You must have me confused with Ann Landers. I don't give dried-vagina advice. I will never tell people to stop doing drugs unless it's idiots like you taking them. Our thirst for adventure can't, and shouldn't be quashed.

You made an awful mistake and now you want everyone else to pay for it. I'm not buying it. Most people who take drugs do them responsibly. You didn't. You fell off the stupid tree and hit every branch on the way down.

I know you're hurting and you genuinely want to help your friends avoid what you went through. But you're never going to do it by becoming a pain-in-the-ass moralist.

Get therapy. You need to find out how can you use this awful experience, this journey into darkness, into something that will help you and the people around you.

I have a vested interest in keeping you guys alive. If you keep dying, book sales will go down and out comes my stumbling drunk of an editor demanding I give back my royalties. And if that happens, believe me, it'll be ME spiking your water with Liquid X.

Look, throughout time people have taken drugs and they're never going to stop. The best advice I ever heard on drugs came from Sister Kitty Catalyst of the Sisters of Perpetual Indulgence: "There's nothing fabulous about a trip to the emergency room. The lighting is bad, the outfits are horrid, and they have no idea what a VIP line is."

Amen, sister.

Hey, Woody!
You moron, I can't believe you said, "I will never tell peo-
ple to stop doing drugs." How can you endorse using some-
thing dangerous enough to kill you or put you in a coma?
                                                    —Pissed off

Dear Pissed off:
I'm an agnostic on the question of whether people should use
drugs. I think people should make up their own minds. You think
that my unwillingness to condemn drug use is tantamount to advocating it. You're wrong.

Hey, Woody!
I've never been more disgusted than when reading your
flippant answer to the guy who almost died of an over-
dose. He deserved your sympathy, not your lame jokes.
                                                    —Shamed of you

Dear Shamed:
I don't do sympathy in this column, asshole. In the dictionary
"sympathy" rests between "shit" and "syphilis." That guy didn't
need my pity, he needed my support, both for processing the horrible event that almost took his life and to find a meaningful way
to stop people from dying or becoming vegetables. He was on
track on the first issue, off-track on the second.

Hey, Woody!
How could you call a guy who almost died of an overdose,
a "pain-in-the-ass moralist" because he's trying to get peo-
ple to stop using drugs? You suck.
                                                    —A former reader

Dear Former:
Because pain-in-the-ass moralists make things worse. They're
the reasons drugs are illegal, which means they're not regulated

like alcohol or nicotine, which means people don't really know what they're taking, which exponentially increases the chance of overdosing.

Pain-in-the-ass moralists came up with teaching abstinence in high schools and what did we get? The highest rate of teenage pregnancies in the world. Pain-in-the-ass moralists gave us Prohibition and what did we get? Increased consumption of hard liquor.

Policies based on moral outrage produce massive failure. If the guy really wants to help people, he'd replace his pious Just Say No campaign with a hard-boiled Just Say Know approach. If we get people to Know their limits, Know the dangers, and Know when to stop, we could actually prevent a lot of needless deaths and injuries.

Hey, Woody!
Would you ever say "I will never tell people to stop having unsafe sex"? Then why would you say it about drugs?

—Amazed at you

Dear Amazed:
Would you really expect me to discourage people from having sex because sex is dangerous? Or would you expect me to preach safety, to use a condom, to be responsible? Why should drugs be any different?

Hey, Woody!
Drugs are *illegal*. I think it's immoral to advocate any kind of use, responsible or not, for something you can get arrested for.

—A legal beagle

Dear Legal:
You pinhead. Homosexuality is illegal too. Check your state's criminal laws and see what they say about sodomy. By your definition, I'm being immoral every time I tell you to use a condom.

Hey, Woody!
There is no such thing as "responsible" drug use. You might as well teach pyromaniacs how to light a house on fire in a way that won't harm the building.
                                                    —A flame retardant

Dear Flamer:
Bullshit. Drugs are not in and of themselves dangerous. It's the way you use them that makes them so. Drugs are like electricity. They can electrocute you or light your house, depending on whether you apply stupidity or intelligence to it.

Hey, Woody!
You are a mean, evil queen who doesn't care that our gay brothers are killing themselves.
                          —Leader of the Logtop Woody Campaign

Dear Leader:
And you're a hand-wringing schoolmarm addicted to the ecstasy of sanctimony. You care more about making people wrong than about reducing injuries.

I spend a lot of time writing about responsible drug use because I'm alarmed at what gay men are doing to themselves. I don't have to do that, you know. Last time I looked this was a sex advice column, not a drug education class.

Hey, Woody!
How can you make "clear-headed" decisions if you're on a substance that clouds your judgment?
                                                    —Wondering

Dear Wondering:
The same way you make responsible judgments when your dick is hard. The same way you make them when you drink. One stroke, one drink, one bump, one hit at a time.

You make responsible decisions BEFORE your judgment is clouded. Sorry, but a hit of ecstasy or a snort of Tina does not automatically cloud most people's judgment (if it does, then halve your first hit).

It *is* true that the more drugs (or alcohol) you take, the less rational your judgment becomes. The trick is to start slow and constantly ask yourself this question: "Can I have one more hit and still stay in control?"

Hey, Woody!
You're acting as if "control" is that easy with drugs. You forget they're highly addictive.

—One who knows

Dear Knows:
Compared to what? According to the U.S. Food and Drug Administration, about 8% of people who drink alcohol are dependent. The FDA did not break out club drugs, but experts believe about 12% of people who use club drugs are dependent. This means about 88% of people who do club drugs don't get addicted.

Now what was your point?

Here's the rest of the FDA's breakout of drug users who are dependent: Hallucinogens 9%, marijuana 12%, cocaine 21%. Nicotine is the drug that has the highest percentage of dependency among its users (80%). My guess is you were smoking a cigarette while you typed your outrage over drug addiction.

Hey, Woody!
I'm with you. It seems to me that the more shrill the warnings become about using drugs, the more people want to do them.

—A fellow sane voice

Dear Fellow:

Ever heard of "The Romeo and Juliet Effect"? Romeo Montague and Juliet Capulet came from feuding families. They fell deeply in love, despite fierce parental opposition, and ended up in a double-suicide. Gee, I wonder what would have happened if their parents had paid no attention?

A lot of psychologists believe they would have broken up. A team of shrinks did a study of 140 teenage relationships. Here's what they found: Those couples who had interfering parents felt greater love for each other and expressed a higher desire to get married. If parental interference decreased, researchers noticed that romantic feelings cooled at a corresponding rate.

What's all this got to do with drugs? That which is forbidden is desired more greatly.

Hey, Woody!
Is it possible that all your lofty speeches about using responsibly are about justifying your own drug use, maybe even a drug problem? You've always been honest, don't stop now.

—Suspecting you

Dear Suspecting:

I'm not ashamed to say that I've had my share of problems with drugs. At one point in my life I couldn't go a day without giving myself a fix. My head would start to pound, my hands would start to tremble, and I couldn't really concentrate without it.

But enough about my morning coffee.

Here's my club drug history: I've had great experiences that make me understand why people take them and I've had terrible experiences that make me understand why people stop. At this point, I only do them at huge circuit events, maybe once every couple of months.

Hey, Woody!
Do you really believe that drugs aren't more harmful than
alcohol?

—Not believing you

Dear Not:

No, I believe drugs are more harmful.

Go from one cigarette to thirty in a night and you'll get sick.
Go from one drink to ten and you'll pass out. Go from one hit of
G to two and you might die.

So yes, drugs are more dangerous. Which is why, if you're
going to use them, you have to be even more responsible than
when you use alcohol.

Hey, Woody!
I'm totally into the circuit scene but I have to admit things
are starting to get a little out of hand. One of my friends ac-
tually died from a crystal addiction and several others
landed in the ER. I'm in control when I do drugs and I try to
get my friends to ease up a little on the throttle, but some-
times they go too far. Last week a friend fell out. As we were
waiting outside, none of us knew what to do for him (he was
passed out). I know this isn't a sex question, but what are
you supposed to do while you wait for the ambulance?

—The helper

Dear Helper:

What should you do while you wait for the ambulance? Another
bump. Never let the selfish flailing of a dying friend get in the
way of a good buzz.

Seriously, I have to compliment you on the intelligent way
you're using drugs and for the compassion you've shown your
friend by sticking with him till help arrived. But enough compli-
menting—it ruins my reputation. Here's what you should do
when He's-Ruining-It-For-The-Rest-of-Us bites off a little more
than he should snort:

1) **Keep him breathing.** If he isn't, then do mouth-to-cock re-suscitation. Put his mouth on your cock and blow. It's al-ways the first thing I do when a cute guy falls out. It doesn't do him any good but it makes me feel blissful, loving and spiritually connected to the brotherhood of man, and isn't that what the circuit's all about?

   If he isn't cute, or if you've already had him, then do mouth-to-mouth breathing. Make sure he doesn't aspirate any vomitus if he upchucks (damn, why can't my medical advisors just say "Make sure he doesn't swallow chunks of his own vomit"? They're always trying to impress me with big words). Anyway, getting vomit chunks in your lungs can cause pneumonia and kill you (no lie) within three days. That's why surgeons don't perform operations for at least twelve to twenty four hours after you've eaten.

2) **Check head-to-toe for unseen injuries.** You're looking for fractures, head injuries, etc. Femur fractures (breaks in the thighbone) can kill because they bleed so much and so quickly. So be sure to check the upper inside thigh. Relieve him of any drugs he's carrying. Consider it your reward for being so helpful. If a neck injury is suspected, stabilize the head, neck, and body. Don't twist or turn it, unless it's to steal his money when nobody's looking. Try to keep him immobilized until you've gone through all his pockets and be sure to check the inside of his socks. I always find an extra $20 bill there.

3) **Do what the EMS workers say.** Answer their questions truthfully—tell them what drugs your friend was taking. The emergency team isn't interested (nor does it have the authority) to arrest you, so don't cop out on your responsi-bility to help. Don't tell them you went through his pockets and filched all the valuables, though. Those EMS vultures hate competition and they're liable to strap you onto the gurney just out of spite.

Once they load your friend onto the ambulance the EMTs will give him some combination of oxygen, heparin (prevents blood clotting) and fluids. Keeping victims breathing is the biggest challenge of any overdose situation. Especially when I'm in the ambulance throttling the victims for being so goddamn stupid.

You know, most people start anti-drug campaigns after seeing some of the tragic consequences of drug abuse. I'm more realistic. I start anti-stupidity campaigns. In fact, my slogan is "Just Say Know." If you're going to party, Know what you're taking, Know your limits, Know what combinations to avoid.

If you can't stay in control, do us all a favor and stay home. Ambulances should be chasing heart-attack victims, not idiots who can't use drugs responsibly.

Hey, Woody!
Have you heard of BetterMan, the new "herbal Viagra" thing that's been in the news? You're such a bastard about herbal stuff, I figure if you give it the okay I'd give it a try.
—Looking for an alternative hard-on

Dear Looking:
I'm a bastard to the herbal industry because they exploit innocent people with wildly inflated, unsubstantiated claims. It pisses me off that they take advantage of male vulnerability for personal gain. That's my job, Goddammit, and I won't be poached.

BetterMan made news because it was the first herbal compound to show results in a rigorous, peer-reviewed study published in a major scientific journal. This is important because medical journals look at herbal claims the way I look at vaginas—with complete and utter skepticism. So for the *Journal of Urology* to state there were "significant results" to the BetterMan study is quite an achievement.

HOWEVER. Before you run out and stock up on the expensive mixture, pay attention to the study: BetterMan helped dicks get hard, but the dicks were hanging off rats, not humans.

Researchers put 24 young rats on a high-cholesterol diet to induce erectile dysfunction. Yes, even in rats, fat makes hard weenies go bye-bye. Oh, this little research tidbit is going to send those Fat Liberation people into orbit. Well, if their arteries are as clogged as my mailbox was after last month's Lard-Ass Sex series, I guess I have nothing to worry about because they're going to die next week anyway.

Anyway, there the rats were—like half my readers—fat and impotent, when two months into the study scientists slipped some BetterMan into the drinking water of half the rats. Those who drank the herbal mixture were later able to achieve erections, while the other eight rats remained impotent.

I am not going to recommend using BetterMan on the basis of a single, well-conducted study on rats. But neither will I discourage use of it since it doesn't seem the mixture has any side effects. But before you plop down $100+ for the mixture, know this: You have to take it daily for three months before you see any effect.

You can get more information about BetterMan at the company's website, which is riddled with wildly inflated claims, unsubstantiated assertions, and eyeball-rolling anecdotes. It's at www.bettermannow.com.

Hey, Woody!
My pothead boyfriend smokes at least every other day and he's got zero interest in sex. He puts the lack in slacker. The only thing standing upright in my house is the vacuum cleaner. Would it help if I slipped him some Viagra? Is it safe for him to take the big blue pill while he's stoned? He just doesn't seem to want me, or anyone else for that matter.

—Begging for it

Dear Begging:
I'm still trying to figure out how you "slip" Viagra into somebody. Like Tang, I guess you could crush it into a powder and mix it with water. But then we'd have to call it Bang.

There are no known interactions between Viagra and pot; as long as he doesn't have any blood pressure or heart conditions, he shouldn't have any problems. But I doubt it'll do any good. Viagra can give you a boner, but it can't give you what comes before it—desire.

Sexual arousal starts above the belt, not below it. Brain cells get activated, which start the blood flow to you-know-where. If brain cells can't process a sexually-exciting image (say, you in "Dance Fever" leotards) because there's enough marijuana haze to make asthmatics long for the cleanliness of Los Angeles air, then what good is Viagra going to do?

A lot of scientists believe marijuana decreases testosterone, sperm count and, consequently, sexual desire. It's been proven in laboratory rats that marijuana changes the chemistry of the nerve cells in the brain affecting sexual behavior, the same cells that regulate hormones producing testosterone and sperm.

But rats, schmats, nobody really knows marijuana's sexual effects on humans. The limited research is contradictory. Some studies show decreases in testosterone and sperm count; some don't.

The studies may be contradictory but don't be a fool. You can't do anything in excess and not have it affect your sex life. I'm afraid you're going to have to give your boyfriend something harsher than Viagra—an ultimatum. It's decision time: Your ass or his pot. Maybe he needs an unbiased source for a decision. Send a naked picture of yourself and a sample of his stash, and let me be the judge.

Hey, Woody!
I haven't had any problems getting an erection since I've been taking Prozac but it takes me forever to cum. The gun's loaded but it won't fire, if you know what I mean. My partner's patience is about as thin as the condoms I wear and I'm not exactly thrilled either. What can I do?
—Pistol-packin' Poppa

Dear Pistol:

With simple once-a-day dosing and fewer side effects than older drugs, people have flocked to Prozac and other SSRIs like gay activists to nauseating rainbow merchandise. Like Prozac, activists do a tremendous amount of good, but not without unwanted side effects. One makes you lose your libido, the other your lunch.

The first studies of SSRIs showed adverse sexual side effects in less than 10% of patients, but those studies relied on unprompted reporting—patients who spoke up during a doctor visit or called their doctor on the phone when they noticed sexual problems (which like you, tend toward delayed ejaculation).

In more recent studies, doctors specifically asked patients about libido or orgasmic difficulties, and found nearly half of patients on SSRIs experienced them. "Oops," you can hear the drug companies saying, "Did we say 10% of SSRI users report sexual dysfunction? We meant 50%." Bullshit, try 90%. I have rarely talked to anyone on SSRIs who didn't experience negative effects.

Exactly how these drugs interfere with sexual desire isn't known. There is one theory that SSRIs bind to the brain's receptor cells convincing single men they're actually married, which as everyone knows, is the fastest way to kill a boner. But not all scientists believe it, particularly because I was on my third martini when I proposed the theory to the NIH.

Here's what you can do to get willie to cough up the goods:

1. Switch to a non-SSRI antidepressant, like the tricyclic Elavil. They don't have as many sexual side effects, but—warning, they carry others, like dry mouth and constipation at much higher rates than SSRIs. Pick your poison.
2. Get off Prozac but stay within the SSRI family. It's hit or miss which ones give certain people certain side effects, but truthfully, they ALL list some kind of sexual dysfunction. One doc on my advisory panel said the makers of Celexa brag it doesn't have as many sexual side effects as other SSRIs (apparently, drug companies don't have piss-

ing contests anymore; they have ejaculation contests). "Personally," said my advisory doc, "I always try Zoloft first. Mainly because the Pfizer drug reps are hotties and they do wonders for MY libido, but also because my patients seem to respond to it better."

3. Stay with Prozac but lower the dose. Warning: Don't do this without your doctor's supervision. There's a right way and a wrong way to do it. Ask him. Or her. Or it.

4. Take a "Drug Holiday." Say you want to have sex on Saturday (it's a stretch, I know, but stay with me). Simply stop taking the drug a few days before the blessed event (maybe longer depending on how long your particular drug stays in the bloodstream). It's sort of like cashing in your Frequent Desire Miles for a free fuck, only you get to decide the blackout dates.

Hey, Woody!
You're the only one I can turn to because I'm too scared to ask anybody I know. Last month my 24 year old boyfriend died while I was fucking him. He sniffed some poppers and suddenly lost consciousness. I panicked. I called 911. The emergency workers burst in asking "Is he on any kind of drugs?"

In my panic I said "No." I was too scared. You see, I got the poppers illegally from a hospital I work at. I figured if I told the truth there would be an investigation and they'd find out. None of my friends who've "fallen out" at circuit parties ever died, so I figured my boyfriend would be okay.

He died en route to the hospital. The autopsy report said the cause of death was unknown, but I think he died because I didn't tell the emergency team he was on drugs. I'm haunted by what I've done—I can't sleep at night, I have trouble eating. I'm too ashamed to go to a therapist. I need a safe, anonymous person, so I'm turning to you. Would the emergency workers have done anything differ-

ently, could they have saved my boyfriend's life, if I had told them he was using poppers?

—Haunted in Texas

Dear Haunted:

This story is so shocking that when I convened my panel of experts they practically gasped. But to a person (including an EMT— Emergency Medical Technician), they all agreed that emergency workers on the scene would have done nothing differently had they known about the use of poppers. The only way the information would have been useful is if it were possible to pump poppers out of his system or if there were an "antidote" for it. There isn't.

Poppers open up your veins and coronary arteries by relaxing the muscles in these vessels. They often plunge blood pressure to dangerously low levels. The EMTs already knew he was in shock because monitoring blood pressure is standard procedure.

The consensus of my panel is that your boyfriend died from unsustainable low blood pressure brought on by the poppers. But there were contributing factors: Anal intercourse stimulates the vagal nerve, which drops blood pressure and slows the pulse. Also, your boyfriend may have had arrythmia (a change in the regular beat of the heart). This common condition could have accelerated the drop in blood pressure.

You didn't kill your boyfriend. He was an adult of sound mind and body who asked you for the drugs he took. Still, you have to face the moral implications of giving someone you loved the agent of their death. It was a horrible accident of chance, but there is no getting around the fact that you contributed to it.

You have to find a way to release the guilt and secrecy haunting you, and create meaning out of this tragedy. Find a therapist you trust and work it out with him. You have some work to do, starting with his family. When you're emotionally strong enough, let them know about the poppers (but not how you got them— it's irrelevant). You owe them that.

You owe your boyfriend, too. You owe him the possibility that some good can come out of this tragedy. Like stopping it from happening to someone else. Devote yourself to helping people make sound drug choices.

For some, it'll be to never use them; for others, to use them judiciously. In the memory of your boyfriend, find a way to forgive yourself so you can make a difference in someone's life.

Hey, Woody!
I was stunned when I read last week's installment about the guy who felt responsible for the death of his 24 year old boyfriend because he had given him the poppers that killed him. I've been doing poppers for about 18 years and am probably addicted to them and the effect they cause.

After reading about this tragedy I was moved to tears and said that for my life and health I would quit. I had just purchased a bottle at the time I had picked up this publication, so I went to the fridge and poured out the full bottle into the sink. I then decided to write you so that maybe "Haunted in Texas" will know that at least one life has been affected by his letter. I am so sorry for his loss that I can't even search for the right words. I hope Haunted finds the wellness that he needs and, please, find a way to let him know that I will pray for his quick recovery.

—Quitting in Texas

Dear Quitting:
Thanks for such an inspiring letter. There's an old saying in addiction circles and I hope you heed it: "You're the only one who can do it, but you can't do it alone." Find someone to help you through this—a therapist, a priest, a friend.

Unlike the potential for scoring at a late nite bar, cutting through the fog of a drug-riddled life ain't easy. Your body is sensitized to poppers and sex will not feel right without it at first. Making fundamental changes takes time, energy, and support from other people.

There should only be two kinds of drug-users: The kind that use drugs intelligently and the kind that don't use them at all. Lord, if we could just quarantine the in-between. They have a drug IQ so low, if you pounded their brains into powder you wouldn't be able to snort an intelligible vowel out of the vial.

Here are a few facts about poppers or amyl nitrate (AM-il NYE-trite). In prescription form it's used by inhalation to relieve the pain of angina attacks. It works by relaxing blood vessels and increasing the supply of blood and oxygen to the heart. There's a popping sound when you crush the cloth-covered glass capsule, hence the street name.

Poppers smell like dirty feet and give me a headache. You can have it. If you do, at least be intelligent about it. Use the dose doctors recommend for their angina patients: Pass it back and forth close to your nose and inhale the vapor several (1 to 6) times. The dose may be repeated within 1 to 5 minutes. Do not exceed a total of 2 doses in a 10 minute period. Again, for the intellectually feeble, let me repeat that: *Do not exceed a total of 2 doses in a 10 minute period.*

In other words, STOP. I know some idiot is out there thinking "duh, that means I can take 2 doses every 10 minutes." No, it doesn't. After 10 minutes the game's over. Period.

If you're on antidepressants, Viagra, heart disease or blood pressure medication, or suffer from anemia or glaucoma and you want to use poppers, write a will because you're as good as dead.

Poppers are extremely flammable. Flick that cigarette anywhere near it and you just signed up for skin grafts.

Hey, Quitting in Texas, do me a favor. Drop me a line in a few months to let me know how you're doing. I'm rooting for you.

Hey, Woody!
Your advice to people about using poppers SUCKED. What the fuck is "intelligent use of poppers"? There is no such thing as an intelligent use of poppers. Why don't you wake up, fool? How about telling people not to use them at all, like any responsible expert would? Well, you're no expert

and you're certainly not responsible with that kind of advice. Poppers damage the heart and fuck up the immune system. I can't believe you'd write an article telling people how to use them. Shame on you, Woody. I've read the last of you.

—An ex-reader

Dear Ex-:

First of all, you must be confusing me with Ann Landers. She's the one who gives the kind of dried-vagina advice you're looking for.

My advice is not directed at children, but at grown adults, the kind who've already made up their minds about whether they're going to use drugs. I have never advocated nor condemned drug use. My role is to haul out the Stupid Meter and call the crowd's attention to it when it goes off. And goddammit, does it goes off in the gay community.

It's a good thing the Stupid Meter doesn't run on batteries—I'd be on a first name basis with the Radio Shack cashier.

Do I think people should do drugs? No. Do I think they shouldn't do drugs? No. I think people should make their own decisions and people like you and me should stay out of it.

We should have the same penalties for drug abuse as we do for alcohol abuse. Namely, if you're not hurting people or property, we should leave you the hell alone. Do something stupid, like Driving Under the Influence, and you should have the book thrown at you. Along with the vase, picture frames and whatever else was on the shelf with the book.

We're exposed to alcohol education all the time (Budweiser "Drink Responsibly" ads come to mind), but you think we shouldn't be exposed to drug education?

No matter what the penalty, there are three things that men will always play with: Fire, drugs, and themselves. And not necessarily in that order. The "Just Say No" mentality was given its chance and it failed spectacularly. Your corner is always yapping about giving it more time, and maybe you're right; maybe we should give it another shot—after all we only gave it a hundred and forty fucking years to work. Maybe that's just not enough time to see results.

Hey, Woody!
They say "don't drink and drive" but what about drinking and DRIVING, if you know what I mean? I don't know about you, but when I drink, it puts me in the mood and I don't care if I'm steering or being steered. Apart from the fact that alcohol can cloud your mind in terms of safe sex, how does it affect actual sex? I say it's an aphrodisiac but other people say it kills their boners. What do you say?
—Toasting your answer

Dear Toasting:
Alcohol is both a boner-upper and a boner-downer, depending on how much you use. The question we all have to ask ourselves about alcohol is the same question we have to ask ourselves about men: At what point does volume get in the way?

A study at Southern Illinois University showed three and a half drinks for a 150 pound guy starts getting in the way. Every measure of arousal the researchers looked at went south after three and a half drinks.

Basically, alcohol can make you as lousy a driver behind the wheel as under the sheets. It impairs your ability to DRIVE the way it impairs your ability to drive. Namely, by dulling the nerves that transmit sensations. So what you see is not what your dick gets. Your eyes see the prize and send out the message "Wake Up. He Wants You to Board Him," but your penis hears "Go To Sleep. This is Boring."

There's nothing intrinsic about alcohol that acts as an aphrodisiac. It's just that it tends to relax you and melt away reservation, inhibition and worry, the absence of which makes for great sex. So yes, alcohol is great for sex. Till you get to the fourth drink.

Hey, Woody!

I'm an emergency medical services worker (EMS) who's just about had it with the gay drug culture. I'm really tired of saving kids who are "falling out" at circuit parties. EMS workers hate "OD" calls (Overdose) because it's always potentially a life-or-death run. They're scary as hell. Sort of like an "MI" call (Myocardial Infarction, a.k.a. heart attack), only worse because at least the heart attack victims didn't bring it on themselves.

Privately, many EMS workers call the gay overdosing "Attempted Suicides." My compassion for these people is ebbing. I'm risking my life for people who are trashing theirs. Emergency calls are fraught with danger for the rescuers. Imagine if we had to send helicopters to rescue people because they fell off a cliff. Now picture sending helicopters to rescue people who throw themselves off a cliff, over and over. How many times can we keep sending the helicopter before you say, "Look, these people obviously want to die, let them."

As you can see, I'm not in a good space about this. Where do I go to get my compassion back?

—Tired of it

Dear Tired:

I cannot believe the homophobic crap you just laid on my living room floor.

Straight overdoses are worth turning the TV off and hopping on your ambulance to save them, but gay ones aren't? Are overdose calls less dangerous when the victims are straight? No? Then shut the fuck up about gay people overdosing and talk about ALL people who overdose.

Another question: Who died and left you fuehrer? How dare you imply that some people are worth saving and some are not? Your job isn't to sit in judgment; it's to save lives.

Apparently intention is part of your equation when deciding who "deserves" to have their life saved. If somebody who never does drugs OD's because someone "slipped" something into their drink—does that buy them enough points to get saved? And how would you decide who gets to live, Adolf, if you can't tell whether the OD case is a victim of his own excess, or a victim of someone's spite until you get there?

According to you, a depressed person who throws himself off a balcony is worth trying to save. But not if he tried to kill himself with drugs. Then it wouldn't be worth getting off your ass and doing your job. Flawless logic.

Let me tell you why your training did not include discerning the worthy from the unworthy in an emergency call: Because this is America today, not Germany in 1941.

But I digress. I see two options for you: Talk to someone in your EAP (Employment Assistance Program) and ask for help. Believe me, you're not the first emergency worker calling because they're burned out. Or, if you truly feel like you can't do the OD runs anymore, ask to be transferred to a different county or simply put in for a change of shifts. I suspect you won't see too many overdose cases on Wednesday mornings.

You have two responsibilities: One, to human beings needing emergency care, and two, to yourself. Both require a high level of compassion and it's your responsibility to generate it within yourself, either through therapy, a change in shifts, or a change in jobs.

I don't want to minimize the danger (or the heartbreak) of drug overdoses. Yes, it's a shame. Yes, it's preventable. But you know what? So are gun shot wounds, and you didn't write in complaining about that.

Your frustration is understandable—I share it—but it's the profession you chose. Saving lives is so much nobler than judging them. Be nobler.

Hey, Woody!
I'm new to the circuit scene and I have a question about circuit party sexual etiquette. Okay, the meth's kicking in, right? The music's tribing, your arms are vibing, your teeth are grinding, and then ... oh, wait. I forgot the question ...

oh yeah! Then you see a guy you've had a crush on for years on the dance floor. Do you go up and tell him you've wanted him all this time? He's friendly and all, but I can't tell if he's interested. I figure if I tell him and he doesn't react well, I can just blame it on the drugs next time I see him. It's only when I'm high that I have the nerve to tell him. Should I?

—Short-circuited at the circuit

Dear Shorty:

No. Talking in a circuit party is like talking in a porno flick. It's annoying and it gets in the way. Groping is the preferred method of communication when you're visiting Circuit Nation. Basically, the rule is "never say with words what you can say with your hands."

Understand the concept of "Buzz Management." Like diabetics, party boys are constantly regulating their Buzz levels and they do not appreciate anyone making the meter go south on them.

If you're going to open your heart to him on the dance floor while you're both tripping, you might as well spray a can of "Buzz-Be-Gone" in his face. No, you're much better off grinding your sweaty teeth over to him when he's at the pre-orgiastic group-dance-hug-huddle thing on the floor, and do the tribal laying-on of hands. That way, you get to cop a feel without unnecessary damage to your ego.

I don't think it's a bad idea to tell him—eventually—but not at a circuit event. There is no room for personal disclosures in the swirling potpourri of dick, drugs and disco.

Hey, Woody!
Who made you the Shell Answer Man/Ms. Manners for us gay guys? I don't know what your credentials are or why you were chosen and anointed for this important position as one of the shamans of our tribe. Your advice to the guy who wanted to know how to approach his dreamboat at a circuit party was way off-base.

It normalized drug use and undermined the ability to formulate solid relationships, effective communication skills, and personal authenticity.
—A pissed off MSW/LCSW at a large gay medical organization

Dear Marie Osmond:
You remind me of one of those hand-wringing, Smell-My-Piety kill-joys spraying Lysol over the slightest scent of libidinal pleasure.

"Personal authenticity" at a circuit party? "Formulating solid relationships" at an intimate gathering of 5,000 shirtless men? What are you, nuts?

There's a time and a place to Smile Pretty And Say Jesus, but a chest-thumping, bicep-ripping, crotch-bulging, sweat-soaked, mind-blowing tribal sex rave in a cavernous, ear-splitting dance hall probably isn't one of them.

You might've had a point if I had advised the kid to take drugs and get screwed without a condom. I didn't. I told him to lay hands upon the wonderment on the dance floor and wait for a decent time and place to spill his heart.

This may come as a shock to you, Nancy Drew, but men like to get laid without using "effective communication skills," or being in committed relationships, or participating in long, drawn-out Victorian courtships. I see nothing wrong with one night stands. Or getting sketchy on meth. Just like I see nothing wrong with committed relationships. Or getting drunk on vodka. My rules for sex apply to one-nighters and all-lifers; namely, be safe, have fun, and keep me in mind. My rules for partying are pretty much the same.

You asked about my credentials. How can I dispense advice on the complicated subject of sex? The same way you can pontificate about gay men's lives so piously, Mr. Seven-letters-after-your-name-but-still-clueless-as-fuck: *Easily.*

I have no psychology degrees, no medical degrees, and no sex therapy training. I don't need them. You know why? Because when I need those backgrounds to bolster my common sense advice, I go to the panel of experts I've set up to make sure I don't say something stupid or untrue. You oughta try it. It might save you some embarrassing press.

Finally, noting that this is, after all, an advice column, I'd like to give YOU some advice: Get off the cross; we need the wood.

Hey, Woody!
My lover and I like to have sex while on crystal meth. He's in his early 50s. Lately, after a few hours of sex, my lover has noticed some blood in his semen. This never happens when he masturbates during the week. It only seems to happen when he orgasms after partying all night, tweaked up. Can crystal or other drugs be responsible for that?
—Bloody mess

Dear Mess:
Your boyfriend is showing signs of prostate or some other form of lower urinary tract cancer. It's highly doubtful that the drugs are doing it. Here's your four-step plan to keeping him safe: 1) Get him to a doctor. 2) NOW. 3) Send me the rest of your crystal. 4) NOW.

Hey, Woody!
I keep hearing about the sex-enhancing power of Yohimbe. I don't have any trouble getting it up but I'd like better, stiffer, longer-lasting erections. Do you know anything about it?
—Looking for more action

Dear Looking:
Yohimbe (pronounced YO-HIM-BEE) is a herbal supplement made from the bark of the *Pausinystalia Yohimbe* tree. Its active ingredient is the alkaloid Yohimbe, which—until Viagra—was the only FDA-approved oral medication for impotence.

Only a doctor's prescription will assure you of actually getting Yohimbe, thanks to the frauds in the herbal supplement business. It's sold as a herbal extract in health food stores, but good luck trying to get a dose that actually contains the active ingredient.

Because they're not regulated, herbal companies aren't under any obligation to fill their bottles with the ingredients listed on the labels, the lying motherfuckers. Studies of products sold in health food stores found most contain little or no Yohimbe when tested. So much for wisdom and honesty from the crunchy, Birkenstock set. They get away with lies corporate America could never get away with, proving you don't have to wear a tie and wingtips to screw the public.

If you can actually get Yohimbe, odds are that it will help. It's been proven in clinical studies to increase blood flow to the penis. Its main problem are the side effects. Yohimbe can cause elevated blood pressure and heart rate, dizziness, headache, skin flushing, anxiety, panic attacks, and hallucinations. It should not be taken, under any circumstances, by anyone with heart disease, kidney disease, or anxiety. Because of its severe side-effects, the FDA classifies Yohimbe as an unsafe herb.

If you don't fall into one of the danger groups, I don't see any harm in trying it. The largest study ever done on Yohimbe showed that the best results came with 42 mg of Yohimbe daily over two to three weeks. But again, good luck getting the right dosage. How the hell are you going to know if you're taking the right dosage when the labels are mostly fiction?

Hey, Woody!
Prozac is killing my sex life. As my shrink gradually increased my dosage to where my depression is at bay, my libido has slowly gone south, along with my ability to maintain an erection. My lover of three years and I have a gleeful understanding of our sexual roles: I'm the pushy top and he's the passive bottom. We won't switch roles, so don't even go there. He's been a model of support, in a Hillary Clinton kinda way—calm on the outside, but when

nobody's around, threatening to start getting fucked by other guys if I can't satisfy him. What can I do?

—Dickless in Duluth

Dear Dickless:

First of all, Hillary Clinton would never say "fucked" to her husband unless she was using the word to describe the future of his marriage.

Second, your boyfriend isn't a passive bottom. He's a passive-aggressive bottom. He needs to know he's got two roles in your bedroom—lying underneath you when things are going well, and standing beside you when they aren't.

We've all been sold a bill of goods about antidepressants. According to the pharmaceutical companies, about 30 percent of users will suffer some sort of sexual impairment—from reduced libido ("yeah, you're really hot, man, but let's watch *Biography* on A&E first") to taking an eternity to climax ("Honey, you keep trying, I'll go and make us an omelet") to outright impotence ("I'm furious and I'm going to start getting fucked by other guys if you can't satisfy me").

The truth is, pharmaceutical companies lie. I don't know ANYBODY who's on an antidepressant who hasn't peeled the banana and had it droop before anybody could take a bite. Prozac and its sister SSRIs are the modern way of selling your soul for a little happiness. Peace at the cost of your piece, as it were.

That being said, it's also true that these antidepressants are often the only things that can overcome crippling depression and anxiety disorders. So pick your poison.

I'm assuming you've picked the pill poison because you've tried everything else: therapy, meditation, yoga, crystal meth, fisting, web design, and they've all failed. Talk to your doctor about other SSRIs (Prozac is one of many, each working on the brain in slightly different ways). There might be others that can provide depression/anxiety relief without making you Noodle Man.

Another way might be to get off pills altogether and try the herbal route—St. John's Wort, which does not seem to have sexual side effects. But do it under doctor supervision—do NOT take both SSRIs and St. John's Wort together. And if you're stuck on Prozac, consider decreasing the dose steadily as you increase a spiritual practice like yoga or meditation. You might find a happy middle ground.

Hey, Woody!
Are there natural alternatives to Viagra? I want a jaw-breaking hard-on, but I have arrythmia which prevents me from taking it.
—Lookin' for a few hard hours

Dear Lookin':
According to Dr. Andrew Weil, the controversial but much beloved alternative guru, Yohimbe bark can put the yo! back in yo' sex life. The only drug in the *Physician's Desk Reference* classified as a sexual aid, Yohimbe is available only by prescription. Dr. Weil also recommends *ashwagandha* and ginseng but he's not popping corks over them either. They're more for "sexual energy" (whatever the hell that means) and their effects are cumulative over many weeks.

Another candidate might be *muira puama*, nicknamed "potency wood" (in honor of my column, no doubt). James Duke, a well-known botanist and author of *The Green Pharmacy*, was quoted in *Men's Health* as saying "I confess that if I had erection problems, I might try this herb." How's that for a resounding testimonial? There's no consistent data showing any of these herbs work to give you a hard time.

Plus, herbs aren't regulated, so the manufacturer is under no constraint to properly label their product's ingredients. You may think you're taking 50 mg of Horn-dog Extract and end up taking 25. Consumer beware.

Hey, Woody!
First of all I have to say that I love your column! I like how
you put humor into some serious questions. I have always
been in some form of relationship only to get hurt in the
end. I'm in my early 30s and find that I am having more fun
than I have ever had in a relationship I'm doing the circuit
scene. I am meeting the hottest men I've ever had.

However, I would like to get back into a relationship
should the right man come along. But my best friend tells
me that that I am doomed to get a reputation and no man
will want me, or, if I do find a man, and he finds out about
my party times, he will dump me. Is this true? It is like, I
am the nice guy that no one wants to get serious with, or
the bar slut that guys only want to trick with. It's a no win
game!

—Confused at the orgy

Dear Confused:
You're having sex with some of the hottest men around? Write
me when you have a real problem, huh?

I think you're doing exactly what you should be doing—taking a break from beating yourself up over the guys who left you.
The attention and confidence you're getting from the circuit
scene will make you stronger for your grapple with the next relationship.

The circuit scene seems to be Pine-Sol for you, disinfecting
all that pining you were doing for love gone wrong. I say, take the
time to stop and smell the disinfectant. The only danger is getting sucked into the circuit culture so far that you start internal-
izing its values and project it on to real life (that the worth of a
man is in the tightness of his muscle vs. the content of his character, that using drugs is always preferable no matter what the
social circumstance, and no matter the loss of time and energy—
Christ, it takes DAYS to get back on track after a circuit binge—
that could be used to build a better life).

I say party, but party with perspective. As for your fear of
meeting guys who'll be turned off by your "rep," so what? There

are plenty of decent, good-looking guys who like to party now and again, and won't be "turned off." The main thing is balance.

Hey, Woody!
Get the splinter out of your ass! Your lack of any warning to the potential harm of meth and other drugs pisses me off. For too long the "gay mainstream" has placed the discussion of drug use in the closet in fear of stepping into judgment. Mister Miller, because you are in a publication that is in the public domain you have a responsibility to inform your readership. You affirm drug use by not responding to its potential harm. You seem to be an angry and self-righteous man. If you step back and set aside your ego, you may find the flaw in your work. We all like sex and lots of it. But the more chances we take with drugs, the less experience we will have.

Your column is filled with half-answered advice and potentially harmful statements. If you are not qualified to give advice, don't. You will do more harm than good. You must be informed to inform. If "Need Wood?" is an advice column, give good advice. Otherwise, place it in the editorial section.

—Spittin' nails at your tales

Dear Spit:
Yours is the kind of hypocrisy shared by society in general—that it's okay to alter your mood with alcohol, but not with drugs. You conveniently took my statement out of context. I said, and I quote, *"I see nothing wrong with getting high on meth, just like I see nothing wrong with getting drunk on alcohol, as long as you're safe."* I stand by that statement.

Like most hypocritical windbag moralists railing about drug use, you probably typed out your letter while drinking a beer. According to your line of thinking, it's okay to numb your senses with wine, but not with K; it's okay to get wired with caffeine, but not cocaine. I defy anyone to tell me the difference between a shot of tequila gold and a snort of crystal meth, other than its intensity and duration.

Compared to alcoholism, drug addiction is a pimple in the ass of substance abuse. According to every shrink's Bible, the DSM-V (*Diagnostic and Statistical Manual of Mental Disorders*), approximately 35 million people have suffered alcohol dependence some time in their life. Know what it is for amphetamine dependence? About two million.

In the last six months, alcohol has probably been responsible for more deaths, divorces, and job loss than drugs have for the last ten years. When men get infected by HIV because they've exercised poor judgment in bed, that judgment is far more likely to be impaired by alcohol than drugs. Yet not a word in your letter showed the least concern for alcohol's potential damage. Why is that?

I'll tell you why. Because you think people should use only the depressants and stimulants that you use. By attacking drugs and not alcohol, you can get buzzed *and* feel superior.

You're pretending that I'm defending drug abuse when I'm really advocating moderation in all mood-altering agents. I'm tired of being denied pleasure because there's a group of idiots who abuse that pleasure. And I'm especially tired of people like you, who think the best way of protecting these idiots is to deny access to the majority of us who are responsible users.

This may come as a surprise, Mother Theresa, but a lot of guys like to have a little buzz when they're going to have sex, me included. I don't see anything wrong with that. Where that buzz comes from—vodka, marijuana, caffeine, dirty underwear—is irrelevant. What's relevant is that you maintain control so that you don't end up making stupid decisions you'll later regret.

And the fact that most people *can* maintain control really pisses off people like you because it derails your drug Armageddon argument. Most people in the circuit scene are not drug addicts, just like most guys at a bar are not alcoholics.

You have a valid point about the growing gay drug culture and I share that concern. But "DON'T" as the last word in advising people isn't the answer. Look how well it worked for alcohol

(Prohibition), teen-age pregnancy, and in our own community, the rise of unsafe sex.

I will continue advocating common sense in whatever mood changers people use. I do not "recommend" drugs anymore than I "recommend" alcohol. What I "recommend" more than anything is staying in control.

Chapter 9

Odds and Ends

"What's the best sexual position if a couple's so fat they can't reach each other's genitals?" "Why does a porn star's dick always look so big?" "How do I make my bedroom soundproof?" "What's the best lube?" "Why do I like to linger in the toilet after I've pinched a loaf?" "Why do I get a headache after sex?"

Why? Why? Why? My readers are a bunch of whybabies. Thank God. How would I know what to ask my medical panel if they weren't? This section is devoted to all the "whying" that doesn't fit neatly into any categories.

The letters in this chapter tend to be more on the medical side, though most are about health conditions that don't affect a large number of people.

On the non-medical side, this is probably one of the most entertaining chapters of the book. If you're like me, you'll look up from the letters and ask yourself, *"Where do people come up with this shit?"*

Like the straight guy worried that his "fake fagging" was unethical (he plays gay to get chicks who think they can "turn" him). Or the guy who bitch-slapped a flight attendant to the ground for not putting out and wanted to know if that was okay. Or the porn star of several gang-fuck videos getting miffed that his real-life boyfriend was "passing him around."

Someone recently asked me if I ever get tired of writing this column. "How many questions about sex can there be," he asked, "before they all start sounding the same?" Only somebody who hasn't been around gay men much could say something so naïve. As Albert Einstein said, "Only two things are infinite: The universe and human stupidity, and I'm not that sure about the former."

Maybe someday I'll get tired of hauling out the Stupid Meter, pointing it at gay guys and watching smoke billow out of it, but as the letters in this chapter prove, it's going to be a very long time.

* * *

Hey, Woody!

My boyfriend and I are, ahm, "weight-challenged." We didn't used to be that way, but we got older, stopped going to the gym and next thing we knew, we started smelling like bacon when it got past ninety degrees. Skip the motivational speeches about getting in shape—we're trying. My question is, until we "try" ourselves into size 38 pants, how do we have better sex, given our amplitude? It's getting harder and harder for our genitals to touch because our stomachs and legs are getting in the way. Any tips?

—Sitting around the house

Dear Sitting:
You bring up a good point—fat people have sex too. Just not with me.

Oh, skip the protest letters, guys. I don't care how politically incorrect it is to say, no one wants to have sex with guys who can sell shade.

There are three things I advise my tubby readers:

1. Duck! Because I'm going to hurl the best of my rock collection at your windows.
2. Invest in dildos. It might be the only way you can plug the beast if you can't lose the weight.
3. Learn the "scissors position." Lie facing each other on your sides. Cross your legs over each other's like scissors, inter-

locking your bodies. Even with the weight of large legs and stomachs, experts agree this is the best position for lard-ass sex.

Look, if you're going into restaurants and they hand you an estimate instead of a menu, you've got some serious issues to deal with. Lose the weight. Not for vanity; for sanity. The more overweight you are, the more likely you'll suffer from some type of sexual dysfunction. You said no lectures, but come on. If you can't reach your boyfriend's banana because your stomach's in the way, I say reach for the phone and call your doctor. You need help.

Hey, Woody!
You anorexic son of a bitch, how dare you describe sex between overweight people as "lard-ass sex?" Your advice to your "truly tubby readers" was the kind of hateful and disreputable intolerance we expect out of Dr. Laura. You are just as much an evil queen as she is.

You think you're funny, but you're actually just a sorry excuse for a queer. You think you've overcome so much, but in your attitudes you haven't achieved anything toward becoming a decent human being. My suggestion to your editors is to have you attend a circuit party in a 250-pound fat suit. Take a walk in someone else's chub before you fling the insults.

I'm enclosing a *New York Times* article about the growing intolerance toward overweight people, how hateful attitudes like yours result in us being denied jobs and housing. I'm part of the Fat Liberation Movement and proud of it. Why don't you just accept that people come in all sizes and that one isn't better than the other?
—Tired of your shit

Dear Tired:
Christ, here we go again—another hand wringing, bed-wetting crybaby who can't stand to be poked fun at. First of all, let me

say this to ALL my readers, not just the porky ones: If you're looking for warmth and compassion you've got the wrong column. Try *Chicken Soup for the Cock*. It's three aisles over.

As for you, Mr. Walking Heart-Attacks Have Rights Too, you're treating fat as if it were a moral issue instead of a health crisis. I'm not buying it. According to the Centers for Disease Control, 55 percent of us are overweight or obese. That's well over half the country.

In some people, obesity can be explained by genetic abnormalities. But that's just not true for most. If it were, then why did the Centers for Disease Control report that obesity among adults increased almost 60 percent since 1991?

That "Fat Liberation" crap smells like it got squeezed out of the joint sphincters of political correctness and compulsive victimhood. You are NOT a victim because you pick up a beer instead of a bike. That logic is as shallow as the breathing in a Bel Ami video.

That obesity in the United States is a serious public health threat to millions of Americans is not my opinion. It's the CDC's. They went so far as to describe obesity as "epidemic," and said that we need to respond to it "as vigorously as we do to an infectious disease."

A few years ago former Surgeon General C. Everett Koop said if he had stayed in office longer, "I would have launched the same assault on obesity that I did on smoking."

By the way, obesity is defined as being at least 30 pounds over your ideal weight. Overweight and physical inactivity account for more than 300,000 premature deaths each year in the U.S., second only to tobacco-related deaths. Obesity and being overweight are also linked to heart disease, diabetes, and other chronic conditions.

Fat Liberation, my ass.

What am I supposed to say to the people I love who happen to be overweight? "Here, dear, have another rack of ribs. You're liberated, you know."

My heart really does go out to people struggling with their weight. The method is simple (eat less, exercise more), but the process is not. Depression, anxiety, eating disorders, body image issues, society's conspiracy (why don't we have fast-food fruit?), all contribute to the difficulty in losing weight.

I stand by my previous advice: If your obesity isn't genetic and you are having problems touching your partner's genitals because your stomach is in the way, the answer isn't to try different positions, it's to lose the weight.

Hey, Woody!
I am a big, fat guy and I get laid all the time. I know you don't like us, but you know what, I don't care. If you don't want to fuck fat men, don't. There are plenty of men who like us. I would love to meet you and see how utterly perfect you are. I'm sure deep down you have a fear of being fat, or you wouldn't project that negative attitude onto the world. The bear movement, Girth and Mirth Clubs, and bear festivals around the globe prove you wrong about the notion that no one wants us. Go to www.bulkmale.com and see what I mean. "Lard-ass sex?" Fuck you.

—Livin' large and lovin' it, babe

Dear Livin':
I have said all I'm going to say about people who yell out the names of condiments during sex. You guys have more impotence problems, you suffer from more chronic conditions, you die younger, and yadah, yadah, yadah. How many times can I say this? Apparently, the floors are going to buckle before your belts will.

You guys just refuse to look at the fact that you're killing yourselves and divert the issue by making me sound like I'm fatphobic.

Obesity is rampant in the U.S. If you want to fetishize a public health threat be my guest, but don't expect me to encourage it. The only thing I encourage is having safe, consensual sex in any manner you choose. It would be irresponsible for me, knowing the documented hazards of obesity, not to say something about losing weight just so I could spare your feelings.

I say lose the weight, period, case closed, end of discussion. I think it's stupid not to. But I also recognize stupidity is not a reason to abstain from sex. So I encourage all obese men—the smart ones trying to lose weight, as well as the stupid ones who aren't—to engage in one of life's great activities.

So yes, visit www.bulkmale.com and other sites like it. If your biggest fear isn't muggers but poachers, this is the perfect site for you. You're sure to yell out the names of all five food-groups when you take a look at the pockmarked fat asses wiggling and writhing away in the galleries and webcams. The site also has personals and classifieds, the latest chubby video releases, a huge list of links to other sites, and resources on the Internet for the chub, chaser, and bear communities.

You might also want to try http://www.geocities.com/WestHollywood/4210/clubs.htm, it has a pretty good listing of girth and mirth clubs all over the U.S. and Europe.

Hey, Woody!
The good news is, I live with a guy so hot my dehydrated plants stand at attention when he walks by. But I have asthma, which means I can't have sex without hanging over the bed and coughing my guts up. How can I get my asthma under control when I'm having sex? Or am I destined to go without being fucked by my beautiful lover?
—Horny but hacking

Dear Horny:
Actually, you ARE getting fucked, but it ain't your boyfriend driving the point home, it's Mother Nature. You're living a Greek fucking tragedy, man. All that wood and no way to burn it.

Anyway, in a recent study two-thirds of people with asthma said their sexual activity was negatively affected by the disease. Well, except for one guy, who used his asthma to great effect whenever he brought a trick home and changed his mind at the last minute. Nothing like coughing up a lung to get someone to leave.

The point, if I ever come around to it—oh wait, it's right here—is that you're not alone. As in 12 million asthma sufferers not alone. They're all wrestling with the same question whenever they're in bed with a hottie: How do you avoid breathing like Jesse Helms when he sees a civil right flaunting itself in broad daylight?

First thing, check your bedding to make sure you don't have dust mites triggering the lung-womping. My docs recommend using a bronchodilator, which relaxes the muscles in the large and small airways, increasing ventilation. This can be taken in pill, liquid, inhalant, or injection form, or you can mash it into a paste, bake it at 350 degrees and . . . oh, wait. Wrong inhalant. Scratch that.

Seriously, try changing the time of day you reach for the stick. According to researchers, lungs function best in the late morning or early afternoon. Also, avoid anything that increases pressure on the lungs. That means no missionary position (you know, man on top/man on bottom). Sucks, huh?

If you have asthma, the only way you can assure yourself of regular sex is to be as passive as you can. You have to minimize anything that can cause shortness of breath. How do you have sex without breathing hard? Hell if I know. Ask a republican.

Hey, Woody!
Don't laugh, but I swear my vision blurs when I'm about to have sex. My vision is otherwise okay. Tell me I'm not imagining it. Tell me it's all my boyfriend's fault.
—Eye-baller

Dear Eye-baller:
Your boyfriend is responsible for your happiness, not for your eyesight. Any good therapist will tell you that.

You're probably suffering from something called a "spasm of accommodation." It's usually associated with an eight-inch dick ramming itself into a two-inch hole. But in this case, it's what happens when you change your focus from something far off in the distance to something up close.

The shape of the lens in your eye changes and allows your eyes to adjust their focus. Sometimes your eye can spasm involuntarily, making your vision blurry for a few moments. Sexual arousal is a potential cause. It's not very common but it does happen. There's nothing you can really do for it, and chances are it'll go away on its own. Unlike some of my tricks.

Hey, Woody!
I've got a problem I'm too embarrassed to ask anyone about. Whenever I go out, especially to the bars, I can't seem to pee if there's anyone next to me, even if my bladder is about to explode. Sometimes I can do it if I go into a stall and shut the door, but when you're waiting in line and the stall is occupied, it's not always possible. The worst is waiting in line, wondering if I'll be able to pee when I get to the urinal. If the place has one of those troughs where everyone pees into a vat, forget it, I won't even try.

I have been humiliated standing there in the urinal with two guys on either side of me, hearing their urine splash and me pretending to pee. I'm horrified that they're going to look over and see that nothing's coming out.

My problem has gotten so bad I refuse to go out to the bars (or really anyplace where there's going to be lots of people and long lines in the bathroom). I want to go out and party and get laid, but I'm too scared of the humiliation I put myself through. Woody, what can I do? How do I get over this?

—Pee shy

Dear Pee:

I know that was a tough letter to write. About as tough to read, if you suffer from being "pee-shy" like I do.

You and I are not alone. About seven percent of the public, or 17 million people suffer from being pee shy, which is a diagnosable condition technically known as "Avoidant Paruresis." It can severely impair people's lives (some sufferers have literally landed in the ER where they had to be catheterized to "void" their urine).

Shrinks classify it as a type of social anxiety disorder. When fear sets in you get an adrenaline rush and your body automatically shuts down the internal sphincter muscle. It's a protection mechanism. When you're running for your life, the last thing you want to do is stop and urinate. With a shy bladder the fear, anxiety and adrenal response spiral until no matter how hard you try, you just can't go.

Some shrinks have tried "disinhibiting" medicine like tranquilizers or antidepressants, but with no real success. You can always go with the gold standard in lowering inhibitions—alcohol. Basically, you drink till you're so whacked, you don't care if the Backstreet Boys are in the bathroom with you, you're gonna piss like a racehorse. And hopefully all over them, too. It'd only be fair. Whenever one of their songs comes on I feel like they're pissing all over me.

But as you know, I don't ever offer alcohol as a problem solver, unless that problem is a potential trick having second thoughts. Then I say pour, pour like the rain.

Seriously, desensitization techniques are the best way to move the waters within. It works like this: You gradually introduce the feared stimuli—other men—until they lose their power to paralyze your body. Hey, wait a minute, this is starting to sound like an Exodus de-gaying program.

Anyway, you do this first with visualization, then in real life. This is how I overcame it. With relaxation, distraction, and visualization techniques I short-circuited the panic, allowing me a great degree of bathroom freedom. Though I have to be honest and say that my shy bladder hasn't gone away completely.

I never sought professional help. Mostly because I was too ashamed, and by the time I tried stuff on my own I got it mostly under control. Don't let shame stop you like it did me. Get help. I could have saved myself years of agony.

Start by going to www.paruresis.com. They register more than 42,000 visitors a month in their discussion site. There are all kinds of helpful links.

BTW, there isn't anything particularly "gay" about being pee-shy. It affects everyone, male or female, gay or straight, at almost any age.

Hey, Woody!
Is it possible for sex to cause headaches? I swear, after sex I get a splitting headache. What can I do?
—Achy-breaky head

Dear Achy:
You're suffering from "coital headache." They're usually caused by tricks who won't leave after you cum. That's what causes mine, anyway. Yours are probably caused by muscle tension.

Some men are sensitive to certain pressures—especially around the head, neck, face, jaw, or shoulders. These pressures can end up hammering your head like a Thai hustler pissed off at the lousy tip you left him. Try positions that allow your head and neck to stay relaxed. For instance, let him get on top, you selfish bastard, and let somebody else have some fun for once. Oh, wait. I've got you confused with my boyfriend.

Anyway, breathe slowly and deeply during sex, and try a hot shower. Ask for a gentle massage after its over (if he's still there and you remember his name). If that doesn't help, your head-aches could be the result of changes in blood pressure. Sexual excitement alters blood flow in the body, enough to cause a headache. If that's what's going on, splurge baby, and buy some aspirin. Take it *before* you have sex. No sense in taking a pound-ing after you've taken a pounding.

Hey, Woody!
As a physician I constantly marvel at how correct your medical and physiological answers are. You research your medical topics well. However, you were off base when you told a reader to take an aspirin before sex for his post-coital headaches. Aspirin is an anticoagulant which promotes bleeding by interfering with platelet function. It can cause gum bleeding and rectal bleeding (sometimes undetectable), increasing the risk of HIV transmission during sex. The better answer would have been to take two Tylenol, as it has no bleeding side effects. Keep up the good work—the advice you give is well-needed!

—Take me and call me in the morning

Dear Take Me:
I stand corrected, though my research shows that the risk you talk about is exceedingly slight. Still, I vote for you. Why take the risk if all you have to do is switch brands? And thanks for the compliment. They're hard to come by in this bed-wetting, hand-wringing, advice-phobic age.

Hey, Woody!
I'm straight. At first I started out using fags as my personal pimps to get chicks. But then I got close with my gay friends. I pretty much act, talk and dress like them. I'm a regular Joe turning mo, man. Except for the sex thing, I'm practically gay.

I even read gay rags like this one, dress well, and I'm becoming more sensitive to chicks. Here's my question. One of my gay friends thinks it's sick that I "Play Gay" to get girls. Well, it works! Every chick I meet at a gay bar thinks she's the one who's going to "turn" me, and who am I to stop them? Do you think this "fake fagging," as my friend calls it, is unethical?

—Mo Joe

Dear Joe:

Unethical? It's brilliant. Christ, you're the straight version of me. There's nothing unethical about lying to get laid. Dishonest? Yes. But it's dishonesty on the level of telling your boyfriend "No, you don't look fat in those jeans, honey."

Everyone lies to get laid. We just don't admit to it. We call it "exaggerating" ("no, really, I have an 8 inch dick"), or "fudging" ("I'm 32, why do you ask?"), or "stretching the truth" ("no, I don't have a boyfriend").

Do you really think when straight men say "I only want you, honey" to their 200 pound wives they're telling the truth? Do you really think when gay men say to their boyfriends "No, honey I didn't have sex with that cruisy hard-bodied 20 year-old because you mean too much to me" that they're telling the truth?

Do you really think when I tell a conservative hottie that I belong to the Republican party that I'm telling the truth?

Please.

There's no difference between your lies and mine. You play gay and I play like I give a shit. You pretend to suck cock; I pretend I'm interested in the other guy's life. Not all lies are the same, of course. A waiter pretending to be a banker to seduce his pretentious prey is not the same thing as a boyfriend pretending to be faithful when he's not.

If you're aiming for a relationship I'd say fuhgedaboudit, don't lie. But if all you're aiming for is a little nookie-nookie, come on, who cares?

I always thought if straight men had any brains they'd seek us out and become our best friends. Nothing turns chicks on more than guys who are comfortable with their sexuality. Straight guys would be up to their dicks in cunt if they could ever get over themselves.

And you, my friend, are Exhibit A.

Hey, Woody!

I know you're not a fan of testosterone patches but is there anything we can do to increase our testosterone naturally?

I keep reading that testosterone is a key ingredient to better sex, so naturally I want to go to Wal-mart and buy it in bulk. Can I? Should I? Any danger in taking supplements?

—Testy when I don't get some

Dear Testy:

The average healthy man has about 1.5 milligrams of testosterone in his bloodstream. That's all you need to get hard, build muscle, and do other manly things like letting the barbell strangle your work-out partner because you're too busy cruising to spot him.

As we grow older, that lousy 1.5 milligrams starts shrinking. Production problems hit the testosterone manufacturing plant. Labor disputes, greedy management, and old equipment take its toll on the testes. Around 40, the average man's testosterone levels drop 15 percent each decade. If that doesn't give you vertigo, I don't know what will.

Patches are good for the one percent of the population that are seriously low in testosterone. Any artificial form of testosterone—patches, injections (and soon, tablets)—poses a health risk because it can accelerate the growth of prostate cancer. There's no evidence it can cause it, but there's evidence it can make preexisting tumors grow.

Studies also show supplemental doses can cause depression. Great. Now you can get harder, fuck longer, and then crawl into a hole and cry yourself to sleep.

Many of us will suffer from *mildly* lower levels of testosterone as we grow older. This can be corrected by following Woody's AssMaster plan:

1. **Get off your ass:** Testosterone levels are greatest after a tough work-out. But not too tough. Too much exercise actually lowers testosterone levels. Weight lifting is one of the best ways to pump up the volume, though you'd never know it from gay gyms, which are basically bottomless sources of estrogen.

2. **Get your drunk ass home:** Too much alcohol destroys testicular cells that produce the hormone. Basically, you should drink as much as it takes to seduce another man, and not a drop more.

3. **Get some ass:** Sex stimulates testosterone production. If you're getting a little on the side, try getting a little more. It'll help.

4. **Eat some ass:** Pig, cow, goat, it doesn't matter which rump, eat it. Studies have shown men who eat meat have more testosterone than vegetarians. Plus they don't have that sallow, sick look the health-obsessed tend to have.

5. **Put your tired ass to bed:** Alleviating stress is the single best way to boost testosterone. Get a full night's sleep.

Hey, Woody!
Why is it that every porn video is filled with guys packing big pieces? There are thousands of porn videos, each with over a dozen men, and they all seem to have specimens that local serpentariums write grants for. And yet, most of the guys I go home with are as average as air. What's up with that?

—Livin' large but lovin' average

Dear Liv:
You know how the camera makes people like Tom Cruise look taller and heavier than he really is? Well, height and weight aren't the only things the camera pastes pounds on. One sex expert estimates that porn penis is about 30 percent shorter than it appears.

It's not just the camera work—there are tricks to the trade that help too. Like trimming pubic hair and temporarily engorging the penis with a vacuum pump (the engorgement is only temporary, so don't start flashing your credit cards—I don't want to cause a run on vacuum pumps).

Not everyone on-screen is average. Remember, producers "audition," and it ain't for "talent" in the ordinary sense of the word.

Hey, Woody!
I'm in my 40s and I've noticed a decrease in my sex drive.
It's not that I can't get it up, it's that I don't want to have
sex nearly as often as I used to. Am I sliding into unwanted
celibacy, or is there something I can do to have Willie
wake up and smell the semen?
                                          —Down but hopefully not out

Dear Down:
Even carpenters get tired of hammering when they get older. It's
normal to have your libido increasingly ignore hot men on the
way to the hammock. But if it's really becoming a problem, there
are things you can do.

The most common psychological reasons for a flagging libido
are stress, depression, and of course, the awful music they play
in gay bars. Fortunately, you can do something about two of the
three.

Stress produces cortisol, a hormone that suppresses testosterone—the nectar to the god of erections. Exercise is a well-
documented stress buster, what with its ability to flood you with
a rush of endorphins. Lots of studies have shown that regular exercise raises circulating testosterone, the hormone most responsible for making Willie do stupid penis tricks. Although the total
level of serum testosterone remains pretty constant as you get
older, the level of "free" testosterone starts to decline once you
hit 40. The equation is simple: Relieve your stress and watch
Willie go bananas.

Another way to race your sexual engine is to lose weight. Fat
metabolizes testosterone to estrogen, turning you from an aggressive top to a submissive bottom. If you believe that last
statement, I've got some ripped condoms I'd like to sell you. But
the truth is, estrogen will sap your sex drive. The more fat you
have, the more testosterone you'll turn to estrogen, and the less
sex drive you'll have.

As someone who likes a good buzz before a good lay, I'm sad
to report that alcohol's favorite sport is mugging libidos. Alcohol

is metabolized in the liver, which is also responsible for metabolizing testosterone. Too much liquor and your liver may start converting your testosterone to estrogen, contributing to a loss of sex drive.

Finally, check your medicine cabinet. Like your hands on a lonely night, medications are known to choke the life out of Willie. For example, Sudafed inhibits the release of histamine, a chemical normally released when you get a whiff of mangina and the blood starts boiling. Tagamet, the heartburn medication, can screw up testosterone metabolism. And antidepressants like Prozac, Paxil, or Zoloft can make your banana droop before it's ever peeled.

Whatever you do, don't ignore your flagging libido. If none of these suggestions work, talk to your doctor. There could be a medical explanation. Like maybe your porno collection needs updating.

Hey, Woody!
I keep meeting these guys that sexually tease me, and then at the last minute they play Sister Mary Magdalene and claim they're "just not that kind of girl."

Last month I met some flight attendant on the way home from a business trip and he agreed to spend the next weekend with me. We had a great dinner and then things got hot and heavy at my place. We're kissing, scratching tonsils with our tongues, and our hands are all over each other. I make my move and I guess he gets insulted that I tried to board him without the proper ticketing or something.

He was like, "I don't have sex on the first date." I'm thinking "Who is this Winged Whore kidding?" and I get even more forceful. I was like, "Nobody spends the weekend with a stranger they picked up on a plane without wanting sex, you fucking Air Mattress." And with that I hauled off and smacked him to the ground.

I would have fucked him right then and there but luckily I came to my senses and just threw him out of the apartment.

So I have two questions: First, why are all these guys such prick-teases? Second, how do I keep my anger about this in check? There's something about a guy refusing to have sex after a heavy make-out session that makes me go berserk.

—Mad as hell

Dear Mad:

Why are all these guys such prick-teases? Because they're going out with such a prick. If I were the Sky Witch I would've opened the emergency door at thirty thousand feet and pushed you off. And if that didn't work, I would have jumped out myself.

Clearly, you're doing something wrong if you can't get a flight attendant to fuck you. I mean, one kiss and it's heels-to-Jesus with those guys.

The reason guys leave you boiling at the bedpost is because, like a fart in a perfume store, you have an odor of entitlement that stinks up the place. Nobody owes you sex even if they've kissed you or fondled your wallet at dinner.

What are you, straight? Let's keep "date rape" in the heterosexual community where it belongs.

Here's why I think you're doing it: You're a spoiled little shit who's been catered to all his life. You're not used to people saying no to you because you've always gotten what you've always wanted. Like a two-year-old, the word "no" ENRAGES you.

Make no mistake about it; you have a serious problem. It's not unreasonable to want sex after a date, even to anticipate it. But the appropriate response to being denied sex is disappointment, not rage. You need a therapist to figure out why sex is the only thing that validates you with other guys. Their company, their kisses, their attention don't seem to mean shit to you. Only their willingness to have sex satisfies you.

If you're not willing to get therapy, then I have three options for you:

1. Wear a red neon sign over your head that blinks "Put Out or Get Out" whenever you go on a date so your victims at least know what they're in for. And, no, you can't have mine. Get your own.
2. Make an attempt to change yourself. Ask yourself why you're so angry. Learn a little empathy. How would you feel if you changed your mind about somebody and they tried to force you to have sex? As a formative exercise, ask guys out and YOU be the one to decline sex. Learn to enjoy a man's company whether he puts out or not.
3. Get better at getting booty. The difference between rape and seduction is salesmanship. With your sales technique you couldn't sell water to the rich and thirsty.

Hey, Woody!
Behind your intended-to-be funny advice to the guy who bitch-slapped the flight attendant ("Air Mattress") because he kissed and rolled around with him but wouldn't have sex, you missed another possibility: Maybe Air Mattress gets off on bringing guys to the brink and then denying them. I've been with lots of people who WANTED to be coerced/pressured/forced into sex.

If you leave your keys in the car to run in for your dry cleaning, only to return to find someone's driven off with your car, sure, you've been victimized and should expect police support—but you're also an idiot who'd do well to examine how your own actions contributed to your misfortune. I'm of the opinion that Air Mattress got what he deserved.

—Been there, done him

Dear Been:
No he didn't. Nobody deserves violence as punishment for being a prick tease.
I agree with your premise that the sky witch enjoys putting

the kibosh on the kielbasas he helps raise, but come on. Smacking somebody to the ground because they won't put out?

Violence is only acceptable when they won't put out for me. The rest of you guys need to lead a principled life. That means no hitting, no kicking, no pushing, no clawing at the eyes when you end up with a "Greet 'em, Tease 'em and Street 'em" seducer.

I believe in the martial arts philosophy: Never attack. Violence is justified only in defense of yourself or your loved ones. Hitting a ding-dong for denying you dick isn't considered a defensive maneuver.

The whole sordid affair reminds me of a North Dakotan saying: "If it has testicles or tires, you'll have trouble."

Hey, Woody!
I stopped smoking after a ten-year, two-pack-a-day habit. I figured the one really good thing is, my sex life would get better. Well, it hasn't. In fact, it's worse. Since I've quit I'm having problems getting it up. Can giving up smoking be bad for your sex life?
—Wanting to blow more than smoke

Dear Wanting:
It's not unusual to suffer a temporary loss of libido after you quit smoking. You're de-toxing, man, and you're getting the heebie-jeebies. Or in circuit party parlance, you're being "chemically inconvenienced."

Smoking is bad for sex. Nicotine constricts blood vessels which leads to hardening of the arteries. As your arteries become harder and narrower they let less blood into your penis, making it harder to get an erection. Quitting reverses the process, but not without some side effects along the way.

It's not unusual for quitters to temporarily feel mentally unfocused and sexually unsettled. If the problems persist, talk to your doctor about nicotine-replacement therapy to help ease the transition.

Hey, Woody!
A while back I heard you speak at a function where you listed the four things you'll never hear a gay man say. I was laughing too hard to write them down. Can you refresh my memory?

—Al Zheimer

Dear Al:

1. "Hey, look at the morals on that stud."
2. "He's hot. I bet he's loyal as shit."
3. "You know, I'd like to see him again, but his dick is too big."
4. "Sex isn't that important, sometimes I just want to be held."

Hey, Woody!
Whenever I run out of lube I usually buy the first thing I see at a sex shop, mostly because I'm too embarrassed to ask the clerk for a recommendation. I mean, do I really want to ask the give-a-shit-help-living-for-their-next-break what they think would help penetrate my ass better? Woody, tell me what to buy.

—Slippery-dee

Dear Slippery:
Picking a personal lubricant is like picking a good trick—you want something that goes down easy, isn't smelly, or hard to get off you.

Like sex partners, consistency varies dramatically with personal lubricants (can somebody please tell me why they're called "personal"? Is there a "public" lubricant?) You want your personal lubricant to be as slippery as your boyfriend when he's confronted with the strange underwear you found in the back of his truck. But not too slippery, because if you can't get a good grip and some floorboard friction, you won't get off.

Another thing to look for is the lube's drying factor. Did it disappear after the first few strokes—like the commitment-phobe you dated last year? Or did it stick around like that trick last night that couldn't take a hint? The best lubes are slick (and stay slick for a long time), don't smell too awful, are easy to get out of the bottle, and wash off without making you feel greasy afterward.

With that in mind, my recommendation is . . . my boyfriend. He's like WD-40—a couple of squirts and everything fits without squeaking. However, the logistics of having him sleep with everyone isn't practical—though I must say it isn't from a lack of trying—so here are my product recommendations:

THE GOOD

ForPlay: Probably one of the longest-lasting lubes. Keeps on lickin' even after it takes a stickin'.

Slippery Stuff: Your spit should work as well, but it gets sticky as it dries out.

ID Glide: Dispenses in drops for easy application. Pungent smell, a good consistency, but has an alarming tendency to make you yell out "Who's Your Daddy?" even when there's no one else in the room.

THE BAD

Men's Cream: oil-based, so it's only good for masturbation (oil can rip latex condoms). Comes in a jar instead of a tube or bottle—a double-yuck factor, since jars tend to collect pubic hair.

Astroglide: Like using saliva from a cotton-mouthed whore.

Probe Thick Rich: Like somebody sneezed on your cock and left a goober trail as hard to wipe off as it is to look at.

Eros: It lasts like a top on Prozac, meaning forever, but it's difficult to wash off, and well, a little smelly.

Wet Oil: Leaves you with that deep-down oily feeling even after you pressure-wash your balls. Save it for underwater fucking.

Wet Light: Like my boyfriend, tends to get creamy and foamy within a few strokes. A slightly medicinal smell, too. The lube, I mean, not the boyfriend.

THE BETTER

Wet Original: Great balance between slickness and stickiness, washes off easily but thickens as it dries.

Probe Silky Light: Feels great, but like your pleas to the Office of Naturalization about your immigrant maid, you have to re-apply often if you want it to stay. Washes off easily, too.

Wet Classic Platinum: It'll slick your Willie for the longest time, but it is so thick, the bottle is hard to squeeze.

THE BEST

Aqua Lube: So good you'll start referring to your Internet start-up as a dotcum. Fruity smell, long lasting, easy to dispense, even easier to clean up.

Pleasure Glide: Great fudge-packing quotient. Long lasting and slippery. A no-frills meat and potatoes kind of lube.

Maximus: Slick but gives lots of friction. Like a gel, a little goes a long—and did I mention thick?—way. It warms up great, making you split-grin happy.

Hey, Woody!
It's been four months since September 11th, and my boy-friend and I have had completely different reactions in bed. We're both running semen factories only mine's work-ing to capacity and he's laid off half his staff, if you know what I mean. Since the attack I've been horny as hell and

he's lost all interest. How do I get me down to normal and him up to par?

—Winging it

Dear Winging:

You're both having natural reactions to stress. Some people, like your boyfriend, suffer from an Armageddon mentality and spiral into a depression where everything in him or on him droops like a wilted flower.

Other people, like you, suffer from an Ahmogetmesome mentality where you want it all the time because, well, because you're a pig.

Seriously, like everyone else, I'm sure the tragedy brought up fears and insecurities in you. In the midst of uncertainty people have a strong need to be connected. Sex is your way of feeling connected. It's a phenomenon psychologists call "Terror Sex." Before September 11th, it used to mean a date with me, but now it refers to people who fuck like rabbits after a traumatic event.

Wait, that still sounds like a date with me.

Anyway, there are documented examples of "Terror Sex." During the bombing of Britain in World War II, for example, people were literally fucking in the London subways. And in Turkey, after the horrendous earthquakes that killed tens of thousands, demographers noticed a "birthday bump" from all the people who wanted to feel the earth move under their feet again.

Stressful times cause a rush of chemicals to course through your body, including dopamine and testosterone, a hormonal cocktail more effective than a Viagra binge at a "Rape the Brad Pitt Look-alike Contest."

But as you know, not everyone reacts to stress in the same way. Shrinks have also noticed the reverse. In the sexual fight-or-flight response to stress a lot of people board the plane, if you know what I mean.

Stress can lead to depression and anxiety, which can de-horn the horniest among us. In one post 9/11 poll, 50% of Americans were having trouble concentrating and 30% weren't sleeping well. That doesn't bid well for sextra-curricular activities.

How do you get your sex life back to normal? The way you get life back to normal after any traumatic event. You anchor yourself. You meditate, pray, you talk things through. And you wait and you wait and soon time works its magic, and your boyfriend eventually looks at your dick and says, "Oh, I remember what that's for," and tries to hide it somewhere in his body.

Hey, Woody!
My parents are coming to visit and our guest bedroom is right next to ours. My boyfriend and I want to have sex while they're here, but I don't want my momma to hear her son squealing like a whore. What can I do to make my bedroom a little more sound proof?
—Thumper

Dear Thumper:
First, seal your crack. Not with your boyfriend's penis; with a weather-stripper. No, wait. That would really hurt.

We're talking about your bedroom door, right? Okay, then put a threshold seal along the bottom. If you can see light through the cracks, sound will go through too, so plug it tight.

Again, I'm talking about the door, not your boyfriend.

Play songs like "Can't Get Enough Of Your Love, Babe," or "Your Sweetness Is My Weakness." Anything with Barry White will help muffle your ruffles. Low frequency noises like headboards banging against the wall can be camouflaged with strong bass sounds.

If your mattress squeaks, Barry won't help. Try Britney. The best thing for squeaky box springs is squeaky music. Though be careful with that. Listening to Britney Spears is like snorting meth. It'll make you all happy and jumpy but in the end it'll give your dick a flat tire.

Next, buy a scrap piece of carpet and place it up against your door. Wait. Did I just say that? Christ, I'm turning straight! Still, heavy carpets and wall hangings are good for absorbing noise.

And if all that fails, do it the old-fashioned way—turn on the shower. They'll hear the water running through the pipes of the house, masking your pig-like squeals.

Hey, Woody!
You know those vacuum pumps advertised in men's magazines that promise to put at least another inch on your dick? Are they a waste of money?

—Wondering

Dear Wondering:
I'm wondering what I'm doing wrong that I'm still getting pathetic letters like this. For the last time, there is no known way to make your penis bigger. Why do you think we build all those nuclear bombs?

These vacuum pumps were originally devised to help men with erection problems. You stick your soft dick into a plastic cylinder and, like a hamster pressing a lever for the treat, you press a lever that pumps air out of the cylinder. This creates a vacuum that draws blood into the penis and voila—an erection! Then you tie a specially designed rubber band around the base of your penis (to hold the blood in place and keep willie saluting for hours).

The boys in the vacuum pump industry got a little ahead of themselves and decided they could repackage it as a way of making your dick bigger. Technically, they're right—the pumps do make your dick bigger. In the same way your mouth can make mine bigger.

Hey, Woody!
A transvestite friend told me he was diagnosed with a yeast infection. My response? "Yeah, right." He girls up everything he goes through so why should I believe him? Now he's hurt that I don't believe him, and I'm confused. Can men get yeast infections?

—A rising bun

Dear Bun:

She ain't lying. The trans has yeast in her glans. Men can and very often do get yeast infections. Balinitis, an infection of the tip of the penis (glans) is often caused by yeast organisms. Symptoms include a red rash and itching or burning in the glans or the foreskin.

Male yeast infections occur mostly in diabetics and uncircumcised men. You can get it through trauma or minor injury to the foreskin and penis. And by trauma, I don't mean the kind where the ugly one in the three-way keeps getting in the way. I mean the kind of trauma that comes from excessive masturbation.

Mostly, male yeast infections come from bad hygiene. To avoid that yummy yeasty feeling, wash your spring-action toy every day with soap and water. If you do end up with a baker's dough, it may require smearing your penis with an antifungal medication, which could be fun, actually, if the doctor's hot and insists on applying the cream himself, but doctors tend to bring up that bullshit about doctor-patient boundaries. I hate that.

If you're not circumcised and the yeast cannot stay deceased, the foreskin may have to be released. Circumcision may be the only way to prevent reoccurrence.

Hey, Woody!
Whenever I make love, my nose gets clogged up. It's embarrassing. I want to blow my partner, not my nose. What's wrong with me?

—Schnozzie

Dear Schnozzie:

There's nothing wrong with you. During arousal it's common for nostrils to flare as much as your underwear. The raising of blood pressure and the accumulation of blood in your genitals often leads to facial flushing, rashes on the chest or a stuffy nose.

Tell your partners they're so hot, they got your nose engorged too. The good news is that orgasms release chemicals that can actually clear nasal passages. You're lucky. The rest of us have to take Claritin.

Hey, Woody!
I'm giving my load to a lesbian! She wants a kid and I want to help her. I want my specimens to be perfect and someone mentioned I oughta stop wearing "weenie warmers," (you know, cotton Fruit-of-the-Looms) and switch to boxers. Why? What difference does it make what I wear? I don't want to give up my cotton shorts. I like them too much.

—Loads on sale

Dear Loads:

The jury is still out in the war between boxers and briefs. There is just no consensus among the experts.

Here's what scientists do agree on: Cooler testicles produce better sperm. In fact, that's why our testicles hang on the outside of our body, rather than the inside like most other mammals. The exception being the guys in Exodus, the gay de-programming outfit; their testicles hang on the mantle of Pat Robertson's fireplace.

And it's also why fertility experts recommend sleeping in the nude and wearing light clothing during the summer. Though I must say, you don't have to be a scientist to see the wisdom in that; you just have to be GAY.

Interestingly, Mizuno, a Japanese clothing company, came up with special underwear that whisks away sweat and body heat. It's got a new fabric mixing cotton with an active ingredient called polyethylene vinyl alcohol. Sounds like you'd be wearing a martini, but the company claims the fabric dissipates heat and keeps the skin one or two degrees cooler than regular cotton fabric. That, or they get your balls drunk, which would be helpful, actually. If my testicles got wind of where you wanted to send their sperm, they'd need at least a round or two before bellying up to the glans.

Hey, Woody!
I just want to jump out of my skin with shame and embarrassment when I go to strip clubs. It's not like I'm turned off by the dancers, I think they're hot. But for some reason it embarrasses me to be in the clubs.

All my friends like to go and I'm making excuses for why I can't. How do I get over this so I can quit being such a stick in the mud?

—Horny but embarrassed

Dear Horny:

Men uncomfortable with their sexuality often freak out when they're around other men who can "witness" their attraction to men. It's called internalized homophobia. Don't worry, you're not alone. I'm no stranger to self-hate. For example, whenever I don't insult pompous queens for saying something pretentious I end up hating myself.

Of course, you might be uncomfortable for other reasons. It could be that you don't like being lumped in with the great unwashed. The more social power you have (money, status, career), the more likely you are to lose it in a strip club setting.

I mean, come on. Complete strangers are looking at you looking at dicks. How dignified is that?

Will they notice you've got half a stock in your jeans, Mr. Millionaire Entrepreneur? Do you look a little *too* turned on, Mr. Corporate Vice President? Wow, you're not very different than the busboy you're sitting next to.

You get turned on and succumb to the feelings everyone else has and that makes you something you think you're not: Common. Not to mention weak. There is no strength in the presence of dancing dicks, you know.

Strip clubs are the great equalizers. They strip every man in the audience to his essential pigginess. So how do you get over your embarrassment? The same way you get over the embarrassment of reading this column: You learn to embrace your inner pig.

Hey, Woody!
Why is it that when I go to defecate I always want to linger
on the toilet? When I sit down I just don't want to get up.
                                          —Not full of it

Dear Not Full:
When you pinch a loaf in the toilet, you stimulate the vagus
nerve, which then drops your blood pressure, creating a peace-
ful feeling. Some people actually pass out on the john because
their blood pressure can drop so low. I shit you not.

Hey, Woody!
I'm not sure how it happened but a few of my friends
ended up sleeping with this guy that just moved into town.
I was the one who ended up dating him, though. Well, one
day we're in the hot tub with a bunch of my friends and he
realizes he's slept with every one of them. Later, he told
me he felt used. "Is this the way this town operates?" he
asked me. "Pass the new guy around?"
   He accuses me of being part of this "lazy Susan" con-
spiracy and he breaks up with me. A few weeks later I
found out this hypocrite did a couple of porn films! Woody,
why are men such hypocrites about their sex lives? This
guy was the pivot man in gang-fuck videos and he gets all
indignant that he's being "passed around"? Please! What
am I missing?

                                   —I'll take a pass on him

Dear Pass:
I love it. A pious porn star. That's a new one, even for me.
   Listen, nobody gets "passed around" unless they want to be
passed around. There are no victims in gay sex, only volunteers.
   There are two issues here: Porn Hole's sanctimony and
hypocrisy in general. I'm not going to say much about him because some things are better left unfucked. I mean, unsaid. But I
will say this about us: We gay men have the chance to redefine

the way we relate to each other but instead we cop the same double-standard, hypocritical stand straight men take.

We're no better than the Rush Limbaughs and Newt Gingrichs—the guys who blather about the sanctity of marriage even though they've all been divorced twice and are on sanctity #3. Well, okay we're better than them but only because we don't use the stink of our hypocrisy to shape public policy.

The premise behind your friend's reaction is that the only way to be perceived as a decent guy is to have "meaningful" sex with someone "special." Bullshit.

Throughout time the greatest men, the men who showed the most courage, the most character, the ones we most admire for what they accomplished, were, well, WHORES. Martin Luther King, Jr., John F. Kennedy, you name the man and I'll point to the vagina factories they plundered during their reign.

That applies to gay heroes too. Like Harvey Milk. It's a well-known fact he wormed his way into more asses than Preparation H. So don't give me that crap that character is in inverse proportion to the number of sexual partners.

The level of your sexual activity says nothing about your character. There are good-for-nothing whores and good-for-everybody whores.

There. I feel so much better now. Now, go. Pass some guy around.

Hey, Woody!
How can I prevent pimples and in-grown hairs after shaving my butt?
—The Barber of Seville

Dear Barber:
There are lots of bacteria near your dipsty dumpster. Shaving the skin allows bacteria to slip through. Pimples and ingrown hairs are the skin's reaction to the bacteria. There's not much you can do about it except maybe use an antibacterial soap like Lever 2000 or Dial.

Hey, Woody!
I think I pulled a groin muscle. My own, I mean. It hurts
like a mother. How long will I have to go without sex?

—Hoping not too long

Dear Hoping:
Sounds like you strained your abductors and now they're making you suffer.

No, wait. That was a scene in one of those bondage videos. I meant *adductors*. They're fan-like muscles in the upper thigh that pull the legs together when they contract. They help stabilize the hip joint.

Groin strains occur when a muscle is stretched too far or meets an unexpected, opposing force. This can happen when you're playing sports or dating me. Anyway, always follow the R.I.C.E.W. treatment plan: Rest, Ice, Compression, Elevation, and Woody.

"Wait," you may be asking yourself, "how did Woody get in my groin?"

Trust me, you wouldn't be the first to ask.

So here's the treatment plan: Avoid aggravating activities for the first couple of weeks. That means no sex, no sports, no reading this column. Once you're well enough to start, ice the muscle after exercise to reduce any swelling. And after applying the ice, wrap the thigh to keep it compressed. Pop some ibuprofen, too. That'll help the swelling.

Hey, Woody!
Why do I get headaches after sex? It doesn't happen all
the time but just enough to know that it's the sex that's
causing it. Have you ever heard of it?

—Heading for a fall

Dear Heading:
Sexual headaches are a common problem: You bring some guy home, manacle him to the bedpost, he loses consciousness, you

don't know what to do with the body and BAM! Just like that: A splitting headache.

Of course, sexual headaches aren't just caused by weenie tricks who can't take a joke, they're also caused by the stress and spiking blood pressure that accompanies sex.

The Solution?

1. Dump the body at a circuit event. Everyone'll think he fell out and leave him alone.
2. Take an Advil before having sex.
3. Let sex build up more gradually. A new study in Germany showed that "quickies" are much more likely to give you a headache than "gradual" sex because the blood pressure spike is so much more pronounced. So start slow and build up.

Hey, Woody!
I've always wanted to dye the color of my pubic hair but I don't know where to start or if it's dangerous. Any tips on coloring the bush?

—Bush-whacker

Dear Bush-whacker:
Pubic hair is notorious for rejecting color like a bad organ transplant. Bleaching almost always turns it orange. And orange only looks good on fruit.

If you still want to go ahead, here's a couple of rules: Dyes made for men's beards tend to work better. Dying pubic hair black works better than any other color.

Be very careful about using any form of bleach or peroxide. Not only will they make you look like you're not just for breakfast anymore; they can cause severe irritation of the mucous membranes. If you're going to have an irritation in bed, better it be a trick that wants to stay the night than a skin condition that wants to stay the month.

I know I don't need to tell you this, but I will anyway because

I never underestimate the stupidity that can come from mixing hope with vanity: DON'T color in between your legs.

Hey, Woody!
This is going to sound like a weird question for a gay sex advice column, but I need advice on how to talk about "the birds and the bees" to my kids. My lover and I are at a loss as to how to bring the subject up and what's appropriate to say.

—**Gay dads**

Dear Dads:
You're looking for something *appropriate* to say to your kids and you came to ME? Man, that kind of optimism should be framed.

All right, here's the "birds and the bees" Woody-style: A man sticks his erect penis in a vagina and that's where babies come from. A man sticks his erect penis in a woman's mouth and that's where jewelry comes from. A man sticks his erect penis in another man's mouth and that's where heaven comes from.

Just in case you wanted something more serious, I asked my grumpy advisors what they thought. Here's what they recommended telling your kids:

1. Talk to them early. Age 10 or 11 is too late.
2. Talk to them often. Like sex itself, once is not enough.
3. Take advantage of "teachable moments"—running into a pregnant neighbor, seeing a TV program—and springboard into a discussion.
4. Tell them to run. When they turn 18 and they see me coming, it's the only advisable thing to do.

Also, use resources like Planned Parenthood's *Talking About Sex* kit, which includes a videotape and booklets (1-800-669-0156; or http://www.plannedparenthood.org/store).

Hey, Woody!
I love having sex when I'm wet, but sometimes it's hard to convince my partners to part the waters with their legs and let me in. Any tips on submerging their objections?
—Slip-sliding away

Dear Slip:
Water is sensuous and relaxing. We're conceived in it, born in it, made up of it. Is there a better sensation than feeling water trickling down your body? I mean, other than Ricky Martin trickling down your body.

Everybody likes water but not everybody likes to fuck in it. For good reasons, too. Like getting a good grip. Also, it's hard to keep lubrication in the cavern, if you know what I mean.

A couple of things you have to be careful of: Hot water damages latex condoms and washes away spermicidal foams, jellies and jams. I mean, creams. Also, keep the ambience in mind. Bright lights and cold tile are boner-busters. Try scented candles, bath salts, or even fresh flower petals.

Don't forget the wine but be sure to use plastic glasses, otherwise you'll end up breaking glass in the tub. Trust me, you want your trick yelling, "Oh, God!" for the *right* reasons.

You might want to try getting him in the shower with a T-shirt and underwear on. Glenn Wilson, the author of *Creative Foreplay* says it's a great way to put some play in your lay. Is there anything sexier than wet clothing that clings to the outlines of the male body?

If you do end up fucking him in the tub (I just know I'm going to get letters saying "I thought you could only fuck men in the ass"), make sure he's on top. The buoyancy will give you a nice rhythm.

Hey, Woody!
I've noticed I get hornier on days near or on the full moon. Am I nuts or could there be a reason for it?
—Baying at moon men

Dear Baying:
Psychologists used to believe the moon caused insanity. The word "lunatic" is derived from the Latin "luna" (meaning "moon"). Of course, today we know the true cause of insanity is too little sex.

A study by the American Institute for Climatology concluded that arson, kleptomania, and other "psychological" crimes showed peaks when the moon was full.

We know the moon causes tides by pulling on the water on the earth's surface. We also know humans are made up mostly of water—it's not that much of a stretch to believe the moon could exert a kind of tidal pressure on us and possibly cause a "lunar libido" effect. But there haven't been any studies proving a correlation.

Before electricity, full moons were our only light bulbs, making it easier to look for sex at night. Maybe we're still carrying that monthly cycle in our psyches. Or maybe it's just in your head.

Maybe you had a couple of hot sessions under a full moon and you subconsciously associated it with sex and romance. But really, who cares? If the full moon makes you hornier, get thee to a man.

Hey, Woody!
Usually when I'm floggin' it (or gettin' it flogged), I drown that stifter in ye ole water-based slip 'n slide. But . . . when I skip the generous slathering of spoo-goo, sometimes my willie gets puffy, swollen and lumpy about 30 minutes afterwards. There's no pain or soreness, but it's seriously freaky looking and totally tweaks me (I've never let anyone else see). It looks like someone with a bee sting allergy, or a sausage full of golf balls. It doesn't seem to be hurting anything and it goes away in a few hours. Is this common, or am I just spankin' it too hard, or what?
—Sad Willie

Dear Sad Willie:

You might be suffering from contact dermatitis, or, an allergy to one of the variety of lubricants you're smearing your love tool with.

Switch to plain K-Y jelly, which is least likely to make your wood burn. If the flare-up happens again (the dermatitis, not the erection), the treatment of choice is to apply an over-the-counter cortisone cream to the affected appendage.

But don't use cortisone cream every day because it can make the skin shrink. With a warning like that, I have a feeling you'll listen. If, as you're suggesting, it's also happening when you yank your doodle dandy without any lubrication, the same advice holds. There might be something on your hands irritating your member.

Hey, Woody!
Can you get acne in your " 'tain't" ('taint' your ass, 'tain't your balls)? It feels like a pimple or two, and it's red and inflamed. Will over-the-counter acne medicine help?
—Pop goes the weasel

Dear Pop:

It's most likely a small cyst or an infected hair follicle. Try a hot compress (sorry, tongues don't count). Warm baths are your best bet. Like a good blow job, heat and moisture will relieve inflammation.

Be sure NOT to put anything in the bath water (Epson salts, oils, etc.). They'll irritate the affected area. If the baths don't work after ten days you've probably got a boil, which needs to be lanced and drained, much like the President himself. But don't try it yourself. He's got too many secret service agents running around. Get a doctor. You'll probably just drive the infection farther underneath the skin if you try to do it yourself.

Hey, Woody!
Please do something about the torso shavers! It wasn't
enough that we all became obsessed with removing body
hair in the early 90s, but almost nobody does it right.
Torso stubble is NOT, I repeat, NOT attractive, and it's
nearly impossible to avoid it. So why isn't a little trim (in
the clipping sense) enough for these people? Are they
afraid guys won't find them attractive for being who they
really are?

                                                    —Will trim 4 sex

Dear Will:
Asking why gay men go through certain grooming routines is
like asking Madonna why she wears skimpy halter-tops. *So you*
can see more, silly.

All in all, I'm with you on this one. There's nothing worse than
trying to get to the middle of the dance floor and having your
chest butchered by the claws of death hanging off shaved torsos.

Guys shave their torsos because they're frustrated that body
hair is covering their hard work at the gym. Wait. Let me put that
in a different, more truthful way. Guys shave their torsos because they think it'll get them laid more often.

I do think there's a little bit of body Nazism going on when
everybody feels that the only way they can get laid is to look like
everybody else. I like your trimming suggestion. That way, you
get a better view of your pecs, without criminally assaulting anybody who accidentally rubs up against you.

Hey, Woody!
I read your column about men shaving their torsos. Well, I
think it's pretty much a myth that everyone wants a smooth
man. I'm in my early forties, slightly overweight, and I
have the hairiest body in town. Everywhere I go—and, no,
I don't get it myself—but it seems everywhere I go I get hit
on. There are men younger and older who love hairy bods.

So, people who think you have to be smooth to get more sex, take my word for it, it's totally a myth.
                                        —His and hirsute

Dear Hirs:

Thanks for trimming the bush around a house obsessed with smoothness. We came out of the closet to escape the oppression of our sexuality, only to step into a room that oppresses our expression of beauty.

Youth and muscle have become the herders of a flock scared that they won't get through the narrowing pen of Beauty. So we line up like sheep, bleating, as scissors and shavers snip and whirr, giving us temporary entrée to an imaginary and totally arbitrary sense of what looks good.

The truth is that men can be beautiful, hot and sexy whether they shave or not. One isn't inherently more beautiful than the other, but we act as if it is. It's true that shaving your body makes you look younger and shows off your muscles better than if you didn't. But so what? We don't look *that* much younger. And hair can often highlight muscles better.

There's a certain element of disrespecting yourself when you refuse to accept natural body contours. I think we should do with body hair what we do with head hair—womp it up to highlight our best features. Trim it, style it, and make it a natural plus, not a perceived negative. Few of us would consider pointing at our heads and telling the hair-dresser to shave it all off, so why do it with our body hair?

Hey, Woody!
Sometimes, when I come, I lose the hearing in my right ear. It comes back after a few minutes, but this can't be right. Am I in for something terrible as time goes by?
                                        —Don't want to hear it

Dear Don't:
Actually, I'd love to have your condition. I hate guys who talk after sex. My tricks always turn into canaries after sex. Why can't they turn into pizzas?

Anyway . . . what was your question again? Oh, yeah. It could be a particular sexual position aggravating a simple condition like earwax buildup or nasal congestion. But it could be the eustachian tubes—the narrow tubes connecting the nose to the ears. They're the site of many vascular changes associated with orgasm.

A faster heart rate and increased blood pressure doesn't just swell your jeans, it also has the potential of swelling these tubes, which could end up causing temporary deafness. Go see an ear, nose and throat doctor and find out.

Hey, Woody!
Is it true that tea is bad for your libido? Say it isn't so!
                                              —Tea for two. Or more

Dear Tea:
Some researchers suspect that the estrogen levels found in tea are as high as the levels found in George Michael's dressing room. Meaning, you won't be able to get it up unless you're in a skanky public toilet waving your dick at an undercover cop.

Researchers suspect, though they have no real evidence, that tea's estrogen levels may be high enough to disrupt male hormones temporarily, causing a loss of libido. The key words here are "suspect" and "temporary." No one knows for sure. But if you've got a hot date planned, I'd stay away from it.

Hey, Woody!
For some reason, I go through these stages when I'm only interested in guys of a particular ethnic background. First it was Asian guys, and I made my way through the entire

continent. Then my friends dubbed me the "Rice Queen" (isn't that racist of them?), and I moved on to Hispanics. I've had every Puerto Rican, Cuban, Mexican, Venezuelan, and Argentinean in town. Then, most recently, African American men are where it's at! But with all the great sex, I'm still sort of lonely. Is the ethnic obsession the problem, or is that just my personal taste?

—Yo quiero taco homos

Dear Taco:

Nice to know the United Nations has a new "piecekeeping" force. I'm not worried about your "ethnic obsessions," unless of course, you move to Kosovo, where the term has a different meaning and a *very* different outcome.

Your loneliness isn't being caused by your sexual desire for men who are different from you. I happen to share your appetite for international appetizers. Black men are sexy, Asians are hot, and Latinos, well, who wouldn't leave home, family and career just to smell their dirty shorts?

But you're confusing appetizers with entrees. One leaves you craving for more, the other fills you up. You sound like you need a little filling up. Stop dating so much and create some emotional magic with one (or two!) of your black/latino/asian/mutant ninja turtle partners.

Your promiscuity may or may not be part of the problem. Personally, I don't believe that promiscuity and loneliness are tied at the hip. Sleeping around doesn't "cause" loneliness anymore than celibacy "causes" emotional fulfillment. But promiscuity will make you more lonely if you're sleeping around to avoid intimacy. Tricking because you're horny and he's hot is different than medicating yourself with dick because you're scared to death of being emotionally close to a man.

There are different reasons for being promiscuous. Some that serve us, some that don't. You've got to figure it out for yourself. My advice: Don't have sex for the next couple of months and try to figure out what it is that's making you lonely. Only by not having sex can you be with yourself long enough without distraction to know yourself better.

Hey, Woody!
I know what "69" means but how did the position get coined with a number?
                                        —Not good with numbers

Dear Not Good:
The term refers to two people going down on each other at the same time.

It was coined by a race car driver who claimed that the top speed of sex was 68 miles per hour, because at 69 you eat it.

Actually, I'm not sure how it got its start, but if you turn the number on its side, it isn't that hard to figure out.

Hey, Woody!
I love jerking off in the great outdoors. My house has a se-cluded lot in the back and late at night I go out there, take my clothes off and, uhm, commune with nature. There's a lot of privacy but I'm worried that someone's going to catch me in the act. Should I stop?
                                —Fooling around with Mother Nature

Dear Fooling:
Only animals do it outdoors. But since men are pigs, we qualify, and therefore I see nothing wrong with squealing under the moonlight. But it sounds to me like you're getting off on the danger of getting caught as much as anything else. I'd be careful. The next time your neighbors have a cook-out and see you grilling your beef without the barbecue they could slap you with a public nuisance charge and win.

Hey, Woody!
After reaching 40, I've felt a big drop-off in wanting to get-off.
I'm considering testosterone shots or patches to help. Any
advice in this area? And who do you have to see to get them?
                                                        —Longing for a Layin'

Dear Long-Lay:
Many men after 40 see their libido plummet like a meteor
marked "special delivery" to Earth. However, the odds that your
drooping sex drive is caused by a testosterone deficiency, are
lower than the odds of Bob Barr staying with his third wife. One
percent, to be exact, according to my medical sources and political spies.

Still, you should have it checked out, because you might fall
into that one percent. Go to any general practice physician and
explain your situation. They'll draw blood and test your testosterone levels.

Understand that a lower sex drive is normal for guys as they
get older. Aging has the same effect on your libido that a lighter
foot has on your car's accelerator—you'll still get there, just
maybe not as fast or as often as you'd like.

But if what you're experiencing isn't deceleration but jammed
brakes, it's most likely caused by fatigue, stress, or depression.
When you go for the testosterone test ask your doc to give you a
test for stress and depression.

Hey, Woody!
A straight friend swears if he beats off before having in-
tercourse, his girlfriend is less likely to get pregnant. Is
that true?
                                                        —Just wondering

Dear Wondering:
No. Research shows the second ejaculation contains just as
much sperm. Tell him there's a technical name for couples who
use that form of contraception: "Parents."

Hey, Woody!
Is it true that a man reaches his sexual peak at 16 and then it's all downhill from there?

—Hoping against hope

Dear Hoping:
If you measure "sexual peak" as the frequency of spontaneous erections, I guess it's true that you're an old man at 18. The question shouldn't be "when does a man reach his sexual peak?"; it should be "when does a man become a better lover?" And I think that's between 30 and 50.

Hey, Woody!
I have this fantasy of being covered in baby oil and doing it with a hottie. I've got a willing guy but I don't have a willing bedroom set. I can't even imagine what my bed would look like at the end of the session. What can I do to keep the mess to a minimum?

—Slippin' & Slidin'

Dear Slippy:
A well-planned fuck is the well-spring of spontaneity. Bathing yourself in lubricants will bring out (and in) things you've never thought about. You're right about taking some precautions. First, if you're not going to fuck, baby oil is fine. But if you are, ditch it. Baby-based products tear condoms. Or is it petroleum-based products? I forget. Either way, the condom's done for by the fifth pump.

So go to your nearest Whore Store and pick up a couple of gallons of water-based lubricant like Wet, K-Y, or Glide. Get a water mister and keep it on hand. When things start to dry out a little you can spray yourselves happy.

If the thought of that much lube on your 300-stitch Neiman Marcus sheets is too much to bear, relax. Go Wet, young man, because there's a solution every parent of a bed-wetter knows about—vinyl mattress covers. If you're too cheap to spring for the cost, you could try Saran Wrapping your bed length-and-width-wise. When you're done, do what I do with all the stupid letters I get—ball it up and toss it.

Hey, Woody!
What are the effects of smoking on sexual performance?
Do cigarettes light up your sex life, like the ads promise?
                                    —Trying to get my boyfriend to quit

Dear Trying:
You're better off striking a pose than a light, according to the latest research. In a study conducted in Kentucky (infuriating the state's tobacco growers no doubt), 290 couples were surveyed on sex and smoking (as opposed to smokin' sex, which we deal with regularly in this column). Results showed that nonsmokers got twice the nookie than smokers. Nonsmokers rated their sex lives better, too. They gave it an average of nine on a one-to-ten scale while smokers rated their sex lives at a five.

Researchers don't really know why smoking would have such an awful effect on sex, but hell, cigarettes poison other body functions, why wouldn't it poison sexual function too? Tell your boyfriend to lose the cigarettes. There's better things to stick in his mouth.

Hey, Woody!
We've all heard the myths before—masturbating makes you grow hair on your palm or grow zits . . . How did shit like this ever come up?
                                    —Hairy Harry

Dear Hairy:
Personally, I think it came out of the church's anti-sex policy, especially the prohibition against "spilling your seed." Which, by the way, I completely agree with. Why spill if you can shoot?

Masturbation starts around the same time puberty hits. The

church, always looking to make people feel bad about something, connected the dots and said, "See? You're growing all this hair and sprouting all these zits because you're beating off. That's God saying, 'Stop It, You Whore.'"

Undoubtedly many Catholic priests took the opportunity to say, "God said to leave your dick alone. He wants me to take care of it."

Can't Get Enough Wood?

Visit Woody's website at www.menarepigsbutwelovebacon.com. You'll find sexually insulting greeting cards, T-shirts, coffee cups, and more with the *Men Are Pigs* logo. You can also ask Woody tender, sensitive questions you're too ashamed to ask anybody else. True, you'll get squashed like a grape at a wine-making festival, but don't be selfish. Best of all, you can sign up for a weekly e-mail alert and have Woody's latest column delivered right to your desk. Remember: www.menarepigsbutwelovebacon.com